What Others Are Saying about This Book . . .

If you have ever longed to hear God whispering a love song into your life, and whatever love language you prefer, you will hear it loudly and clearly in the pages of this compelling and honestly written book.

—Gary Chapman, Ph.D., *New York Times* best-selling author, *The Five Love Languages* and *The Love Languages of God*

In this most beautiful memoir, Greg Hunt invites us into an unsettling time in his life, exposes the fault lines of his faith, and describes the path he walked into and out of the dark. Thanks to the trail markers he leaves along the way, he makes it easier for us to find our way, too.

—Susan M. Heim, co-author, *Chicken Soup for the Soul, Devotional Stories for Women*

If you've ever felt perplexed by God's silence, then you will find this book utterly fascinating.

—George Mason, Ph.D., senior pastor, Wilshire Baptist Church, Dallas, Texas

Sometimes raw, always honest, and ultimately hopeful, **Blackbird Singing in the Dead of Night** *speaks to the spiritual longings of the human heart. It offers not a tidy spiritual prescription, but a ragged record of the quest for God and the pursuit of a purposeful life. It's as much about the search for truth as it is finding it.*

—Julie Pennington-Russell, senior pastor, First Baptist Church, Decatur, Georgia

As Greg Hunt shows in his thought-provoking account of faith under stress, we don't have to give up when God seems elusive. His own experience provides a trail to follow, with unforgettable things to learn along the way.

—Dr. Robert A. Schuller, Crystal Cathedral Ministries, Chairman, FamilyNet Television Network, and *New York Times* bestselling author, *Walking in Your Own Shoes*

Thought-provoking, soul-searching, and honest.

—**Dr. Allen Walworth, president and principal, Generis**

When I read Greg Hunt's intelligent but accessible book, I felt as though I took the journey with him. It is an affirmation for us all on God's presence and supreme guidance in our lives—if only we are still enough, patient enough and trusting enough to see and feel them.

—**Christine Belleris, president, Beyond Words, Inc.**

None of us are free from the experiences of doubt, obstacles, even hardships in our lives, and thus we turn to God for guidance and direction. But what if God doesn't answer? As this compelling book shows, just as when Pastor Greg Hunt's journey took him to the edge of his faith, the journey itself is often the destination in disguise.

—**Donna Schuller, Television Host, Great Health, and co-author,**
Woman to Woman Wisdom: Inspiration for Real Life

Blackbird Singing in the Dead of Night *is a beautiful book of Hunt's reflective journey from pathos to passion. The lessons he learns along his path of listening for the voice of Christ give insight useful to all of us who might be questioning how God is moving in our own lives.*

—**Barbara Metzler, author,**
Passionaries* and *The Gift of Passionaries

Greg Hunt could be described as a 21st Century pioneer in the field of communications. Rare is the person, particularly a pastor, who will admit a disconnect between themselves and their Creator. **Blackbird Singing in the Dead of Night** *tells about a very personal quest he shares with his congregation over a period of months, and now on a larger scale through this remarkable book.*

—**Linda C. Fuller, co-founder, Habitat for Humanity International and The Fuller Center for Housing**

I'm not sure which is more frightening for a clergy person, confronting a crisis of faith or telling the world about it! Greg Hunt does so with a clarity and grace that takes you along on his pathway, draws you into his story, and illumines your own similar struggles.

—Bo Prosser, coordinator for Congregational Life,
Cooperative Baptist Fellowship

Blackbird Singing in the Dead of Night *is perhaps the most honest book I've read in a decade... From his lived experience of the soul's dark night Greg Hunt, like a contemporary Job, asks many of the questions no-one is supposed to ask and so finds his way to realities we all need to hear. This is one of those rare books that really could change your life. Don't miss it.*

—Christopher Webb, president, Renovaré

This book is a fascinating combination of things: a memoir, a testimony of faith questioned-tested-restored, a description of a specific scripture engaging practice to address struggles in faith, and, an invitation for others to engage on a similar journey. It was Carl Rogers, I believe, who noted that when one is most personal then one is most universal. It is on this personal-thus-universal note that I find the book most effective. There is offered a vital engaging and candid account of a grueling spiritual crisis and journey through encounter with Jesus' words back to faith. It is indeed a story of transformation, a fascinating read, filled not only with Greg's "aha's," but with some for each new reader. I commend it to you.

—American Baptist Quarterly Reviewer: Richard P. Olson,
Ph.D., distinguished professor, Pastoral Theology,
Central Baptist Theological Seminary, Shawnee, Kansas

Greg Hunt joins the ranks of the spiritual seekers whose journey toward God crosses the desert of doubt and uncertainty. His story of pressing through toward a deeper understanding of himself, his vocational calling, and his faith provides an engaging and inspiring look at a topic that is too often ignored or swept under the carpet in many 21st century churches—accepting and remaining faithful in times of unbelief.

—Joan Ball, author of *Flirting with Faith:
My Spiritual Journey from Atheism to a Faith-Filled Life*

BLACKBIRD SINGING
IN THE DEAD OF NIGHT
What to Do When God Won't Answer

GREGORY L. HUNT, Ph.D.

BETTIE YOUNGS BOOKS

www.BettieYoungsBooks.com

We would like to acknowledge the following publisher for permission to reprint the following material: **BLACKBIRD,** © 1968 Sony/ATV Music Publishing LLC. All rights administered by Sony/ATV Music Publishing LLC, 8 Music Square West, Nashville, TN 37203. All rights reserved. Used by permission.

About the Cover: The cover photo of a blackbird in the dark captures the nature of the author's experience during the two-year struggle of faith from which his book emerged. The lonely bird, the leafless branch, the cloud-covered nighttime sky—matched his sense of spiritual isolation during those days. Despite his apparent loneliness, the bird looks up in hope; although the clouds are thick and foreboding, a light shines through.

Cover design and photography by Tatomir Pitariu of GraphEye and Jane Hagaman of Quartet Books

BETTIE YOUNGS BOOK PUBLISHERS
www.BettieYoungsBooks.com

Distributed by SCB Distributors
15608 South New Century Drive
Gardena, CA 90248
800/729-6423
www.SCBdistributors.com

If you are unable to order this book from your local bookseller or online, you may order directly from the publisher.

Library of Congress Control Number: 2011922971

ISBN: 978-1-936332-07-6

10 9 8 7 6 5 4 3 2 1

Contents

Part I: The Journey Begins

Part II: The School of Discipleship

Part III: Getting Stretched

Part IV: Mountains and Molehills

Part V: Downward Spiral

Part VI: Dying for Life

Acknowledgments

I owe much of my faith's formation to my parents, my brothers, and the churches of my childhood. Madison Baptist Church, Madison, New Jersey, stands first among these churches. I also owe a debt of gratitude to every congregation that influenced my faith even as I led them: First Baptist Church, Knoxville, Tennessee; Sanders Baptist Church, Sanders, Kentucky; Graefenburg Baptist Church, Graefenburg, Kentucky; First Baptist Church, Shreveport, Louisiana; Holmeswood Baptist Church, Kansas City, Missouri; First Baptist Church, Norman, Oklahoma.

This book took shape in stages, and I am grateful to those who encouraged its development. Members of First Baptist Shreveport responded positively when I began teaching the Gospel of Matthew using my journal notes. They were the ones who introduced the idea of turning the material into a book. When I completed my first draft, I put the book in the hands of reliable first readers: Gary Baldwin, Mary Gurski, Terry Hamrick, Michael Tutterow and Allen Walworth. Their feedback gave direction to early revisions.

Midway through the writing process, an old friend came back into my life and had a significant impact on the book's development. Fred McCormick's perceptive feedback as a writer and a student of biblical faith pushed me to new depths of self-awareness and faith reflection. His input further clarified what I needed to say and how to put it in words.

I first approached Bettie Youngs for leads about a literary agent, knowing her as a successful writer, not as a publisher. I am grateful that she saw my book's potential and agreed to publish it. From the beginning of our literary relationship, she has nurtured the project with attentive care. Integral to this care was Bettie's most excellent staff and associates. Elisabeth Rinaldi's review editing raised perceptive questions and prodded me to enhance the narrative thread that runs through the book. Line editor Christine Belleris worked with great kindness and skill to help me polish the manuscript. I also want to thank designer Jane Hagaman and the many others who helped bring these words to life.

Throughout this book I pay tribute to people past and present. I feel the imprint of their influence profoundly. I want to express particular appreciation to Dr. E. Frank Tupper who, over the course of M.Div. and Ph.D. work, influenced me more than any other single person in the shaping of my theological perspective.

I would not have been able to see this process through to publication without the support of contributors to Directions, Inc. Their commitment to Priscilla and me and the work we do with organizations, couples and individuals has been a lifeline.

Most of all, I want to say thanks to Priscilla. Not only has she been the great love of my life, she has been an endless source of wisdom and encouragement. She lived this story with me and kept me sane. She offered essential input as the book took shape. I dedicate the book to her.

it started here: God in the Echoes

"Lord, if you won't speak to me, if you won't come to me directly and reveal yourself, then I will listen—I will watch and wait for you—in the echoes of your words gone by. I will listen for you in the words of Jesus."

Thus began my journey through the "red letters" of Matthew's Gospel.

The material in this book originated in a sometimes desperate experiment of devotion. I was a pastor at the time, and I had built my life and work around relationship with a Living God. I had always counted on some sense of God's presence. At the time of these "conversations" with Jesus, I particularly longed for vocational guidance from God. What I got instead was neither—neither God's guidance nor God's presence. At a time when the interior question of my life had been, "Which way should I go?" the sense of God's silence began raising an even deeper question: "Are you there . . . at all?"

A Generative Time

A confluence of factors brought me to this crossroads of my vocational and spiritual life. I had been leading First Baptist Church, Shreveport, Louisiana, since late summer 2002; first in the role of interim pastor and, beginning March 2003, in the role of senior pastor. It felt like particularly important work in one of the grand old churches of Baptist life. It was a church that was still a force to be reckoned with in the city, among other Baptists and beyond—despite its recent struggles.

The church had reached an apex of strength and growth forty years earlier and had found it difficult to maintain that momentum in the ensuing years. In 2001 a storm of conflict culminated in the departures of its senior pastor, three other key staff people, and a significant number of its members—many of them younger adults with families, the lifeblood of the congregation. I had been invited into the pastoral role a year after this congregational tempest, and the church had used the intervening year to good effect. It had worked on relational rifts, confronted the underlying causes of conflict, and begun outlining a new course for the future.

For my wife Priscilla and me, the arrival in Shreveport came as a return engagement. We had first come to First Baptist Church, Shreveport, in 1985 with two young children. I was a freshly minted Ph.D. grad from seminary, and I had served as the church's associate pastor for four years before accepting an opportunity to serve as senior pastor of Holmeswood Baptist Church in Kansas City. During that time we forged a connection with the people and the community of Shreveport that defied distance and time. This relationship made the return there all the more compelling. The church would have a leader with whom it already had a connection, and we would be making our home in familiar territory among people we already knew and loved. Robert Frost once famously wrote, "Home is the place where, when you have to go there, they have to take you in"[1]—his pithy way of celebrating the power of life's enduring and unconditional relational ties. That's what our return to Shreveport felt like; it felt like coming home.

I plunged into the work of the church and the life of the city with great enthusiasm, grateful to be in a cultural context that still welcomed clergy into significant roles of leadership and that looked to First Baptist Church as an influential force for good. In addition to guiding the congregation toward the fulfillment of its goals, I quickly found myself involved with the downtown Rotary Club and on the boards of some outstanding local organizations that were addressing the social, economic and spiritual needs of Northwest Louisiana. Priscilla and I picked right back up with old friends and enjoyed developing new friendships as well.

On the larger front, years of involvement in Baptist life had expanded my network of relationships and opened doors of involvement at a regional and national level. I served on the executive committee of the Board of Central Baptist Theological Seminary and in a variety of roles with the Cooperative Baptist Fellowship, a progressive movement that focuses its missional energies on being the presence of Jesus in some of the toughest and neediest places around the world.

I say all of this to accent the fact that these years in Shreveport brought me to a particularly fertile time in my vocational life: a kind of vocational primetime, when all of my training, experience and relationship building came together in productive ways.

Disquiet

Why, then, the disquiet? What could possibly have disrupted my contentment at what, on the face of it, should have been a fulfilling time in my life? The simple pleasures of this time were disrupted by an internal "push-pull": the "push" of stress related to congregational leadership and the "pull" of my attraction to new possibilities elsewhere.

Pastoring First Baptist Church proved particularly challenging. Progress came slowly. Deaths and departures continued to outpace new participation. Differences lingered over worship (traditional, contemporary or eclectic?), denominational affiliation (Southern Baptist, Cooperative Baptist or none of the above?) and congregational priorities (would we be internally focused on the interests of members or externally focused on the needs of people in the world around us?).

It wasn't all about the church, either. The congregation's continued stress fed my own stress, and I began to wonder about my effec-
tiveness. A sense of divine calling had brought me to First Baptist.
That calling, I thought to myself, could possibly have reached its
expiration date. I wondered if the church might need a new leader.

This internal question about my future with First Baptist both
fueled and was fueled by a larger theme of vocational ambivalence
that had waxed and waned over the full course of thirty years in
ministry. Despite decades of often gratifying work, I had never settled fully into my vocational skin. I had long imagined that I might
transition out of pastoral ministry before normal retirement age to
pursue under-expressed interests in writing, speaking, and consultation. When returning to Shreveport in 2002, I allowed for the possibility that circumstances might change that—that life and work
might prove so fruitful and enjoyable that I would decide to extend
my time in the pastorate. On the other hand, I just as easily imagined
that I would, after a period of time, shift into different work.

In fact, my wife Priscilla and I had created a nonprofit organization
in late 2001—Directions, Inc.—for just that purpose and had exited
pastoral ministry in what we thought would be a permanent change
of vocational focus. During a one-year interval between pastoring
First Baptist Church, in Norman, Oklahoma, and coming to First
Baptist Shreveport, we gave the organization what turned out to be a
test run. We named it Directions, Inc., because of the organization's
mission to serve people as they found direction for their organizations, relationships and lives. I provided consultation services to a
small number of for-profit and nonprofit organizations; Priscilla and
I coordinated the Marriage and Family Initiative of the Cooperative
Baptist Fellowship and led couple-related conferences, retreats and
seminars; and I did some life coaching. Our one-year experience gave
us confidence that we could make it work financially, and we loved
being back in metro Kansas City, where we had lived for the ten years
I served as senior pastor of Holmeswood Baptist Church. Only the

unique nature of our relationship with First Baptist Shreveport and our sense of God's specific calling had diverted us from the course we had set the year before.

Which Way Should We Go?

Now the future became uncertain again. All of the factors—the satisfactions and stresses of the current situation and an alternative waiting in the wings—created an internal conflict over life direction. Which way should we go? Priscilla played an integral part in conversations about this question, but she also knew that the dilemma was an especially personal one for me. She gave me space to wrestle with the matter while we carried on the life we were creating right where we were. I felt like I had a head full of voices clamoring for my attention, each with its own ideas of what was best. In circumstances like these I had learned to lean into my spirituality, a spirituality centered in the love and guidance of a Living God. I wanted to take my cue from a single mastering voice that could sweep up all of the competing voices into the simplicity of a unified, clear way forward. In other words, I was counting on one of the core benefits of what Christians call "a Spirit-led life."[2]

Things became further complicated at precisely this point. As I focused in on seeking God's guidance, I became uncomfortably aware of a "silence" between us that had actually begun before I noticed it.

How could this have happened? How could I have gone any length of time in the absence of a sense of God's presence and not noticed it? How could this happen to someone for whom spirituality lay at the heart of his life's work, someone who carried on regular patterns of prayer, meditation and spiritual study? I can only answer this by saying that my spirituality had never rested on the premise of an unbroken experience of emotional intimacy with God. I am not a mystic; I haven't lived with a pulsating sense of God's constant presence. I am okay with this to a certain degree. I was taught from the earliest stages of my life to live by faith, not feelings, which meant that though my feelings of God's nearness might ebb and flow, I would continue the patterns of life that faith had inspired in me.

Honesty forces me to acknowledge something more, however. The delay in my awareness of a problem in the divine-human connection also related to other realities: the habits of my spirituality had become somewhat routine, and the busyness of life had drawn me outward into the world of action more than inward into the world of the soul. I had allowed a certain spiritual thinness to develop.

Are You There at All?

When the time came for wrestling my vocational issues to the mat, I became acutely aware of this more fundamental problem. I experienced a kind of "dead silence." The closest I can come to explaining it is by way of analogy: it felt like the spiritual version of what happens if you're in a room when the air handler shuts down. The hum in the background stops. The air grows still. The room gets stuffy. While before you had become desensitized to the sound of the hum you now are acutely aware of its absence.

It's not an accident that in both Hebrew and Greek, the birth languages of Judeo-Christian faith, the word for Spirit can also be translated as "breath" and "wind." God's Spirit breathes life into us—not just once, at our birth,[3] but continuously. As the apostle Paul stated to one of his audiences, "In God we live and move and have our being."[4]

The sense of this became apparent to me again when I no longer felt the breeze of the Spirit. Not only was God not "speaking" into my situation about the future; God was not "speaking" into my life at all.

Now I had a disturbing double quandary on my hands. Had it been about a cloudy future only, I could have dealt with it much more easily. But it wasn't just a cloudy future; it was an unnerving now. In spiritual terms—in terms of my impression about that moment—I was alone. The Breath of Life was no longer breathing in me.

These were the circumstances in which I carried on my life, work and relationships. My public persona persisted for the most part unfazed; but under the surface of my calm, engaged, usually upbeat demeanor, a disquieted, sometimes even terrifying sense of things took hold.

The Past Is No Predictor of the Future

At previous vocational turning points I had experienced God's presence and guidance in a variety of ways: through conversation with others, through reading, through times of reflection, and always also in what the Bible refers to as "a still small voice"[5]—moments of clarity that seemed like God communicating directly into my inner ear. In 1995, for instance, the search committee of a well-respected church in another city—I was pastoring Holmeswood Baptist Church at the time—asked if it could present me to its members for election as senior pastor. Priscilla and I wrestled long and hard over our decision, and I finally had a breakthrough of clarity after conversation with a confidant. My confidant simply asked a series of questions to help me think out loud, and I couldn't get one of the questions out of my mind—"How is this flirtation with another church similar to an affair?" The question burst the romantic bubble that had clouded my considerations. Soon thereafter I experienced what felt like God's answer to my prayers for guidance. Interestingly enough, my experience of the inner voice was really more like a wordless and settled sense of divine direction, and it came not so much as a "No" to the invitation but as a renewed "Yes" to Holmeswood.

I had never experienced anything as dramatic as the cross in the sky that led to Emperor Constantine's conversion but I had, a time or two, actually heard an inward whisper. My calling into ministry as a sixteen-year-old happened like this; I actually heard a voice in my head saying, "Greg, be a preacher." Furthermore, I had always counted on the fundamental confidence that I was floating on a sea of grace. Even in the emotional ebb and flow of my life I assumed God's nearness.

Not this time. Despite constant pleading, all I experienced was God's silence. Days turned into months. Months became seasons. Seasons added up to a year, then two.

I asked God for strength to press into the challenges of my life. I asked God for grace to enliven the church I served. I asked for clarity of direction for all of us. I asked for insight into what was wrong and how to make it right. Ultimately, I asked for some word—any kind of message—that would tell me whether God wanted me to hang in there or move on. I got nothing.

What Was Wrong?

If you've been a lifelong skeptic or if for any other reason you've not lived with an underlying impression of God's nearness, the idea of God's silence may make you shrug your shoulders. "So what?" you might say.

For me, the sense of God's absence caused real distress, sometimes even panic. Eventually, it led me to question the basic framework of my faith. Having spent a lifetime talking with God, I found myself seriously considering the possibility that I had been talking to the ceiling, the stars, the sky.

I begged. I pleaded. I bargained. I shouted. I cried. I confessed and asked for mercy. Nothing.

Depending on one's faith tradition there are different explanations for what I was experiencing:

- *Faltering faith?* There's a story in the life of Jesus in which he encounters a father desperate for his son's healing.[6] "If you can," the father says, "please heal him!" Jesus responds almost indignantly, "If you can! All things are possible to those who believe!" The father's reply has become a classic: "I believe. Help me in my unbelief!" Did my dilemma originate in a weakness of faith?

- **Some moral obstacle?** The prophet Isaiah records God as saying that our patterns of moral life can separate us from God.[7] I had to allow for the possibility that my choices in life had created a barrier. Indeed, I did take this possibility very seriously and had plenty of material from an imperfect life to confront.

- **Dark night of the soul?** The sixteenth-century mystic, St. John of the Cross, wrote of periods like this as a Divine gift, strange as it may sound. These periods of dryness purge us of dependence on emotions. They cleanse us of pride, greed, anger and ease. They enliven the cardinal virtues of faith, hope, love, prudence, justice, self-control and courage. They draw us more deeply into a mature life of the Spirit. He called these experiences "the dark night of the soul."[8] Did this explain my dilemma?

- **Faith development?** My Ph.D. dissertation focused on the idea of faith development, with special attention to pioneering faith development theorist, James Fowler. Fowler, who defines faith as "the quest for meaning,"[9] argues convincingly that our faith develops in stages and can alternate between periods of relative stability and unsettling periods of instability, when one stage of faith gives way to the next. We can reach points in our human experience when our faith, as constructed, no longer proves adequate, no longer works. Had I outgrown the structure of my faith? Did I need a more mature framework for a new stage of life?

- **Projection of the imagination?** German philosopher Ludwig Feuerbach concluded that our notions of God are nothing more than figments of our imagination projected onto the backdrop of the universe.[10] In one way or another, all atheists tell us that there is no God, no Divine Other at the opposite end of prayer. Was I simply confronting a reality I had resisted all my life? Was I finally waking up to the unpleasant discovery that God does not exist?

  I will say that I have never wrestled with this possibility more seriously, more deeply, and more personally than I did during the long, dry spell in which the journal entries in this book were first penned.[11]

I couldn't know for sure which of these explanations made the most sense for me and, at one time or another, I tried them all on for size.

The Red Letters of Jesus

In the meantime, I settled on the only strategy I could think of for making contact with God. I had grown up hearing the Bible called "God's Word." I had grown up Baptist, a tradition that thinks of the Bible as the revelation of God's will and way, and even as God's very self-revelation. According to this conviction, the Bible is not just a record of God's words and deeds in the past; it is also a living expression of God's presence and purpose today. God's Word, including that recorded on the pages of the Bible, is "alive and active, sharper than any two-edged sword."[12]

Furthermore, this tradition of faith places special significance on the words of Jesus, whom it believes to have been God in human flesh, the defining self-revelation of God. So valued are Jesus' words that certain Bible publishers set them off in red ink so that they stand out all the more.

Contemporary scholars debate whether Jesus actually spoke all of these words. As a trained Bible scholar and theologian, I was aware of this debate; but, in the crucible of my existential crisis, I decided to cut through all of the complexities of academia and settle on a simple strategy of simple faith.

I would experiment with the possibility that I could have a personal encounter with Jesus through his words. I would look to the Gospel of Matthew for the pure and simple reason that Jesus' words first appear there in the Bible. If I could not hear him speak directly into my inner ear, I would listen for him in the context of the stories of his life, allowing my imagination to transport me to the times and places in which his words were first spoken. In keeping with the tradition of which I am a part, I would allow his words to "come alive again," to speak directly to me in the here and now.

As a means of response to his words each morning, I would continue my practice of journaling, a habit I had formed during high school years. Journaling would give language and form to my thoughts and feelings. Usually addressed to Jesus, these entries would preserve my prayerful journey of faith, uncertainty, longing and hope.

The Shape of What Follows

What follows are short clips from forty of my journal entries during my experiment with the red letters of Jesus and forty accompanying reflection pieces, written after my crisis. For practical reasons, the red letters have been converted to bold print. I have selected the journal entries carefully to capture the flow of my eight-month excursion through Matthew. I chose the number forty for a couple of reasons. First, including all 200-plus journal entries would have made this book too long. Second, the number forty has an honored place in Judeo-Christian tradition, signifying a time of seasoning and preparation. For Moses, Jesus, and countless others across the centuries, forty represents a "wilderness" interval, the suspended animation between what has been and what is to come. Given the nature of my experience, the number forty seemed particularly appropriate.

The accompanying reflection pieces open up deeper conversation about themes that arise in the journal entries, themes related to the pursuit of God and the quest for what Jesus called an "abundant life"[13]: a life rich with love, joy and ultimate meaning. These pieces look more closely at my experiences during my spiritual struggle. They convey the questions and hard-earned lessons that came during what was a perilous journey of faith. The tone throughout is confessional and autobiographical rather than detached and all-knowing.

Here's my rationale. I cannot pretend to have a dispassionate interest in these topics. Yes, I bring my theological training and years of preaching, teaching and counseling to the conversation; but I also bring my hopes and fears and personal struggles. I carried on my experiment not as some ivory tower intellectual pondering abstractions, but as a person of faith in the throes of a faith struggle.

There are any number of wonderful books on theology and biblical faith that you can read without knowing the personal stories behind them. I would be happy to supply you with a bibliography upon request. But if Italian film director Frederico Fellini was right— and I think he was—that "all art is autobiographical,"[14] doesn't it make sense to apply this to the art of conversation about matters of ultimate importance? Doesn't it sound like a worthwhile experiment to take the autobiographical element out of hiding and thread it openly into the flow of the conversation?

That's what this book does, which accounts for the fact that what follows isn't a tidy prescription for spiritual seekers, but a ragged record of the quest for God and the pursuit of a purposeful life. My particular struggle, as recorded here, isn't just about answers; it's about questions, too. In fact, this book is as much about the search for truth as it is finding it. Sometimes, it turns out, the journey is the destination in disguise.

A Note to the Reader

I conceived this book, not only to capture my experience during a transformative time of my life, but also to invite others into deepened reflection about their own life and relationship with God. I encourage you to flag words and phrases that strike a responsive chord. I also encourage you to pause between chapters and ask: What thoughts, feelings, wants or actions does this chapter evoke in me?

Some will decide to read the book straight through. Others will prefer to read one chapter per day, turning their reading experience into a forty-day process of personal development. Some may even decide to give my red-letter experiment a try for themselves. Reading groups will find much to discuss over the course of this book. A set of questions has been provided at the end for personal use or group conversation.

Part I

The Journey Begins

To take Jesus seriously means to listen when he speaks, to consider his extraordinary version of reality, and to take to the road with him toward who knows where. Who can say in advance where it will lead? I will confess that as I launched the journey, hope and doubt walked as hand-holding companions most of the way.

one

Look no further: You come to me . . . in your Word.

I will accept this. I will allow my heart to make this one dimension of your presence a feast of fellowship. You will stand before me in the things you say. Your Word will be more than an echo on the page, more than the vapor of an earlier presence. Speak, Lord Jesus, your servant receives you into his life—your servant listens.

I found my first Bible on the shelf in my office at church and brought it home with me yesterday. It's the only red-letter Bible I have in my collection. Grandmother and Granddad Standridge gave each of my brothers and me the same kind of Bible for our birthdays in 1960. My name is embossed on the black faux leather cover. It's a King James Version Bible with onion skin paper and Bible-story pictures interspersed among the pages. I can still see the tell-tale signs of what happened to the Bible soon after I got it: While racing to the car through the rain, I dropped it in the runoff water at the curb. Resting on the arm of my leather chair is my permanently wrinkled red-letter Bible.[15]

Matthew 3:13–17

(13)*Then Jesus came from Galilee to the Jordan to be baptized by John. *(14)*But John tried to deter him, saying, "I need to be baptized by you, and do you come to me?"*

(15)*Jesus replied,* **"Let it be so now; it is proper for us to do this to fulfill all righteousness."** *Then John consented.*

(16)*As soon as Jesus was baptized, he went up out of the water. At that moment heaven was opened, and he saw the Spirit of God descending like a dove and lighting on him. *(17)*And a voice from heaven said, "This is my Son, whom I love; with him I am well pleased."*

Jesus, your red letters begin here. You speak to John the Baptist in response to John's objections about baptizing you.

The NIV translates your words to John as, "Let it be so now." The King James Version says, "Suffer it to be so." I think the Elizabethan translators got it right: To yield to your inexplicable command is to *suffer.* To "let it be" is to experience the exquisite pain of relaxing my grip on the situation.

"Just go with me on this," you say; and, I who have knots because of my tight-fisted grip on life, must relax and stretch, must "un-contract," until I feel the release.

It's interesting to be considering this spiritual discipline this week, having just gotten past a scare in the rehabilitation of my knee after reconstructive surgery. Bending my knee by sliding my foot down the cabinet door in our bedroom, stretching the quadriceps muscles that had been drawn tight for nine days since surgery, I pressed into the pain and experienced a pop that scared me because I didn't know what it was. I feared that I had reinjured it! It turned out to be a breakthrough rather than a breakdown; the release of muscles that had become knotted by unrelenting contraction.

You engage me in your purposes, and in doing so, you exercise me toward these kinds of breakthroughs, stretching me to relax the knots that form because of the relentless effort to keep a grip on life. "Suffer it to be so." Push into the pain . . . or more to the point, relax your self-contracted control over life as I press and stretch you. Don't fear the "pop." I know what I'm doing.

Father-Son-Holy Spirit God, I ask that you meet me in the stream where I stand and draw me into your action. Work with me to participate with abandon in your life and work. I am ready and willing to be a servant of your will, however small or large the part—wanting to be found faithful in the "few things" so as to be entrusted with more.

Into the Light of the Dark Black Night

[The titled portion of each chapter was written after the crisis of faith and calling.]

Looking back at my crisis of faith through the lens of the Beatles song "Blackbird," I realize how deeply the lyrics resonate with the longing of the human heart when lost in the darkness of what the sixteenth-century mystic, St. John of the Cross, termed "the dark night of the soul":

Blackbird

Blackbird singing in the dead of night
Take these broken wings and learn to fly
All your life
You were only waiting for this moment to arise.
Blackbird singing in the dead of night
Take these sunken eyes and learn to see
All your life
You were only waiting for this moment to be free.
Blackbird fly Blackbird fly
Into the light of the dark black night.[16]

This Lennon-McCartney song captures the longing I felt during those months in the absence of the sense of God. Honestly, it captures a longing that, though deepened by the crisis of my faith, has been there most of my adult life. When I signed on as a follower of Christ, I was particularly captivated by Jesus saying that he had come that we might have Life and that we might have it more abundantly.[17] I knew he was talking about life before death just as much as he was about life after death. Eternal life, truly understood, is all of this. It begins now and goes on forever. It is life at its best, life animated and blessed by God. I knew Jesus was inviting me into an experience that would amplify all that was best about being alive.

Given my sense of faith's possibilities, I have had an uneasy awareness of the gap that often opens between its potential and my actual experience. Thomas Kelly, author of A *Testament of Devotion*, expressed perfectly what I have often felt:

> Strained by the very mad pace of our daily outer burdens, we are further strained by an inward uneasiness, because we have hints that there is a way of life vastly richer and deeper than all this hurried existence, a life of unhurried serenity and peace and power. If only we could slip over into that Center! If only we could find the Silence which is the source of sound![18]

Life. God's promised Life. Elusive, daunting, irresistible Life. It has for most of my life been the pearl of great price I would give anything to possess.[19]

During the dark night of my soul, this yearning became an almost unbearable ache in my chest, an obsessive interest, a bleeding desire. I felt my brokenness. I recognized my blindness. I strained to notice and move toward any evidence, any sign of light.

By light, of course, I mean the presence of God. By light I mean any illumination on a path ahead. By light I mean security, warmth and joy.

My journey into the Red Letters of Jesus was my great, desperate attempt to find this light in the only place I had hope of finding it. When I opened the Bible each morning, I was blackbird singing in the dead of night, with the broken wings of a wounded follower, and the sunken eyes of a blind believer.

To sing a song, any song, in the dead of night is to defy what the evidence suggests. To talk to God when God seems absent is the foolishness of God's kind of faith. To keep believing, to keep trying, to refuse to give up even when you fear that God has given up on you; that's blackbird singing in the dead of night.

two

Matthew 4:1–11

(1)*Then Jesus was led by the Spirit into the desert to be tempted by the devil.* (2)*After fasting forty days and forty nights, he was hungry.* (3)*The tempter came to him and said, "If you are the Son of God, tell these stones to become bread."*

(4)*Jesus answered,* **"It is written: 'Man does not live on bread alone, but on every word that comes from the mouth of God.'"**

(5)*Then the devil took him to the holy city and had him stand on the highest point of the temple.* (6)*"If you are the Son of God," he said, "throw yourself down. For it is written:*

> *"'He will command his angels concerning you,*
> *and they will lift you up in their hands,*
> *so that you will not strike your foot against a stone.'"*

(7)*Jesus answered him,* **"It is also written: 'Do not put the Lord your God to the test.'"**

(8)*Again, the devil took him to a very high mountain and showed him all the kingdoms of the world and their splendor.* (9)*"All this I will give you," he said, "if you will bow down and worship me."*

(10)Jesus said to him, "Away from me, Satan! For it is written: 'Worship the Lord your God, and serve him only.'"

(11)Then the devil left him, and angels came and attended him.

For forty days and nights Jesus fasts. For forty days and nights he concentrates all of his loving attention on you, his heavenly Father. For forty days and nights he delves into the Oneness that so uniquely defines your relationship.

The *Son* is "led by the *Spirit*" into close company with the *Father*. Matthew's wilderness temptation story is a story of you, the Triune God, experiencing forty days and forty nights of undistracted, intimate Oneness.

I can't separate Jesus' response to the devil from this intimacy of relationship, this avid interaction, this feast of love that defines your Three-in-Oneness. This intimacy has such force that it eclipses every other pleasure, every other/lesser necessity.

Jesus' responses to the devil don't just reveal his impressive knowledge of the Scriptures;[20] they reveal—and flow from—the immediacy of his relationship with you. When he turns back the first temptation, he doesn't just repeat the teaching of Moses; he speaks as one who, for forty days, has lived on, been nourished by, and been saturated with your word—that is, you speaking directly into his life. When he responds to the second temptation, he doesn't just battle the devil's misuse of Scripture with a better interpretation; he rests in a relationship with you that is so secure that it will withstand the assault of all naysayers and even a death shrouded in doubt and dismissal. When he responds to the third temptation, he doesn't just assert your Lordship over every other lord; he kneels at the throne of heaven in an immediacy of devotion that gladly gives itself away.

I want to experience a personal relationship with you and completely devote myself to you, and by faith I'm postured in a ready and waiting mode. I want you to step forward and meet me.

Today, Lord, today. Present yourself. I respectfully plead with you:

present yourself alive and loving. Or remove the cataracts from my spiritual eyes so that I can see you already standing before me and in residence within me and in Lordly glory above me. Let me feel your strong shepherd hands beneath me, and I will gladly rest myself there. I will gladly let you be my strength and my sustenance.

Bargaining with God

Looking back now, I laugh to think about how easily I, a supposedly sophisticated Christian, can succumb to unstudied notions of faith. You'd think that my upbringing in a dedicated Christian home, my years of theological study, and my longstanding practice of contemplation would immunize me against this tendency. You'd think that having prepared carefully for Christian ministry followed by decades guiding others in the direction of spiritual maturity, I would have weeded out the immature voices that play in a child's head.

Not so. Here's the truth: I can "know" better at an intellectual level, but that doesn't mean I have truly internalized all I know.

As is true of various kinds of crises, a spiritual crisis throws us back to our faith's most primitive level. At crunch time we really get to see what we believe and how deeply rooted we have gotten in a life of the Spirit, a life characterized by love, joy, peace, patience, kindness, goodness, faithfulness, gentleness and self-control.[21]

Take the matter of bargaining with God. As a preacher and teacher I have confronted this tendency for years. I don't remember exactly when I came to recognize the fruitlessness of it, but it struck me years ago that New Testament faith puts us beyond the pattern of *quid pro quo*.

Quid pro quo. It's a legal term, from the Latin, meaning "something for something." Behind it lies the idea of fair exchange. We practice this principle on a daily basis when we purchase something or sign a contract or return a favor. It's the principle of "tit for tat." It's the idea of "you scratch my back, I'll scratch yours." It finds application in blessings and curses, rewards and punishment.

How does the principle of *quid pro quo* work with God? Well, at a certain level, we have biblical precedents for striking up a bargain with God. We see Abraham negotiating over the fate of Sodom.[22] We see Jacob promising lifetime loyalty to God in exchange for God's blessing and protection.[23] We see Moses resisting the command to lead the tribes of Israel farther into the wilderness until he has assurances that God will go with them.[24]

Furthermore, God actually encourages us to put God to the test. Consider, for instance, God's challenge regarding tithing. "'Bring the whole tithe into the storehouse that there may be food in my house. Test me in this,' says the Lord Almighty, 'and see if I will not throw open the floodgates of heaven and pour out so much blessing that you will not have room enough for it.'"[25] What is this if not an invitation to hold God to a bargain? God makes a promise and dares us to trust. God encourages us to put our money, our things, our very lives on the line and suggests, in so many words, that we hold God accountable to keep God's side of the bargain.

On the face of it, the pattern of *quid pro quo* lies at the heart of covenanting, which is one of the foundational dimensions of biblical faith. To establish a lasting, loving relationship with us, God makes promises and demands, creating expectations from our side and from God's. God calls for obedience and trust on our part and promises blessings or curses, depending on our response.[26]

I've used Old Testament texts so far, but this pattern of covenanting, of promise making and promise keeping, this "if-then" of faith ("If you'll do this, then I'll do that") carries over into the New Testament ("Testament" literally means "covenant"). Jesus calls for obedience and trust and promises eternal life, the kingdom of God, the presence and power and peace of Father, Son and Holy Spirit in exchange.[27]

It's not coincidental that you can find books of biblical promises on the bestsellers' lists. Promise making plays a prominent role in God's ongoing relationship with us. From Genesis to Revelation, God makes promises that you can "take to the bank":

- "I will not fail you or forsake you."[28]
- "Delight yourself in the Lord, and he will give you the desires of your heart."[29]
- "Trust in the Lord with all your heart, and lean not on your own understanding. In all your ways acknowledge him, and he will direct your paths."[30]
- "If you confess with your mouth Jesus as Lord and believe in your heart that God raised him from the dead, you will be saved."[31]
- "Listen! I am standing at the door, knocking; if you hear my voice and open the door, I will come into to you and eat with you, and you with me."[32]
- "Seek first the kingdom of God and his righteousness, and all these things will be added to you."[33]
- ". . . And surely I am with you always, to the very end of the age."[34]

At a certain level, then, I was justified when I took God to task for what seemed to me like failed promises. God had said my prayers would be honored. God promised finding at the end of my seeking.

So, what's the problem with *quid pro quo?*

Actually, there's more than one problem from the perspective of biblical faith. For one thing, this mindset is legalistic: holding God to a standard of fairness that really isn't in our best interest. Were God actually fair in this regard, giving us what we have coming to us, we wouldn't like the outcome. The apostle Paul reminds us that the wages of sin is death[35] and that all of us have sinned.[36] Do we really want God to be fair? What we really want is the unmerited gift of God: eternal life in Jesus Christ our Lord.[37]

For another thing, when things aren't going as we prefer, we can't say with certainty that God isn't being true to God's promise. Look at my situation during my dark night of the soul. I felt God's absence but couldn't say for sure that God actually had deserted me.

And though I had the impression that God wasn't responding to my request for clarity, I couldn't say for sure that God was ignoring my request. I had to allow for the mystery of God's method and timing. I had to allow for the fact of my impatience and the ways God might need to ready me and my circumstances before lifting the fog from the landscape ahead.

Still further, the *quid pro quo* mindset quite easily becomes an attitude the God of Scripture condemns. Jesus, when tempted by Satan to put God to the test, recited words from the book of Deuteronomy. "You shall not put God to the test . . ."[38] God is not a genie who comes to us saying, "Your wish is my command." God's generosity as a promise maker should never lull us into thinking that we can manipulate God. God is Lord; we are not. We dare never forget this.

How easy it is to turn the promises of God into presumption, to act like religious consumers, becoming demanding, insistent, transactional. The essential elements of a covenantal relationship—love, trust and mutual self-giving—get lost in the exchange. Empowered by God's promises we treat God as if God were our cosmic butler, doing our bidding, rather than the other way around. We forget our place.

We also forget our limits—the limits of our insight, our patience, our perspective. We jump to conclusions about what we simply must have, forgetting the difference between wants and needs. We jump to conclusions about how and when God must deliver on the things we expect. Frustrated when our assumptions, presumptions, expectations and demands aren't satisfied, we work up a stew of righteous indignation.

Despite having cautioned Christians against this for years, I still succumbed to these very reactions at times when, after years of waiting for clarity, I found myself seriously wondering if God's promises could be trusted. I felt like I was holding up my side of the bargain; why wasn't God holding up the other side of the bargain?

These inward eruptions of indignation came most often in the privacy of morning devotion, and I would spill out my feelings in my journal. They would occur at times in the middle of the day and in the company of others; but I could tell when they were coming and knew how to cap them off, lest innocent bystanders get slimed. I found safe places in the company of my closest friends where I could lift the cap and experience the temporary relief of my venting. They got to hear me, and sometimes join me, in a plaintive expression of indignation about God's mysterious ways.

Don't misunderstand me. I knew better than to think that I had achieved some level of goodness that secured God's favor. I knew that any hope I had of God's favor rested in God's goodness, not mine. But hadn't God in God's goodness offered the promise that "you will seek me and find me when you seek me with all your heart"?[39] And hadn't I been seeking God for an extended period of time— diligently, urgently? So where was the finding? Hadn't God in God's goodness said that if I trusted God with all my heart and resisted the temptation to lean on my own understanding and acknowledged God in all my ways, then God would direct my paths?[40] And hadn't I done just that?

Oh, wait a minute. No, I hadn't. My exasperation itself gave me away. Nothing about questioning God's promises qualified as trusting God with all my heart and resisting the temptation to lean on my own understanding. Even in the midst of my flights of frustration, a more sensible side of me knew how to pipe up and remind myself that I wasn't being fair.

Where did this leave me? It left me with wonderful promises from God and the challenge to trust and obey God. It left me with a reminder to be grateful rather than presumptuous, focusing on the ways God's good was coming to me rather than on the ways I didn't think God had delivered yet.

Quid pro quo makes our relationship with God a utilitarian thing rather than a relationship rooted in love. If we've got a contract in hand every time we come to God, we thwart the experience of intimate oneness that Jesus, the Son, enjoyed with his heavenly Father and that he extends as a possibility to us.[41]

"Claiming God's promises" isn't an invitation to call God to task. It's an invitation to relax in faith-filled confidence, trusting that whether God's promise-keeping is conspicuous or currently hidden, it's happening either way.

I know this at a certain level, by faith. I simply find it difficult to remember when times get tough.

three

Matthew 4:18–20

(18)*As Jesus was walking beside the Sea of Galilee, he saw two brothers, Simon called Peter and his brother Andrew. They were casting a net into the lake, for they were fishermen.* (19)**"Come, follow me,"** *Jesus said,* **"and I will make you fishers of men."** (20)*At once they left their nets and followed him.*

Matthew says Jesus finds Simon Peter and Andrew doing what they do, being who they are. They're casting a net . . . because they were fishermen. And what he's saying to them when he calls them is, "Come with me and I will transform what you do best. I will give you a way to take your identity, your well-known work, what you know and do best, and play it out for God's pleasure. Rather than rip you out of your life and work, your strengths and passions, I will give you a way to engage these very things with redemptive purpose."

You meet me where I am. You make the connection between what I do—my occupation(s)—and what you have in mind for me to do—my vocation. You invite/command me to follow, to take your lead, to come along with you, to find my vocation somewhere in the context of your vocation.

Here's your message for me and every would-be follower: Who we are and what we do will become metaphorical—a way of seeing, understanding, and living out the redemptive-relational purpose for which we were born. Peter and Andrew, in keeping with their occupation, would cast the net of the kingdom and draw people in. They would hook people on the kingdom of heaven—on Christ. Fishermen become fishers of men. At your invitation, I become . . . (Lord, give me a personalized metaphor for my calling).

Vocation and the Silence of God

The silence of God is doubly disturbing when one is straining to hear God's direction vocationally. My crisis of faith related directly to calling.

I have had a lifelong fascination with the subject of "calling," the idea that God takes initiative and directs us in the use of our gifts and interests as partners with God in the healing of the world. As the bestselling author Frederick Buechner puts it, "The place God calls you to is the place where your deep gladness and the world's deep hunger meet."[42]

Note that according to the biblical idea of "calling," or "vocation," everyone, not just clergy, has a calling. Also note that this calling extends well beyond what one does to earn a living. As James Fowler puts it:

> The shaping of vocation . . . involves the orchestration of our leisure, our relationships, our work, our private life, our public life, and of the resources we steward, so as to put it all at the disposal of God's purposes in the services of God and the neighbor.[43]

To illustrate this understanding of vocation Fowler turns to a mentor of his, Carlyle Marney, who liked to tell a story from his own childhood to clarify the concept. During his boyhood years, Marney's family owned a contrarian cow named Daisy whose milk production offset her disagreeable temperament. Unfortunately, the genetic gift that made her such a great source of milk came with a price. Each time she calved she developed life-threatening mastitis.

She would have died more than once had it not been for Mr. Adams and his unique sense of vocation. President of the small town's bank and elder at the local Presbyterian church, he lived just across the alley from the Marneys. When Carlyle's father called, even in the middle of the night, Mr. Adams would come running, bicycle pump and ointments and hot water in hand, ready to pump and soothe Daisy into production for another season. *This*, according to Marney, is vocation!

> But who is Mr. Adams? Was he neighbor, elder on a Christian mission, banker serving a very modest customer, or a cattle-loving veterinarian with a sympathy for a hurting beast whose name came from the side of a churn? Answer: He was all of these at once. But in the arrangement of the scenery of his life's drama, he was living out his identity, using the special gifts, interests, experiences that gave him a role as a means of relation. And his work, his energy in relation, were all serving a proper relational end. The term for the whole—role, work, proper end, is *vocation*. And from which of these roles and ends is his identity derived? Answer: From none of them. He is *all* of them at once.[44]

This is an understanding of life that captivates me: the idea that God can weave the many-colored threads of my life into something of beauty and grace. Life is not something to compartmentalize into separate, unrelated parts, nor is it only a succession of days to check off the calendar. Life is a gift from God, meant to be lived:

1. in responsive relationship with God;

2. in loving relationship with neighbor;

3. with a noble sense of purpose;

4. in a way true to our own individuality;

5. with a sense of wholeness, every part of our life related to all of the other parts; and

6. in a way that continues to unfold, and even evolve, over time.

Two additional facets of calling remain important to me as well:

1. The term suggests that God *communicates* this direction into our lives; and

2. God *gives particular focus* to our vocational pursuits, which has implications for what we do for a living.

My own sense of vocation dates back to age sixteen. Sitting in prayer with a group of other youth on a hillside outside Madison Baptist Church in Madison, New Jersey, I heard God whisper in my inner ear, "Greg, be a preacher." That singular event has sustained me through years of schooling and ministry, through bright days and dark nights both personally and professionally.

It didn't take me long to conclude that the words themselves didn't confine me to the pastorate. "Be a preacher" was just a way of telling me to be a proclaimer, an open advocate of the good news that is Jesus Christ. Nonetheless, God's gravitational pull kept me pastoring through long chapters of my life, and even when I stepped away in 2001, it turned out to be what one friend called "an unintentional sabbatical." Less than a year later I was pastoring again, convinced that God had called me back into congregational service.

So here I was, seven years later, at what felt like another vocational turning point, drawn toward the nonprofit my wife and I had created in 2001 and toward my passion for writing, but not sure whether it was God or fatigue talking. Discerning which of these lay behind my discontent mattered greatly to me, given my conviction that it mattered greatly to God. Either path would be consistent with my general sense of calling. I simply wanted to move at God's specific prompting. I wanted to stay centered in God's unfolding purposes for my life. I believed that the wellbeing of my family, my church and my own life depended on it.

In other words, this was a big deal to me, one that called for clarity. I needed God to speak his direction into my life. I needed an inward resolution of my uncertainty.

What I got instead was silence.

While I waited for God to reveal his chapter-turning or chapter-continuing purpose for my life, I made the simple commitment to follow his clear guidance about daily life—to live, in other words, the wisdom of his way. I would, I told myself, stick as closely as I could to the way of Jesus so as to position myself best to hear God when clarity came. I would trust God to give vocational meaning to my daily life and relationships, even if I couldn't see it.

Without fully appreciating the fact, I was actually operating by another dimension of calling. Faith doesn't always take us up to the 30,000-foot level for a big-picture look at the trajectory of our lives; most of the time, we live down in the details, demands, duties and distractions of our daily existence. Faith asks us to live obediently, trusting God to weave something meaningful and whole, maybe something even beautiful out of the seemingly incidental and accidental elements of our daily lives. That we don't always see it doesn't mean it isn't happening.

One of the implications of this realization for me was to redeem myself from the danger of the "purpose-driven life":[45] the danger that I would become so obsessed with the big-picture purpose of my life that I would find myself unable to embrace the little moments of each day, the danger that I would not be fully present to the here and now, which ultimately is the only life any of us will ever get.

four

Matthew 5:8

(8)"Blessed are the pure in heart: for they will see God."

[I spent seven days with the Sermon on the Mount, Matthew 5–7, reading it through each day and then interacting with Jesus about some facet of it that struck me on that particular morning. I have included portions of four of my entries from that week. This is the first.]

The Sermon on the Mount lays out the contours of what Richard Foster calls "the with-God life,"[46] a life in and under God's dominion. Today, I ask for your ongoing work in me toward purity of heart, that I might see you, and seeing you, follow. I'm not seeking the thrill of encounter as much as the clarity—the 20/20 vision—of being where you are and doing what you are doing. For me, your nearness is not just a matter of reassurance; it's the possibility of knowing and living *my* vocation—that is, *your* vocation for *me*.

Heavenly Father, wash me, and I will be whiter than snow.[47] Refine me and remove all dross.[48] Under the influence of refining fire, precious silver is separated from dross, and when the dross is skimmed off the top, all that's left is a metal so pure that the Refiner can see his reflection, undistorted. That's what I want in spiritual terms. I want you to see yourself reflected in me.

A Values-Oriented Life

Jesus challenges us to align our lives, in purity of heart, with his. He makes it clear that our hearts will drive our habits and thereby shape our destinies. He encourages those of us who choose this way by telling us that we will see God.

That's quite an inducement, and given my longing for just this kind of experience, it's not surprising that Matthew 5:8 grabbed my attention. It left the following question lodged in my brain: How was I doing?

As I reflected on the question, it drew me into a reconsideration of my life as measured against the basic principles of a values-oriented existence. It also drew me into a reconsideration of my life as measured against some very personal priorities that had gained prominence at an earlier defining moment in my life.

Serendipity at a Nashville Airport

At the end of a business trip to Nashville in 1993 I found myself having to cool my heels at the airport for four hours. With time on my hands, I wandered through the terminal and into a bookstore, where I came across a book with an intriguing title: *The Soul of a Business: Managing for Profit and the Common Good*. I bought it and settled into a seat near my departure gate for a leisurely read.

The book captivated me from the first page. Its author, Tom Chappell, shared the story of his own pilgrimage toward a new way to think about and run his business, Tom's of Maine, an enterprise focused on all-natural health and hygiene products. Despite the success of his business, Chappell reached a point in his life when success for its own sake couldn't satisfy him. He decided to turn over the day-to-day management of the company to others and enroll in Harvard Divinity School. There, he got back in touch with his own deeply held values and the original sense of purpose that had inspired his wife and him to found Tom's of Maine. He decided to return to the day-to-day management of his company and reshape the way it did business so as to become more self-aware and values-oriented. He was convinced—as the subtitle of his book suggests—that he could manage for profit *and* the common good.

I was particularly struck by Tom's discussion of values and the story of his efforts to get everyone at Tom's of Maine on the same page in terms of them. I could imagine having a similar conversation with the people of the church I was pastoring at the time, and I found myself wanting to pause and reflect deeply about my own personal values.

I set the book aside, pulled out my legal pad, and before going any further, asked God to illumine me. Inwardly quiet, I listened for Spirit-guided insight into the core convictions that anchored my life. I wanted to narrow them down to the few most significant and all-encompassing ones.

Key words came to mind: creativity; balance; adventure; nature; rest; challenge; excellence; testing limits; leadership; integration; integrity; influence; wholeness; essential worth; service; goodness; calling; grace.

Eventually, five core values surfaced as the dominating values of my life. With pen in hand, I tried to express in simplest terms what each of them meant to me:

- **Worth.** I believe that every person and all creation have essential worth. I believe that who I am, as created by God, is fundamentally good, delightful and unique. I believe this is true of others and of creation, too. I believe that the purposes of my life are rooted in who I am and who I am becoming. I believe that the value of my relationships and my work is utterly dependent upon my honoring my true self.

I believe that when I am cut off from my true self I limit and even obstruct the potential of both.

- **Relationship.** I believe that there is nothing that matters more than my relationship with God, family, friends and strangers—even with enemies. I believe that these relationships should be characterized by love, celebration, respect, commitment, service, grace, forgiveness and growth. I believe that these same things should characterize my relationship with creation.

- **Purpose.** I believe that fulfillment is impossible apart from a sense of purpose that is larger than self, a sense of purpose connected with the purposes of God, in partnership with others. I believe in calling, God speaking direction into my life. I believe there is special/ultimate purpose in promoting the fulfillment of others in the context of meaningful relationships. I believe that one's life purpose is a co-creative process with God.

- **Growth.** I believe that life has a built-in growth principle. Living things are growing things. For me this translates into ongoing learning, ongoing development, ongoing progress.

- **Balance.** I believe that the "good life" is a balanced life: one that modulates between activity and rest, community and solitude, other-care and self-care, seriousness and playfulness.

By the time I finished my exercise, a sense of deep satisfaction had overtaken me. I felt like I had been able to get in touch with the strongest convictions of my life. These five beliefs truly did represent the values that anchored me when I was living life most fully.

An afternoon of unscheduled reading had turned into a life-transforming experience. A "Pike's Peak" kind of climber had gained a new and life-altering interest in a "Rock of Gibraltar" kind of life. Someone who had always wanted to soar with the eagles found himself with fresh appreciation for the steady plodding of the turtle. In a life-redirecting way I came to understand that I needed an anchor as well as a sail.

How Was I Doing?

During my extended time in the spiritual wilderness, the life-forming work I did that day in Nashville became something of a North Star for keeping my bearings when every other reference point seemed lost in the dark. I couldn't see God but I could see goodness as reflected in these core values.

Each value, in its own particular way, kept calling me back to my better self. When I gave into feelings of inadequacy because of the church's inability to develop positive momentum, my inner compass pointed me back to my worth, separate and apart from my work. When loathing crept into my attitude toward difficult people, the inner compass put me in touch again with my commitment to love and respect. When I found myself more driven by the desire to prove myself than by a passion for God and others, the inner compass reminded me to get over myself and rediscover the joy of giving my life away. When my dissatisfaction with the world as-it-was kept me from savoring signs of progress all around me, the inner compass restored my sense of gratitude for victories large and small and encouraging milestones along the way. When my obsessive-compulsiveness kept me working past the point of productivity, the inner compass sounded a bell saying, "Time to balance seriousness with a little celebration!"

My compass didn't work flawlessly, despite my knowing my core values by heart and consciously referring to them on an almost daily basis. I remember more than once, for instance, coming to the end of the day feeling constitutionally disabled for the work I was getting paid to do. I'd like to say that the inner voice of my values readily got my attention at times like these, reminding me of my worth. In truth, I put my head on my pillow many a night with doubts and misgivings still firmly in command. My attitude and outlook ebbed and flowed.

I fell short, in other words, of always living up to the values that guided my life. I fell short, and when doing so, I consoled myself in the fact that Jesus had pronounced a blessing on the poor in spirit as well as the pure in heart.[49]

I knew that these values continued to have a hold on me, that they captured the longing of my heart. Expressing dependence on the Spirit, I rededicated myself to a life in alignment with them. I had the sense that I was taking the apostle Paul's advice and claiming his promise, a pledge consistent with the very one Jesus had offered in his blessing of the pure in heart. Here's what Paul had to say:

Finally, brothers and sisters, whatever is true, whatever is noble, whatever is right, whatever is pure, whatever is lovely, whatever is admirable—if anything is excellent or praiseworthy—think about such things. Whatever you have learned or received or heard from me, or seen in me—put it into practice. *And the God of peace will be with you.*[50]

five

Matthew 5:10–12

(10) "Blessed are those who are persecuted because of righteousness, for theirs is the kingdom of heaven.

(11) "Blessed are you when people insult you, persecute you and falsely say all kinds of evil against you because of me. (12) "Rejoice and be glad, because great is your reward in heaven, for in the same way they persecuted the prophets who were before you.

Your teaching is a little tough to take because I am a pleaser. Let me clarify that. I am an autonomy-loving, do-my-own-thing pleaser. The combination of these characteristics has created an odd life for me: I seek both to satisfy and escape the expectations of others. I hear this morning's "blessing" through the filter of this odd kind of pleaser mentality. I'm not proud of this, but here's how I'm feeling right now: I don't want to be hated, excluded, insulted or rejected; at the same time, I don't value inclusion, affirmation, love or acceptance deeply enough to sink my soul into human community. At the end of the day, I want people to like me and admire me and respect me and let me do my own thing, accountability-free. I like my injections of friendship but I like my independence more.

This sounds kind of harsh, but honest self-reflection requires me to admit it. The admission also sounds contradictory, and I guess it is. One impulse in me is drawn toward human community. An opposite impulse in me is drawn toward personal freedom and self-sufficiency. I enjoy being with people and making them happy. I also enjoy going my own way. At one and the same time, I care what people think and yet don't like them second-guessing me. Being high on the empathy scale, I tune in carefully to people's feelings and wants. Being high on the autonomy scale, the feelings and wants of others become wearisome to me.

I'm a walking contradiction; but this realization doesn't lead to resignation. I continue to want to learn how better to integrate the polarities of empathy and autonomy into healthy relationship with friends and adversaries alike. Properly finessed, empathy and autonomy can act like complementary partners rather than the battling competitors they too often are.

As a congregational, civic and organizational leader I have experienced only small doses of the despising that you describe in this beatitude. How, for instance, can my brushes with antagonistic members and those disdainful of religion compare with the life-and-death dangers faced by those to whom your words were first addressed? Still, I know I need your Spirit's work to help me reverse my internal operating system. I need to learn the soul's freedom from a need to be liked, while at the same time engaging true self in true fellowship. This feels like learning to pat my head and rub my stomach simultaneously. I need to learn your ability to blend deep love for people with freedom from their opinions, your ability to invest in fellowship and friendship while experiencing immunity to the constraints and dings that come with it.

I know of no way to do this other than to be centered in you.

Unless I see the world as you see it and experience it as you experience it, unless your mind and heart and will direct mine, I will not be able to pull this off.

Nonanxious Presence

Jesus tells us that we can live in a stressful environment without letting it get to us. He offers a way to experience the anger and anxiety of others with good cheer. In circumstances of persecution and open hostility, this insight comes as a lifeline of encouragement. It also serves us well under lesser circumstances of relational stress.

The morning I came to Matthew 5:10–12, it was that lesser relational stress that registered most with me. As a leader in the context of organizational change, I felt the stress of members on a daily basis. The church was an organization in transition, having to set aside some of its old ways and try out new ways in order to remain relevant in the twenty-first century. This kind of change can be hard on a church, especially one with the deep, historic roots and diversity of a First Baptist. Disagreements prove inevitable. Innovators and traditionalists don't yield ground to one another without some fussing and griping. This "fight" response has a classic counterpart: the "flight" response. Those made uncomfortable by unsettled conditions sometimes choose to leave.

As an empathetic leader, I carried the accumulated stress of church members inside me, and not just the stress directed at me. I knew my only chance for survival, let alone success, as a leader of transition was to take Jesus' words to heart and manage my own emotions. Jesus' words that morning put me in mind of family systems theorist Edwin Friedman's idea of "nonanxious presence," and I turned to his book, *Generation to Generation*[51] for a refresher course on the concept and its practice.

"Nonanxious presence" is a way of living that remains relationally connected to others without internalizing their anxiety. It has a certain paradoxical character about it in that our tendency is either to stay connected by absorbing people's stress or to manage our emotions by distancing ourselves (physically and/or emotionally).

The trick, according to Friedman, is to remain calm and present, to center ourselves apart from people's emotional agendas while hanging in there with them. By refusing to over-function or under-function, we make it easier for people to own issues that belong to them and work through them. We also keep our cool more effectively and introduce an ease of heart that can offset the affliction of over-seriousness that comes with anxiety. In fact, Friedman suggests playfulness as a strategy in emotionally charged social settings. This "often can do more to loosen knots in a . . . relationship system than the most well-meaning 'serious' efforts."[52]

Some of this playfulness of spirit comes through in Jesus' beatitude. "Rejoice and be glad," he says. "Consider yourself blessed!" What sounds ridiculous on the face of it actually begins to make sense once we understand the dynamics of true relationship.

Jesus encourages us to see ourselves not as victims but as people of influence. In case we need an incentive, he tells us that our suffering through relational stress puts us in good company and opens us to the rewards of heaven.

Jesus modeled this capacity to the nth degree, and the author of the Gospel of John helps us understand his secret. We're told in John 13 that only hours before his arrest, Master Jesus washed his disciples' feet; but first we're told the basis on which such behavior was possible: "Jesus knew that the Father had put all things under his power, and that he had come from God and was returning to God."[53] In other words, Jesus was able to act in a calm, selfless manner because he knew who he was, whose he was, where he had come from, and where he was going. Centered in God his Father, his identity and destiny weren't in doubt, so he could relax into self-giving love.

This pattern of inward ease and love appealed to me, but quite frankly I struggled to sustain it during these days in the spiritual dark. Without a sense of God's presence, I began relying on my own strength to remain poised in the midst of relational pressure, and my strength suffered as a result. I had arrived as pastor of First Baptist Church five years earlier feeling physically, emotionally and spiritually ready for the non-anxious-presence balancing act. I could deal with members and their agendas and not get hooked. I could inject a lightness of heart and hope into debates over congregational direction. I could maintain perspective when my role as a facilitator of change made me a target for people's anger, knowing not to take it personally.

Without a kind of restorative spirituality working for me, the cumulative toll of leadership compromised my capacity to keep doing these things. I felt more vulnerable as people's moods came at me from all sides; I let their emotions get to me. I managed my temper, I'm grateful to say. I had experienced a defining moment in high school when my temper got the best of me, causing me to wound my parents emotionally by lashing out at them; I had been determined ever since to guard against this. I kept my temper in check, but that just made me more prone to internalize things. I let the tensions of leadership weigh me down.

A heaviness of spirit replaced my lightness of heart. In private, with Priscilla and a few close friends, I let the sadness and anger and self-doubt seep out. They allowed some of the weight of my stress to fall on them. In professional and social situations I kept this masked as best I could. My innately cheery disposition, carefully cultivated over time, provided me the cover I needed to do so. Occasionally, however, people could see through me. "You look tired, Greg. Is everything okay?" For attentive people, my eyes opened a window into my soul.

My soul was hurting. I needed strength beyond my own. That strength, unfortunately, seemed in short supply. Having lived by the conviction that the Holy Spirit supplies supernatural grace for facing difficulty and that God uses stress to make us stronger,[54] it troubled me that relational stress wore me down rather than built me up.

It became one more factor making me question God's providence. It also made me question my capacity to lead a congregation like

First Baptist. If I couldn't manage my internal response to relational stress, I had no business serving as pastor. It wouldn't be good for me or those I led. What was the message in what I was experiencing? Was God saying, "Grow," or was God saying, "Go"? To use a card-playing metaphor, did I need to hold 'em or fold 'em?[55]

In the push-pull of vocational decision-making (the push being unpleasant forces at work in me and at First Baptist; the pull being forces attracting me to the idea of transitioning out of pastoral leadership and resuming my ministry pursuits through Directions, Inc.), I didn't want to choose a path based on "push"; I wanted the decision to relate to a "pull." I didn't want my decision to be driven by fear, anger or exhaustion; I wanted my decision to be driven by God-given vision, giftedness and passion—by an authentic sense of calling.

In my journey of discovery through the red letters of Jesus, I was coming to terms with my part in the problems I faced. I was coming to terms with the way my carrying others' stress kept me tied in knots and compromised my ability to lead with calm, joy-filled confidence. I had to decide whether I needed to toughen up or alter my course. I knew the stress of interpersonal conflict was wearing on me. I didn't know which remedy to choose.

Here, then, is my report from the trenches. I love the idea that I could keep my head when everyone else is losing theirs. I love the idea that I could manage my stress without checking out physically or emotionally. I find the idea of non-anxious presence irresistible. I also find the actual practice of it much easier said than done.

One of the prayers written in my journal during the months in the red letters of Matthew seems a fitting conclusion to this part of the conversation. It captures the spirit of my praying during those days of stress and God's apparent absence: "Lord, keep me centered in you. Except I see the world as you see it and experience it as you experience it, unless your mind and heart and will direct mine, I will not be able to pull this off." Would God answer this prayer? Time would tell.

six

Matthew 6:25–34

(25)"Therefore I tell you, do not worry about your life, what
you will eat or drink; or about your body, what you will
wear. Is not life more important than food, and the body
more important than clothes? (26)Look at the birds of the air;
they do not sow or reap or store away in barns, and yet your
heavenly Father feeds them. Are you not much more valuable
than they? (27)Who of you by worrying can add a single hour
to his life?

(28)"And why do you worry about clothes? See how the lilies
of the field grow. They do not labor or spin. (29)Yet I tell you
that not even Solomon in all his splendor was dressed like one
of these. (30)If that is how God clothes the grass of the field,
which is here today and tomorrow is thrown into the fire, will
he not much more clothe you, O you of little faith? (31)So do not
worry, saying, 'What shall we eat?' or 'What shall we drink?'
or 'What shall we wear?' (32)For the pagans run after all these
things, and your heavenly Father knows that you need them.
(33)But seek first his kingdom and his righteousness, and all

*these things will be given to you as well. (34)Therefore do not
worry about tomorrow, for tomorrow will worry about itself.
Each day has enough trouble of its own."*

Beyond worry. Living into the peace, confidence, rest and easy
living of trust. Experiencing and relaxing into the presence, power,
grace, provisions, pleasure and guidance of God—God, the decisive
presence at the heart of the kingdom. Seeking you first. Everything
you say in the Sermon on the Mount rides on a God's-eye view of the
world and an invitation to trust the truthfulness of what it implies
about the character, compassion and wherewithal of God.

When I see things from your vantage point I hear my own inner
voice saying, Greg, it's safe to put your life in this One's care. You're
in good hands. You don't have to pretend to be better or anyone
other than who you are. Simply set your affection on your heavenly
Father. Lean into God's love and guidance. Learn God's ways. Allow
this to become the instinctive, habitual way of your daily life.

Here I am, Father. If I am in your hands I am living the kingdom
dream. I love what Jesus' message tells me about you—about who
you are and what you value and how you operate in my world. I am
going to trust everything his message implies about you and relate to
you accordingly.

The Emperor's New Clothes

Given the strength and sincerity of the God-confidence I registered in the journal entry for Matthew 6:25–34, it's a little jarring to
note how quickly I lurched back and forth between trust and distrust.
In the quiet of pre-dawn devotion, Jesus' words convinced me of
God's faithfulness. Then life happened, and I experienced the stress
of God's elusiveness. By the end of the day, the idea of God's providence often felt much less certain than it had when I first greeted the
morning. I struggled to match the faith of the morning to the facts
of the day.

At times, this struggle led me to a courtroom in my heart where I filed formal charges against God for nonperformance. My complaint would go something like this: "Honestly!" I'd say, "Let's deal with the realities of Christian faith in comparison with the claims of Christian faith:

- Your providence or lack of it;

- Answered and unanswered prayer;

- Your presence or absence.

The Emperor's New Clothes or *Overpromise; Under-Deliver*—either one of these could be the title of a book on the subject."

I didn't really want to admit my misgivings, even to myself, but I found myself dealing with a disturbing dilemma: I couldn't explain the universe without God, *and*, at the same time, God's claims didn't wash. I didn't agree with the old complaint in the face of human suffering that God could be either good or all-powerful, but not both. Conceptually, I was willing to accept that ultimate goodness and ultimate power could co-exist in God, despite evidence to the contrary. Still, I felt compelled to complain that God's was a strange goodness and a fickle power.

With these misgivings, how could I do what Jesus challenges us to do in Matthew 6:25–34? How could I lean back into God's arms in trust? How could I yield myself to God's control and God's providence when I felt so strongly that God hadn't proven trustworthy? God, for me, was the father who says, "Jump; I'll catch you" and then sometimes let me fall. God was the superior who held me accountable but didn't want to be held accountable in return.

My mind would take me to stories Jesus told to reinforce his message about the providence of God, stories like the one about a man giving into a late-night appeal from a neighbor. The neighbor knocks on the man's door at midnight needing bread to feed a guest; the sleepy-eyed man gives into his request just to get him out of his hair so he can go back to sleep. The implication of the story is that if even a resistant, irritated householder will share when asked, how much more can our loving God, who never sleeps and always stands ready, be trusted to respond favorably to our requests.[56] I would think of stories like this one and wonder how it sounded to the couple of friends I knew who had both just lost their jobs or to the civilians in theaters of conflict in Darfur, Afghanistan, and Palestine? Was the real truth closer to this? "Don't worry about what you shall eat or what you shall drink or what you shall wear . . . some of the time. It's possible that I may step in and protect and provide for you in response to your prayer; but then sometimes the normal course of human events will press ahead anyway. Your prayers may or may not make a difference. You may or may not starve. You may or may not save your home. You may or may not suffer violence. You may or may not be exploited or enslaved."

I couldn't explain the world without some kind of Intelligent Designer/Manager; but neither could I explain the world with the kind of Personal, Faithful God that was portrayed in the Scriptures. In my reality at the time, God seemed way too passive sometimes and seemingly indifferent.

How, I thought to myself, can we honestly rest in the arms of a laissez-faire Father?

Like it or not, that's exactly what life and my reflections on the world aroused in me under the cloud cover of that disquieting time. I wasn't ready to give up on God—not yet; but neither was I willing to pretend that I didn't notice what looked like a gap between the world Jesus described and the world as I experienced it.

I wanted a better, stronger faith. I wanted to trust God. I wanted to enjoy complete confidence, whatever the circumstances. I couldn't honestly say I did.

seven

Matthew 7:13–14

(13)"Enter through the narrow gate. For wide is the gate and broad is the road that leads to destruction, and many enter through it. (14)But small is the gate and narrow the road that leads to life, and only a few find it."

You tell me there are two roads, one I know too well and another I know in part. This second road far exceeds the other, though I really still feel like I know this mostly by faith. Your Sermon on the Mount, now nearing its conclusion, comes as one long lesson about these two roads, and I see myself at times on one and then the other.

A mere sampling of your teaching in Matthew 5–7, when set over against my life for comparison purposes, highlights the point. I hunger and thirst for righteousness, I really do; but I also hunger for other things—a good steak and a little success, for instance—and these other hungers often crowd out my hunger for you.[57] I do indeed try to treat everyone—friends, neighbors, and enemies alike—with dignity and respect; but I have also felt murder in my heart (or at least taken secret pleasure when misfortune has befallen someone who has made my life miserable).[58] The pursuit of material wealth has never driven me—it certainly hasn't entered significantly into the calculus of my career choices; but I have done some stewing lately about how our investments are doing and what this will mean for our financial future.[59]

When it all comes down to it, I still feel like a novice, taking three steps forward and two steps back. I fully appreciate what the brilliant British apologist G. K. Chesterton meant when he wrote, "The Christian ideal has not been tried and found wanting. It has been found difficult and left untried."[60]

You are honest about this way.

You tell me *it is hard* (literally, "small"; "narrow"). Not complex as opposed to simple, but hard as opposed to easy. Sometimes I have to admit I want life like I want to play the guitar: I'd like to wake up with the ability magically infused into my fingers. You tell me that won't do. This way costs me everything, and I must pay that price if I hope to experience what your way promises.

You tell me *few find it*. I have to allow the shattering possibilities of this to sink in, lest presuming myself to be on the narrow way, I discover to my chagrin that I have joined the crowd on the wide and populated road to destruction. I can always point to anecdotes from my life that reassure me—*Remember when I helped a homeless man find a job? Remember those times I waited patiently in line or those times I responded with kindness to a rude employee? Isn't it encouraging that I am learning to embrace the present moment and get my head out of the clouds?*—but a nagging question remains: What does the prevailing reality of my life reveal?

You tell me this way is hard and that few find it; but you also tell me *it is the way that leads to life*. You tell me that with you at the helm I can actually navigate this path and experience its full potential, beginning right here, right now, with ultimate fulfillment in a future beyond time. I would like this very much![61]

Follow the Directions

My kids, now adults, make fun of my efforts to perfect the art of biscuit making. I will admit that it has been a struggle. My first several tries ended badly, with flat, chewy imitations of the real thing. I tried multiple recipes. I learned to go easy on the kneading. Nothing seemed to work . . . until my son found a recipe in GQ *Magazine* that sounded like a can't-miss solution to my quest.[62]

Lo and behold, the recipe worked. The secret, it seemed, was to keep the flour frozen until ready for use and to fold the dough in thirds, four times, while lightly kneading. I succeeded several times in a row in producing fresh, fluffy biscuits, almost as good as the ones I remember growing up.

Recently, however, I experienced a perplexing setback. I pulled out the recipe, studied it carefully to refresh my memory (it had been a while since my last batch), got out all of my ingredients, and went through all of the steps, as indicated. To my chagrin, when I added the milk to the dry ingredients, I ended up with a thick gravy rather than nice, bouncy dough. I had to add a good dose of extra flour to get the dough where it needed to be. I felt relieved when the biscuits rose the way I wanted them to and tasted great, once baked.

The recipe hadn't suddenly gone wrong, had it? After breakfast I studied the recipe to see if I could solve the mystery. I saw my mistake almost immediately. The recipe called for two cups of flour and one cup of milk. I had used two cups of both.

Here's a cook's basic rule of life: don't expect things to turn out well if you don't follow the recipe.

A Reason for Rules

Funny, isn't it, how obvious this sounds in the kitchen and how confining it sounds in life. One side of human nature resists rules, whatever their source. One side of us wants to make the rules up as we go. We improvise according to convenience, or because of laziness or inattention. Then we get upset when things go wrong.

The great film director, Cecil B. De Mille, once said, "It is impossible for us to break the law. We can only break ourselves against the law."[63] Rules, at their best, are really just explanations of the way things are and how best to get along in light of this.

I have found this to be true particularly of guidelines for living in the Bible, starting with the Ten Commandments and reaching their apex in Christ's guidance in the Sermon on the Mount. We can ignore these lessons if we like, but we'll have no one to blame but ourselves when things go predictably wrong.

I have experienced the built-in consequences of my choices all my life, the good ones and the bad ones. And during this period in the spiritual wilderness I experimented with my own recipes for life without God.

It usually began and ended in my imagination. I might be driving to work, say, or sitting at the desk in my study at home, and the notion would come to me to try on for size a world without God, with life after death stripped from the equation. I would let the idea take form in my mind, and see what was left. How did such a world feel? What did it look like? How might it affect my daily life: my moral choices, my relationships, my work? Oh, my work, I would laugh to myself. It would definitely affect my work! The employment contract of a pastor usually includes the proviso that he or she believe in God!

Furthermore, without God or a final judgment as "carrot and stick" to induce good behavior, the moral universe took on a different flavor. If there were no All-Seeing Eyes watching me and no consequences to my moral behavior beyond the grave, then the only considerations left when deciding on do's and don'ts were considerations rooted in the material world. Could I murder, steal or commit adultery? Could I tell people to jump in a lake if they bugged me? Could I spend the rest of my life indulging myself, like the author of Ecclesiastes, who in describing one chapter in his life, wrote, "I denied myself nothing my eyes desired; I refused my heart no pleasure"?[64]

In truth, the freedom-loving side of my imagination met disappointment when I followed its line of reasoning to a logical conclusion, even in a world without God. I didn't need the author of Ecclesiastes to tell me that "this too was meaningless, a chasing after the wind."[65] I could see that I would still have to respect the boundaries of others and live faithfully within my own, unless I wanted to land in jail or die a very lonely man. Even without God in the picture I could see the wisdom of ethical integrity. Its principles had an enduring power that crossed all cultures and faiths across the full length of human history. This moral wisdom was woven into the fabric of the universe, with or without God. Not only would it continue to stand guard at the boundaries warning me not to cross; it would continue to inform my highest aspirations and feed a healthy sense of shame when I fell short of its ideals.

What these flights of imagination left me with, then, was simply a world without a Great Heart at the center of it. And what that led to in terms of my real-world experiments were simply days of relentless routine and trivial amusement, the magic having been stripped from the universe. Get up. Get dressed. Go to work. Fulfill your duties. Eat out. Eat at home. Watch some TV. Go to a movie. Prepare for the next Sunday. I had been socialized so thoroughly in the Christian culture that I had lost a hearty sinner's instincts. My inhibitions kept me from running wild, so I slowly folded in. I felt increasingly like a well-crafted shadow of a self—no fevered ambition; just a quiet desire to walk away.

Two sources of light remained: reading a good book and companionship. At night, before turning out the light, I could still count on a novel or a biography to take me to another world, a world in which I could forget how much I cared about the unresolved issues of my life. Companionship also continued to mean something—actually, it came to mean more to me than ever. Priscilla; some good friends; ever-reliable family—time with these provided an oasis of joy in the desert that remained.

My excursions into and out of a God-permeated world made one thing clear: Removing God from the recipe didn't produce satisfying fare. It was worse than feeling like God had taken a hike or decided not to speak. There was an emptiness unmatched by anything I had ever known.

Living "As If"

My morning devotions in Matthew and my conscious practice of Jesus' teachings from day to day served as an intentional antidote to the recklessness of my spiritual disillusionment. Noted author and conference leader Rebecca Manley Pippert, in her book, *Out of the Saltshaker*, provided me with the pattern that inspired my strategy:

> Based on my understanding of the gospel I now say to nonbelievers, "Tell God (or the four walls if that is the one you think you are speaking to) that you want to find out if Jesus is truly God. And that if you could feel more certain you would follow him. Then begin to read the Gospels, every day. Each day as you read, something will probably hit you and make sense. Whatever that is, do it as soon as you can."[66]

Pippert suggests this faith experiment because of the transformative effect of obedience. I tried it for another reason, too: I hoped that diving into the Gospels would have a relational effect. My hypothesis went like this: When we experiment with the possibility that Jesus is alive and well and Lord, when we live into the notion that he loves us and wants us to find him and enjoy him forever, we place ourselves in the best possible position to notice his presence and his power.

There was an underlying assumption that prompted my hypothesis and the experiment that grew from it. The assumption was that an experience of true faith was much less likely to happen for someone who sat back in philosophical detachment and demanded evidence or a sign. Relational transformation called for an immersion experience. It called for living "as if" the convictions of faith were true.

My descent into the dark night of the soul left me wondering about the very reality of the One who called himself "the Light of the world." But I found that my anxious skepticism (I didn't really want a world without God, but was prepared to accept it) did nothing to prompt God into a doubt-dispelling appearance, nor did it take me to an alternate way of life worth wanting. My experiment with the red letters of Matthew and with continuing to walk "the narrow way" was a willful suspension of disbelief growing out of a willingness to believe again, a willingness to experience God's nearness again, on God's terms.

In a sense, this was about alignment. It grew out of the conviction that the best way to put God to the test was to rearrange one's life around God's claims and God's promises. It was about the belief that 20/20 vision comes when the "left eye" of trust and the "right eye" of obedience come into focus together, when they become "synoptic."

For better or worse, I remained committed to learning and leaning into the narrow way of discipleship, until or unless life convinced me to do otherwise.

Part II

The School of Discipleship

Is discipleship an all or nothing thing? Must we have it all figured out and everything settled to keep company with Christ? I certainly didn't have it all figured out as my red-letter devotions continued. But the Jesus of Matthew's gospel kept challenging me to:

- admit my need,
- push past my fears, and
- act on the kind of compassion that defined his life.

He clearly wasn't interested in making me comfortable.

eight

Matthew 8:1–3

(1)When he came down from the mountainside, large crowds followed him. (2)A man with leprosy came and knelt before him and said, "Lord, if you are willing, you can make me clean."

*(3)Jesus reached out his hand and touched the man. **"I am willing,"** he said. **"Be clean!"** Immediately he was cured of his leprosy.*

In this story I can experience you and hear you from three perspectives:

As the leper, I can come to you in praise, in need, none too proud to beg, none too careful to keep my distance. I can come confessing my faith and hope, urgent, openly pleading. I can express to you the cry of my heart.

As a disciple, I can stand with you in observant, spellbound discipleship, wearing the easy yoke. Being an apprentice in the first stage of training I can: learn by watching, see how you see things and hear things and relate to others—especially those in need, those not on my care list, those I would avoid—see how you act, witnessing your love expressed in power.

In your steps, I can claim my identity, my authority, my power—
"as the Father sent me, so send I you"[67]—and be missional; that is, I
can be your presence here—your graciousness, your authority, your
healing, redemptive power.

As I appreciate it, I am in all three positions simultaneously. At
one and the same time I am needy, learning and missional. I don't
have to wait until your healing is complete to heal others. I don't
have to wait until I've mastered the lessons of the master to put your
lessons into play. I can be a practicing apprentice. I can allow as
much of my day as possible to be a conscious practice of your way—
how you would be and do if you were in my position.

Finding My Place in the Story

Entering into the story of Jesus each morning necessitated that I
choose a point of view. Would I identify most closely with a person
in need, coming for healing or forgiveness? Would I number myself
among Jesus' disciples? Did honesty force me to see myself in the
company of those Jesus condemned? Or did I connect most closely
with Jesus himself? Did the story in some way evoke my awareness
that I, as a part of the believing community, as a part of what the
apostle Paul called "the Body of Christ,"[68] am the ongoing presence
of Jesus in my world?

There were mornings when my own need drew me closest to those
suffering physically, socially or spiritually. I was the leper, the paralytic, the blind man. I was the parent begging for a miracle on behalf
of my child. I was everyone who ever came to Jesus longing for a
word of blessing or forgiveness. Whether prompted by my feelings of
spiritual vulnerability or the daunting challenges of congregational
leadership or the troubles of others in my circle of concern, these stories gave me permission to say, "Here, Jesus, do what you do so well.
Make things right again. Take the pain of the world away—starting
right here, right now. Comfort the family of my dear friend, whose
sudden death has taken joy and laughter out of our world. Heal this

city, too divided, still, by race and economics. Steady me in my fear, conscious as I am of my limitations as a leader."

In the stories of Jesus, I found permission to confess my sin, acknowledge my hurts, and throw myself on the mercy of God. I could claim the truth Paul discovered later: that God's strength is perfected in my weakness.[69] I could put down the burdens of my life and rest in Jesus. I could feel the renewing warmth of his touch, the ennobling love in his smile, the compassionate concern in his undivided attention. I could step down from my roles as pastor, husband, father and neighbor and acknowledge to Jesus that I would be lost without him. I could give voice to the cries of my heart—cries of sorrow, cries of pain, cries of disappointment, cries of confusion; and yes, cries of ecstasy, gratitude, devotion and praise.

At other times I identified most closely with the disciples. Jesus' power and authority would leave me almost speechless. His words would send an electrical current surging through me.

Sometimes his words would call me up short, as when he lambasted Peter for second-guessing his predictions of an untimely, ignominious and excruciating death.[70] I saw myself in James' and John's ambition.[71] I heard my own uncertain heart when Peter wondered what was to become of those of us who had left all to follow him.[72] And though I generally like to think of myself as a spiritually attentive soul, I had to allow for my own dull-wittedness—my inability to make sense of parables without Jesus' help[73] or the difficulty I had recognizing the connection between Jesus' feeding of the 5,000 and his ability, a little later, to tend to the needs of 4,000.[74]

I knew better than to distance myself in smug judgment from Jesus' hard-headed disciples. I had the benefit of looking backward through time; they had to live in the uncertainties of the moment, not knowing how things would turn out. Furthermore, even with the benefit of retrospect, hadn't I, just like they, asked *why* Jesus had to die on the cross (surely, I had thought to myself, an infinitely creative God could come up with a better solution than this)? Wasn't this just like the disciples? And hadn't I asked, just like they, *what* was to become of me, having decided on Christian discipleship and ministry as my way of life? I knew there were other alternatives. In my fantasies I had even imagined some of them: other professions—architect, artist, attorney, telephone company man (like my dad)—and other lifestyles—adventures around the world, epicurean self-indulgence, or just staying home on Sundays instead of going to church! The decision to center my life in Christ, to give control of everything to God, to devote eight years to theological education and decades to professional ministry—all of that represented the calculated risk of faith. Just like the disciples, I wondered from time to time if I had made a huge mistake. I, like they, needed Jesus' reassurance.

As a disciple, I hung on every one of Jesus' words and deeds, wanting to learn my way into life in this kingdom about which Jesus had so much to say and do. I heard his demands of would-be followers and had to examine my readiness of heart. I heard his charge to tell others about the possibilities of a God-saturated world and had to assess my courage, my commitment, my faith.

I felt the rise and fall of emotions: the early excitement, the mounting tension, the poignancy in the cries of those in need and their ecstasy upon their healing, the gathering gloom, the shock and terror of Jesus' arrest, the fear and disorientation of Friday and Saturday of Holy Week, the surprise and joy of Sunday.

As presumptuous as it was to do so, there were also times when I identified most closely with Jesus. I empathized with him as he battled temptation in the wilderness.[75] I had no difficulty imagining his exasperation with his disciples, given my own occasional frustrations leading would-be followers in the twenty-first century. I felt prophetic indignation well up in me when he overturned the money changers' tables at the temple.[76] I knew myself to be commissioned and empowered by Christ to act with his authority in my world today, and I knew it to be a bracing and exhilarating possibility. Jesus, at these times, was my Exemplar, the model for what my life was meant to be.

I brought memories of playing this role into my devotional experiences, memories like the one of leading a group of adults in a study of the Sermon on the Mount and coming to Jesus' appeal to love our enemies.[77] Everyone in the group had been a Christian for years. Every one of them, supposedly, had decided long before this study to live Jesus' way, even when it turned conventional wisdom on its head. At a bare minimum, every one of them—so I thought—had learned to give the "right answer," even if it contradicted their true beliefs and practices. Nonetheless, one of the men in the group—a father whose adult son had been murdered five years earlier—piped up to say, "There's no way this works in the real world. Until the day I die, I will hate the one who killed my son!" I felt his pain and imagined how excruciating it would be to lose my daughter or my son this way. At the same time, I remained deeply convinced that Jesus' call to love one's enemy—an invitation requiring forgiveness and grace—really was best for everyone concerned, including this father who had locked himself in a prison of inconsolable grief. I had empathized with him openly that morning, but kept Jesus' perspective in the center of the group conversation. As our discussion continued, Jesus' perspective prevailed.

In my morning excursions into the stories of Jesus, I was particularly moved by Jesus' compassion, the degree to which he empathized with others, and the lengths to which he was willing to go to address their need. I found myself praying the persistent prayer that God's Spirit would cultivate this compassion in me, this unconditional, sometimes irrational, ultimately life-giving love for the greatest and the least.

I must also say that it didn't seem right to me to bypass the opportunities for self-examination in Jesus' acrimonious relationship with the scribes, Pharisees and Sadducees. I had to allow for the resistance in my own heart to his claims. I had to own up to my legalism and my hypocrisy. Some mornings with Jesus forced me to confess my religious posturing, my spirituality for show, my vulnerability toward debates over the non-essentials of faith to the neglect of the weightier matters of justice and mercy. I could see in myself the makings of a skeptic, my vulnerability to the pressures of an adversarial crowd, my resistance to change, my demands for proof positive.

I even had to allow for ways I might prove worse than disloyal, ways I might betray Jesus in heart, word or deed. I had to allow for a little bit of Judas in me.

The tendency of others to put me, a clergyman, on a spiritual pedestal actually conspired with my own pride to make these confessions more difficult . . . and necessary. My role in ministry actually heightened my temptation to think and act like the hypocritical, self-righteous people Jesus condemned. How often had I, in my public prayers, thought more about the impression I was leaving with others than the connection I was making with God? How many times had I joined the judgmental crowd in taking cheap shots at a public figure whose fall from grace had created tabloid headlines? Jesus hadn't plucked me out of a scandalous life to follow him; I had grown up in a Christian home and on a steady diet of the Bible's moral teaching. This set me up to lean on my practiced goodness rather than grace when carrying on a relationship with God or comparing myself to others. I cautioned against this in my preaching, knowing all too well how it could infest my own way of thinking.

What's more, I could see the growing ill will of Jesus' antagonists in my own escalating feud with the silent God. Yes, it was true that there was more provocation than dismissal in my outbursts of anger—I wasn't writing God off yet—I was still hoping to get a rise out of God. Nonetheless, I could *imagine* writing God off, which *would* make me an antagonist, indeed. It would even open up a possible Judas in me. Were I to turn from my faith, I would betray Jesus to every person I had ever influenced, beginning in high school when I first became an open advocate of Christian faith. I found that thought particularly sobering.

I much prefer to stand among Jesus' loyal followers when he is matching wits with his adversaries. We can smile and wink to one another, knowing that Jesus will get the better of every occasion. We can roll our eyes disapprovingly, feeling superior to demagogues and blowhards. Few satisfactions match the quiet satisfaction of watching the deflation of an inflated ego. There's something gratifying about being a knowing insider against those who, because of pride or prejudice, don't have a clue.

But the truth is, life has given me enough smack-downs to know that I am not immune to the ugliest elements of human nature. And I am humbled by the realization that signing off on the claims of Christ wouldn't have been nearly as easy were I alive then, in the time of Christ, rather than now. One giant factor changes everything: I live on this side of the cross and resurrection. Religious people of that day had to come to terms with Jesus without the benefit of his entire story and ultimate destiny. His identity remained in doubt and his actions defied important customs of the day. There was more than a little room for sincere doubt about the claim that he was the long-awaited Messiah.

My vantage point shifted from day to day. As the preceding reading shows, there were days when I felt prompted to reflect on Jesus' words from multiple perspectives. I was the person in need. I was the disciple. I was the ongoing presence of Christ in my world. There were opportunities of discovery in each of these points of view, and I wanted the excursion into Jesus' life to prove as productive as possible.

The key was that I find myself somewhere in the story, that I enter into each moment as a participant. Closing the distance between myself and first-century Jesus was, from day one, a core agenda in this journey of faith. If Christ would not come to me, I would go to him.

There were times, however, when the best I could manage was a place in the crowd, looking on with a skeptic's thoughts or a disappointed seeker's heart. The things Jesus said or did would raise questions for me or prompt an argument I had with his claims. Even then, the key was engagement. Reading these stories wasn't an academic exercise or a detached morning discipline; it was a deeply personal encounter with Christ, an opportunity to spend time together—at least in my sanctified imagination.

Would Jesus actually come to me in my Now as I carried on this pattern of prayer? Would he, in response to my going to him, return the favor? I certainly hoped so.

nine

Matthew 8:18–20

(18)When Jesus saw the crowd around him, he gave orders to cross to the other side of the lake. (19)Then a teacher of the law came to him and said, "Teacher, I will follow you wherever you go."

*(20)Jesus replied, **"Foxes have holes and birds of the air have nests, but the Son of Man has no place to lay his head."***

Your response to the teacher of the law confronts him with the homelessness of those who would keep company with you. You carry on an itinerant lifestyle—no home of your own, and thus without the stability or security of steady shelter (one of humanity's three core survival needs). Not that you worry.[78] You trust in God's care for your need to clothe yourself, to nourish yourself, and to rest your head at the end of the day. You have utter confidence in Jehovah-Jireh.[79]

Do I?

There's a lesson here for me: Don't make vocational decisions in life based on security needs. It's not that these considerations don't have their place; it's just that their place succeeds rather than precedes the vocational decision. "How will we make ends meet?" isn't a question to determine whether God is prompting me/us along a certain path; it's a question that follows the ready response, "I/we will follow." And as a question, it is to be worry free. It is to be asked under the banner of confident trust that where God leads, God will supply all we need.

Nomads and Nesters

In preparation for a talk in 2009, I came across a fascinating reprint of a *New York Times* column by Francis Greenwood Peabody dated October 17, 1920.[80] In the column, "A Religion of Adventure," Peabody decried what he saw as a decline of the spirit of adventure in the religion of his day. "Instead of being prized as a discovery, a decision, an achievement, religion has often been commended as a retreat, a rescue, a harbor from storms, a place of rest."

While acknowledging that these facets of religion offer needed comfort for "sick souls," Peabody pointed toward the healthy heart's desire for the religion of Abraham, Pilgrims and Jesus. "Religion is more than a medicine, and a church is more than a hospital . . . It is a Way; it is an Adventure; it is a Pilgrim voyage."

Life Is an Adventure

Readings like Matthew 8:18–20 reinforce the truth of what Peabody wrote. They remind us that Jesus cared very little for settled existence. He stayed on the move throughout his public ministry and, in asking people to follow him, he let them know that they would be exchanging the security of the harbor for adventures on the open sea. "Take up your cross and follow me," he said, daring would-be disciples to risk the life they knew on a more abundant (and daunting) life beyond what they could imagine.

I have no trouble understanding this invitation. It actually appeals to my native temperament. I've always loved big dreams and big adventures. Aiming at the next mountaintop gets my adrenaline pumping. I have a low tolerance for routine. I'm a catalytic leader who likes to get things started and move on to the next challenge. Christ's invitation to risk an adventure with him matches up nicely with the way I'm wired.

It also matches up nicely with my itinerant history from childhood forward. The son of a successful corporate executive, I moved with my family eleven times before my twelfth birthday. New cities, new homes and new friends inspired me. Then came my college and seminary years, during which I moved another six times, followed by five moves in succeeding years as studies gave way to professional life.

Native temperament and itinerant history predisposed me to respond with a hearty "Yes!" when I sensed God tugging on me in a new direction.

It just so happened, in fact, that the word "adventure" played an integral role in the decision Priscilla and I made in 2003 to accept the pastoral invitation of First Baptist Shreveport. "Life is an adventure," we had told ourselves when launching a nonprofit in 2001. We made the conscious decision to take more risks, embrace unexpected opportunities, and live at the edge of our comfort zone. For Priscilla, who prefers predictability over spontaneity, this was a particularly significant shift of perspective.

When I was asked to become First Baptist's pastor, it was Priscilla, in a reversal of roles, who coaxed me into seriously considering the invitation. "Remember," she commented, "we said we wanted to live life as an adventure. Something about this feels very much like an adventure to me." As soon as she said it, I knew she was right.

Bloom Where You're Planted

Mark this, then: My problem during my spiritual wilderness experience wasn't with adventure, but with settling down. The impulse to pull up stakes and move on had become a growing impulse, and my recognition of life patterns reminded me to regard this impulse with skepticism. I didn't want to project my impulses onto the backdrop of the universe and pretend that God was the one leading me. I wanted some convincing intrusion of God's guidance that didn't feel like auto-suggestion.

There's actually an important counterpart to the motto "life is an adventure," and it has its roots just as deeply in biblical faith. "Bloom where you're planted," the popular version of this wisdom goes, and it reminds us to sink our roots into the soil where life takes us.

Addressing those displaced and despondent because of Babylonian captivity in the early sixth century B.C., God urged them to:

> build houses and settle down; plant gardens and eat what they produce. Marry and have sons and daughters; find wives for your sons and give your daughters in marriage, so that they too may have sons and daughters. Increase in number there; do not decrease. Also seek the peace and prosperity of the city to which I have carried you into exile. Pray to the Lord for it, because if it prospers, you too will prosper.[81]

God challenged those who felt stuck in their circumstances to see God at work and embrace their situation with hope. "Bloom where you're planted," God was saying, and the message remains relevant for restless souls across time.

One of my favorite movies is *Groundhog Day*. Bill Murray portrays an arrogant Pittsburg weatherman who gets stuck in a time warp while covering Groundhog Day in the little town where it all began: Punxsutawney, Pennsylvania. Seemingly doomed to repeat the day over and over again, Murray moves through stages of anger, deviousness, destruction and despair.

Finally, he accepts his circumstances and turns his attention toward making the most of the little strip of time and place that fate has handed him. He learns to play the piano. He masters the art of ice sculpting. He comes to the aid of people in need. He finds a place in his heart for others, and they respond in kind. He transcends his original vision of life and, in the process, finds the freedom he had sought all along.

Writing about the movie in an op-ed piece, syndicated columnist Donald Kaul captured the message of the film beautifully. "All of us who feel trapped in dead-in lives," he wrote, can ultimately find our escape by means of "enrichment of the commonplace." He then added that "if it seems simplistic, it is at least as profound as such American icons as 'Our Town' and 'It's a Wonderful Life,' both of which tell us that happiness lies in paying attention to the texture of life rather than its grand design."[82]

So, Which Is It?

"Life is an adventure" versus "Bloom where you're planted." Which is it? In actuality, both principles have their place. Let nomads beware of their wanderlust. Let nesters beware of the complacencies of home.

In my journey through the starlit night, it seemed to me that the key was to live with a willing spirit, engaged in each "here and now" while remaining open and responsive to the Spirit. I would continue to operate by the conviction that God plants us and uproots us and transplants us as God sees fit.

I came to appreciate the dynamic tension in this kind of faith years ago. Under the circumstances of my spiritual dilemma, I remained caught in suspended animation between the two. God was going to have to break through with insight about the path ahead. In the meantime, I remained fixed in my commitments right where I was.

ten

Matthew 8:23–27

*(23)Then he got into the boat and his disciples followed him.
(24)Without warning, a furious storm came up on the lake, so that the
waves swept over the boat. But Jesus was sleeping. (25)The disciples
went and woke him, saying, "Lord, save us! We're going to drown!"*

*(26)He replied, **"You of little faith, why are you so afraid?"** Then
he got up and rebuked the winds and the waves, and it was completely calm.*

*(27)The men were amazed and asked, "What kind of man is this?
Even the winds and the waves obey him!"*

What's the reward for getting in the boat with you? A life-
threatening, boat-tossing, ship-sinking storm at sea! Jesus, your "pay-
offs" for following are confounding! They confound us emotionally,
even if they make a certain amount of sense in light of the way the
world works *and* the way you work. You're not about to cater to the
naïve notion that following you comes with a promise that we will
enjoy smooth sailing the rest of the way.

Our reward for following you is to have our faith immediately tested. Our reward for following you is to get pressed beyond the limits of our current capacity to cope. You have called us, it turns out, not into a comfort zone but into a wild ride: a death-defying, faith-stretching, expectations-shattering, self-confidence-destroying, totally terrifying, ultimately exhilarating Great Adventure.

We weren't bargaining on this. It's what we get anyway!

Waking from your steady, rock-solid rest, you size up the situation and us. "Why are you so fearful?" Jesus, you know the answer; but you ask the question to prod us toward life-altering awareness, toward a new way of being in the world. Because you are with us, we can transcend our fear. We can rest as the waves batter our boat. We can call on you with quiet, steady confidence rather than frantic desperation. If we can lay claim to your power and authority, we can relax wherever we are.

At this point I can't help but think of one of the great stories in aviation history. The test pilots who first approached the speed of sound backed off before reaching it because their planes' violent shakes seemed to confirm fears that the "sound barrier," like a brick wall, would destroy their craft and them along with it. Chuck Yeager risked his life on a different hypothesis. On October 14, 1947, Yeager—then an Air Force Captain and later a Brigadier General—powered his jet toward the speed of sound (Mach 1) and experienced the predictable rattling. Rather than back off, he pushed through and became the first person to experience what he suspected: suddenly smooth sailing on the other side. Describing the moment, he said, "We smoked it out to 1.07 [Mach] . . . I was surprised. There had been such a tremendous amount of anxiety about what the hell would really happen to the airplane at the speed of sound. But all the buffeting quit and the airplane flew very smooth. Nothing happened."[83]

Nothing happened; stillness, not disaster.

Okay, think of life as difficult because it's a training program. Lean into the difficulty, hang tough, with expectancy. When approaching life's versions of the sound barrier, don't let the rattling and shaking unnerve you. Don't back down; press through. When you let go of your fears and relax into the grace of God, you'll experience the extraordinary on the other side.

That's where you're taking me, Lord, and that's where I want to go. That's where I want to be.

Facing One's Fears

Fear may well be my number one enemy. It comes as a voice in my head forecasting failure. It stands like a guard at the door of opportunity warning me against risk. It sidles up to me as if it is my one true friend and interprets the words and deeds of others as rejection.

Fear of failure and fear of rejection have been particularly regular and unwelcome companions most of my life. Son of a gifted, perfectionist mother and high-achieving father, and sibling to three bright and accomplished older brothers, I dreaded falling short of their standards. My own internal drive propelled me, too. In fact, it led others to see me as a person of promise, a notion that in the hands of fear became anxiety that I would fail to deliver on my promise.

Moving almost every year as a boy gave my fear of rejection added opportunity to muscle up. The prolific author, ethicist and theologian Lewis Smedes, in *Shame and Grace*, suggests that the fear of rejection is actually everyone's ultimate fear.[84] Whether this is true or not I don't know; I do know that at some point it got its grip on me. I learned early on how to make new friends; but given that we moved almost every year, I never got to test my capacity to sustain friendships, once made. I worried that I would wear out my welcome. Fear whispered in my ear that to truly know me was to tire of me.

Given that one can't live long without making mistakes and experiencing disappointments in relationship, there's plenty of fuel to keep fear's fire burning. I made it to adulthood with a stockpile of true failure and rejection with which to feed the fire of irrational fear.

My family's move from Oklahoma City to Chatham Township, New Jersey, when I was twelve years old provided a particularly sobering lesson. My new classmates laughed at my accent and didn't care at all for my reluctance to share my homework with them. They excluded me from games and conversation on the playground. They made jokes at my expense. I won them over in time but the memory of those early days in the Northeast left a singed spot on my psyche. I knew what rejection felt like—and I didn't like it at all.

Fortunately, I had an even bigger stockpile of success and love and friendship to fuel a healthier fire. How could I ignore the love of my parents and the loyalty of my brothers or the good fortune of friendships that had stood the test of time? How could I fail to see a hopeful message in grades that came easily or my ability to press through to the completion of a Ph.D.? I had taken on major projects in church, city and denomination, and the feedback was consistently positive, suggesting that when I put my mind to something it usually worked out just fine.

More importantly, I had experienced what felt like God's grace. It happened most powerfully for me my final year at seminary, while working on my dissertation. As the fall of that final year began, I was suffering from disillusionment and failure. Two years after being called to what for a seminarian was an exceptional opportunity for congregational leadership—the pastorate of Graefenburg Baptist Church in Shelby County, Kentucky—the experience had ended badly. A staff member had led an attempted revolt against my leadership, losing his job in the process. I had then resigned, emotionally exhausted by the battle and faced with the prospects of pastoring a church that had become divided over my ongoing leadership. Back in Louisville, grateful for the financial and emotional support of my parents, the love of family and friends, and the encouragement of the seminary community, I pressed forward to complete graduate work.

My dissertation focused on faith development, the evolution and revolutions of a person's faith through time. It drew me into the writings of several people whose spiritual wisdom spoke to my wounded soul. The juxtaposition of my own success and failure—the heady experience of becoming pastor of Graefenburg Baptist Church followed by a deflating departure—made me a willing student, ready to take their wisdom to heart. Elizabeth O'Connor was one of those writers.

On a crisp winter's day, with my back to the sunlit window of my upstairs study at home, I read what O'Connor had to say about a way beyond the struggle to claim a place for myself, a way to enjoy the place that was already mine, "prepared for [me] when the foundations of [my] life were laid." In this place beyond striving and competition, "the ordinary is transcended and one is surrendered to the creative force that moves through all things."[85] I could feel my creative juices flowing again as I took her words to heart. It felt like grace, a hand-delivered message of encouragement from God.

Because of experiences like this one, I knew (in the sense that my faith told me) I didn't need to prove my worth, that God loved me separate and apart from achievement, just as a mother loves her child even before she feels him move in her womb. I knew that God accepted me without reservation, even given the contradictions of my good, bad, beautiful, and sometimes ugly life. I knew all of this but still could forget it in a flash—the flash fire of fear.

Fear played a stress-inducing role during this dark night of the soul. It stole joy from achievement. It cast shadows of doubt across the brightest of moments. It compromised my capacity to know whether God was provoking me or the provocations were coming from some other source (say, a clash between my inner voices of fear and foolish courage).

I knew from grim experience how fear could immobilize me. I knew how it could lead me to minimize risk. I knew how the pleaser in me could keep me from standing firm in the face of opposition or resistance to change. I knew how it could make me run away before I could get run off.

As I struggled to lead First Baptist Shreveport toward renewal, was fear what kept me from leading more aggressively? Did I simply need stronger doses of calm-the-water conviction? Was God the one prompting me to transition out of pastoral ministry, or was I hearing siren songs trying to divert me from the course on which God had put me?

Further complicating things was my awareness that fear isn't all bad. Fear of failure can fuel achievement. Fear of rejection can motivate a person to act in more socially acceptable ways. And sometimes we are right to fear. Fear can serve as a healthy warning of real danger, and sometimes flight can prove just as wise as fight.

What were the lessons in all of this for me? I still wanted to cultivate courageous faith. I wanted to push past fear and attempt things that could only happen in the strength of God. I wanted to silence the nay-saying voice within me. I wanted to overcome the fear of rejection that sometimes hindered me in my relationship with others. The Bible assured me, in fact, that "God did not give us a spirit of fear, but a spirit of power, of love and of self-discipline."[86]

At the same time, I also wanted to face and accept my limitations so as to yield to the actual life that was fighting to be heard, my life separate and apart from what I had manufactured it to be. I didn't want to waste my life trying to be someone I was not or attempting to do what was not in the cards for me to do.

It all sounds complicated, doesn't it? It certainly seemed complicated to me at the time, and I knew of only one way to sort through the complications. If I had any hope of distinguishing my healthy fear from the irrational fear that was working against me, I needed a breakthrough of Divine wisdom and guidance.

eleven

Matthew 9:1–8

(1)*Jesus stepped into a boat, crossed over and came to his own town.* (2)*Some men brought to him a paralytic, lying on a mat. When Jesus saw their faith, he said to the paralytic,* **"Take heart, son; your sins are forgiven."**

(3)*At this, some of the teachers of the law said to themselves, "This fellow is blaspheming!"*

(4)*Knowing their thoughts, Jesus said,* **"Why do you entertain evil thoughts in your hearts?** (5)**Which is easier: to say, 'Your sins are forgiven,' or to say, 'Get up and walk'?** (6)**But so that you may know that the Son of Man has authority on earth to forgive sins. . . ."** *Then he said to the paralytic,* **"Get up, take your mat and go home."** (7)*And the man got up and went home.* (8)*When the crowd saw this, they were filled with awe; and they praised God, who had given such authority to men.*

This is one of the most curious and fascinating of your healing stories. Faith plays a critical role, as it often does in these stories; but it's the faith of these friends that proves decisive. "Seeing *their* faith," you forgive the paralytic's sins; "seeing *their* faith," you give him back the strength of his legs.

It would be worth it for me to consider my dependence on others, the galling and potentially liberating fact that I am not self-sufficient, that my salvation story is not a one-man show, that my hope involves help, that I must in some way let others carry me to you.

The paralytic couldn't hide his paralysis; I do a very good job of hiding mine. I do well tending to the needs of others; I don't do well at all acknowledging my own—letting others know my need and serve me in my need. I don't even do well acknowledging my need to myself!

So Jesus, in my need I am carried to you. I am placed in your presence daily on a bed of prayers, conveyed by the faithful who lift me up to you for a variety of reasons, virtually all of them good.

Carry Me to Jesus

A trifecta of native temperament, personal history, and accident of birth into American culture has predisposed me toward the love of autonomy. I prefer having the steering wheel in my hands (and, yes, the remote). I pride myself in my resourcefulness. I prize self-sufficiency.

The neediness of others doesn't bother me in the least. In fact, I take great pleasure in providing emotional and practical support. The combination of my joy tending to the emotional needs of others and the difference it has seemed to make in their lives convinces me that I have the gift of mercy.

Authors Maria Beesing, Robert Nogosek, and Patrick O'Leary confronted me with the spiritual vulnerability of my life-pattern in their book, *The Enneagram: A Journey of Discovery*.[87] Noting that every personality type has a particular focus of avoidance, they singled out avoidance of need as a central theme for some. As I've already noted, I would say the fear of failure remains my central avoidance but the fear of need would follow close behind.

I hate feeling weak. I can't stand it when I hear myself whine. Though I have no problem stopping to ask for directions—unlike the stereotypical male!—things generally have to get *really* bad before I ask others for help.

Yet that's precisely what my devotional reflections on Matthew 9:1–8 invited me to do. Sometimes I have to admit my weakness, accept my dependence on others, and place my wellbeing in someone else's hands.

The apostle Paul learned this lesson through his struggle with a mysterious "thorn in the flesh." Praying repeatedly for deliverance, he finally got this response from God: "My grace is sufficient for you, for my power is made perfect in weakness." Paul finally accepted his condition and decided to "boast" in his weakness. "For when I am weak, then I am strong."[88]

Biblical faith tells us that God's strength often comes wrapped in human flesh, that God sends people our way to ease our pain, offer us encouragement and supply our need. We can't "do life" alone.

I like the way the author of Ecclesiastes puts it:

Two are better than one,
*   because they have a good return for*
*   their work:*
If one falls down,
*   his friend can help him up.*
But pity the man who falls
*   and has no one to help him up!*
Also, if two lie down together, they will
*   keep warm.*
*   But how can one keep warm alone?*
Though one may be overpowered,
*   two can defend themselves.*
A cord of three strands is not quickly
*   broken.*[89]

My wife and I experienced a powerful breakthrough some sixteen years into our relationship when a counselor helped me confront my inner resistance to my own need. Loathe to admit any dependence, I had done a poor job of calling on Priscilla's complementary strengths, and I harbored unexpressed wants out of some perverse notion that I should be able to get along fine without asking that these wants be met. I was a big-idea person who sometimes struggled to translate my big ideas into workable action plans. I would have benefited from a partner who could bat around ideas with me, and Priscilla was just this kind of practical, action-oriented person. I sometimes felt like I was a little boy locked in the body of a grown man. At times like those what I wanted was tenderness, and Priscilla, without my seeing it, had wells of pent-up tenderness to share.

When I finally opened myself to her love and strength and got better about expressing my wants, I discovered to my relief and pleasure that she was more than happy to respond with warmth, wisdom and understanding. She had actually felt frustrated because I wouldn't let her nurture me. She wanted to feel needed!

During my dark night of the soul, I felt my need acutely. Still, I had a hard time reaching out because my struggle seemed so private and even threatening. On the other hand, I didn't resist my need entirely, and I am grateful for everyone who helped keep me going.

Priscilla was there for me on a daily basis, and she listened with a loving and attentive heart when I processed my pain. She managed her anxiety about our clouded future so that I could talk out loud about my own uncertainty. She boosted my spirits by pointing out my strengths and helping me keep things in perspective. I remember in particular one of the things she told me when my faith was weakest: "I can tell you this," she said. "You may be struggling with your faith but your preaching and teaching is stronger than ever. Something really vibrant is coming from the way you are wrestling with God."

It wasn't all seriousness with Priscilla, either. She made sure we kept fun in our lives. "Let's take a ride on the motorcycle and experience the countryside," she'd say. "Let's spend the night in Dallas and have dinner on a patio somewhere," or, "Let's give our friends a call and invite them over for steaks."

Priscilla's support mattered most to me; but I benefited from other support as well. What, for instance, would I have done without the group of Louisiana pastors from as far as 120 miles away who gathered at my initiative for monthly interaction? We did talk shop, to be sure, comparing notes on issues like preaching, pastoral care and the latest books we had read on leadership. More importantly, we shared our stories and our struggles, our joys and our frustrations. We let our guard down and talked about our foibles and our doubts. Every one of us had times when we needed to put our circumstances in front of other items on the agenda, and I found a safe and welcome place to do that, repeatedly. What I remember most about these times is not some breakthrough of insight that came through what they said to me. What I remember most is their supportive presence. They affirmed my worth. They sustained me with their unconditional acceptance. They made me know that I was not alone.

Other friendships provided additional encouragement. I had confidants in Shreveport and in other cities with whom I could process life over lunch or by phone or e-mail. Networks of relationship forged over time—a childhood friend, a brother-in-law who was more like a brother by blood than by marriage, friends from earlier pastoral settings, and colleagues in local and denominational life made it possible for me to share my struggle and keep as much of it as possible from spilling out inappropriately in the church.

I am also grateful for others who, without even knowing how badly I needed it, "carried me to Jesus" on the strength of their prayers. Here's one of those prayers, written on a prayer ministry card and placed in my office mailbox by someone at church who had no way to know how timely their prayer and encouragement were:

Greg, today I am thanking God for you and your leadership and for all the ways he has prepared you to lead this church at this time. I pray for your spiritual and physical health; for your ability to pace yourself and your church; for renewal of soul, body and mind; and for encouragement when you need it most.

There were, indeed, times when the only thread of faith holding me was the faith thread of friends. My own had come unraveled. Theirs, I suspect, sustained me. When I couldn't muster the confidence, conviction or hope to go to Jesus, they, by prayer, kept doing the job in my stead.

I'm still slow to admit my need but as a recovering independence addict I am learning to savor strength beyond my own. I can count more than my fair share of faithful friends whose love and loyalty have stood the test of time.

twelve

Matthew 9:20–22

(20)Just then a woman who had been subject to bleeding for twelve years came up behind him and touched the edge of his cloak. (21)She said to herself, "If I only touch his cloak, I will be healed."

(22)Jesus turned and saw her. **"Take heart, daughter,"** *he said,* **"your faith has healed you."** *And the woman was healed from that moment.*

Jesus, it doesn't take a great leap of the imagination for me to project myself into the mind and heart of someone who for twelve years has been dealing with a problem that creates:

- physical distress,
- emotional shame and embarrassment,
- social ostracism, and
- spiritual/religious alienation—problems for relationship with God and the community of faith (given Jewish purity codes at the time, which would make this woman unclean and untouchable).

I can imagine this woman making her way through the crowd, full of desperate desire and terrifying fear. In her urgent need she was willing to risk condemnation, having calculated the odds of exposure and judged that the risk was worth it. In the midst of a jostling crowd, what were the chances, anyway, that you would notice a touch of your garment?

Hers was a premeditated breech of propriety, totally out of step with the stringent codes of the day. It was also an act of faith and hope right in the wheelhouse of your pleasure. Though she didn't know it, she was lunging into the style of living you were trying to promote. She was exemplifying the kind of life into which you invite us all.

You weren't about to let her think that she had stolen a blessing. Lest she slip away misunderstanding what had happened, you define the experience for her and reveal to everyone in earshot something of your understanding of the world as God sees it and guides it. It is a world centered in compassion and unconditional love.

"Take heart, daughter; your faith has healed you—[has made you whole]." In saying this, you embrace her with words and announce the wholeness that comes with God's compassion. It brings to my mind the explanation of a judge when I was being considered as a juror in a civil trial. He defined the standard of judgment in a civil case as what it would take to "make the plaintiff whole"—what it would take to return the plaintiff, as closely as possible, to his or her condition before things went wrong and, barring that, to be compensated in terms that fairly reflected the financial value of damages.

You do something better than "compensation." You use your power and authority to reverse irreversible destruction, pain and suffering. Court systems try to figure out monetary equivalents for pain and suffering, a ridiculous effort, an apples-for-oranges—or better, a peanuts-for-diamonds—exchange.

Lord, thank you for your extraordinary power and good will, your loving reversals. I'd love for you to turn some of that on me!

Like the woman in this story, I find my desperation for you mounting, Lord. I know my need for something more than self-constructed spiritual development, and I appeal to you for the one, decisive thing I can't muster: your supernatural power, your intervening Spirit, your initiating grace. Unless I have this to hope for, I'm all out of hope. I know I don't have the capacity to produce the transformations I need and for which I long. I'd be satisfied merely to touch your garment!

Second Naiveté

Karl Barth was one of the towering theological figures of the twentieth century and author of a thirteen-volume systematic theology, *Church Dogmatics*. One of the well-traveled stories about him relates to a question asked of him by a journalist. "Dr. Barth, how would you summarize what you wrote in those thirteen volumes of theology?" Barth thought for a moment and then answered: "Jesus loves me, this I know, for the Bible tells me so."

This is second naiveté.

Coined by the philosopher Paul Ricoeur, the term "second naiveté"[90] describes an experience of renewed simplicity that comes on the back side of critical engagement with Scripture and religious thought. Unlike the original naiveté of a child who accepts things at face value, second naiveté comes as a gift to those who have:

- reflected deeply on the mysteries of existence;

- lived their way into their complicated lives;

- seen beyond pat answers;

- developed a more nuanced, sophisticated faith.

Second naiveté embraces complexity without getting tangled in its threads. It finds a way to integrate complexity into a new kind of wholeness, while remaining open to life's and God's mystery.

I have often thought about warnings I heard before going off to seminary (these warnings came not from family but from well-meaning acquaintances). "They'll undermine your faith there. They'll cause you to question the things you've been taught. They'll expose you to other belief systems. They'll introduce doubt. They'll ruin you."

It turns out they were right that seminary would challenge my convictions and expose me to foreign ideas. They were right that this intellectual journey and the life that has flowed from it has had a lot less certainty than it would have had I gone to an indoctrination center rather than the seminary I chose. Doubt has played a bigger part of my life than it probably would have, and the complications to which I was introduced along the way have at times left my head spinning. But that's only half the story (actually, given my gratitude for seminary, I'd have to say it's far less than half the story).

Yes, with theological education came questions—but new possibilities as well. It coaxed me into wrestling creatively with questions like these: What's with the idea of the Trinity, anyway? How can God be three and one? What accounts for the differences of worldview between the Old Testament and the New Testament? How, for instance, do you deal with Joshua 6 and the destruction of Jericho in light of the non-violent teaching of Jesus, and what does this say about the nature of God? And how about the differences between the four gospels? Did Jesus really speak all of those long discourses that appear only in John? I actually went through a period of time when I lost confidence in the gospel of John because it was written later than the other gospels and seemed so odd by comparison. But ironically, from the perspective of someone who would use my lapse of confidence to illustrate the danger of theological education, further study restored my confidence. It actually deepened my appreciation for the richness and depth of John's portrayal of Jesus.

I wouldn't change my decision to go to seminary for the world. Yes, education can be dangerous. It's not mere coincidence that someone who has gotten a little education under their belt is called a sophomore, which literally means "wise fool."

The fact of the matter is, learning complicates things and forces one to deal with the more complex mechanics of life and faith. But when you plunge into this you go on a journey that can bring you out the other side richer in appreciation for the breadth, depth and mystery of it all.

For all the struggle that came in my dark night of the soul, one of the daily satisfactions was entering into the life of Jesus with this second naiveté. Having learned the disciplines of the historical-critical method of biblical studies, having wrestled with divergent theological schools of thought, having lived my way into the difficulties and complexities of twentieth/twenty-first century life, I found myself able to relax with simplicity into the text, trusting myself and releasing myself to the experience without a critical scholar's detachment.

This experience is something like what happens in golf when you've practiced the mechanics of your swing until the sum total of all the mechanical components of head, arms, elbows, hands, shoulders, hips, legs, feet, and swing become second nature. You no longer have to think about each piece in an awkward, self-conscious way. It just flows.

No one would say, "I don't want to spoil the innocence and purity of my golf game by taking lessons." We know that to get the most out of our game, we need to learn the mechanics and practice them until they become more natural. We accept that there is a stage in the process when it all feels un-natural. But if we stick with it, the breakthrough comes, and when it does, we find ourselves enjoying the game as never before.

It may sound like a logical impossibility for someone suffering from doubts, as I was, to experience the stories of Jesus this way. All I can say is that during these morning exercises I was able to suspend disbelief and keep my doubts in perspective enough to let Jesus' stories and words speak for themselves. I was able to meld all that I had learned through years of biblical studies into something more direct and personal than scholarly analysis.

Based on my experience as a lifelong student of faith and Scripture, I can, without hesitation, encourage anyone to cultivate their interest, explore broadly and deeply, remain open to new and divergent perspectives, and invite God to use it all to bring you into closer, more fruitful relationship together.

There's no need to resist the stages in the process that seem disorienting or mechanical. There is a time, as well, for stepping back in critical analysis. All of it has its place.

But for my money, the best part is on the back side of thoughtful, faithful growth, when all that one has learned and experienced converges in this second naiveté, the renewed wonder and simplicity of a child of faith. That I could experience it to a degree during my dark night of the soul was a real "God-send." Being able to do so in my morning engagements with Scripture kept a spiritual trail uncovered in the direction of my hope that this might, one day, become the prevailing experience of my whole life.

Life presents many formal and informal lessons to learn; and if we're open to scholarship and the challenges of science and politics and competing truth claims and people from all walks of life—if we're a receptive, inquisitive, teachable person—we will go through periods that challenge our convictions and reorient us. The more we know, the more we will be humbled by all we don't know.

This won't defeat us. Instead, we will find ourselves holding life loosely and gratefully. And when we come to the Scripture, we won't ignore all the scholarly lessons that sharpen our engagement with Scripture; but we will find ourselves coming to the text with a child's simplicity and openness of heart.

My morning experiences with the Red Letters of Jesus felt this way. I wasted little time questioning the historicity of miracles or second-guessing which sayings were the original words of Jesus and which were elaborations of the early church. My interests weren't scholarly—despite the fact that I had my scholarly toolkit nearby—they were deeply personal. I simply wanted to touch the hem of

Christ's garment. I wanted to experience the warmth and power of his love. There was very little detached or analytical thought about this, though I didn't check my mind at the front door. I simply let the child in me come out to meet the One who has always had a special place in his heart for children.

I would never tell someone to steer clear of scholarly disciplines or to turn their back on the search for truth, wherever it leads. However it remains a worthwhile aspiration for the journey of discovery to bring us to a place that feels like home, where we relax and release ourselves into our faith. That's where the immediacy of life with God becomes the strongest possibility. I didn't just want to learn more about Jesus; I wanted to know Jesus, up close and in a personal way.

thirteen

Matthew 9:35–38

(35)*Jesus went through all the towns and villages, teaching in their synagogues, preaching the good news of the kingdom and healing every disease and sickness.* (36)*When he saw the crowds, he had compassion on them, because they were harassed and helpless, like sheep without a shepherd.* (37)*Then he said to his disciples,* **"The harvest is plentiful but the workers are few.** (38)**Ask the Lord of the harvest, therefore, to send out workers into his harvest field."**

Matthew 9:36 offers an observation that touches me deeply. You are moved with compassion as you look on the multitudes. You have become a magnet for people in need. Once the word gets out that there's someone with the authority and desire to address your problems and defeat them, conquer them, set you free, you are going to drop everything and come running.

You are looking out at a sea of human need. You are looking out at an endless ocean of people whose sense of privacy, shame and guilt is no match for their hope, their longing, their faith. Your compassion gives you eyes to notice. It also sends a signal that *they* notice. It makes it safe for them to come running to you.

My reading of the situation is colored by a comment a colleague of mine made to me recently about an openness he had seen in unchurched people to talk about their problems. In the founding days of his church he was surprised and moved by how willing people were to show up and confess the nature of their needs.

What I'm thinking, what I know, is that compassionate people—which is what I aspire to be—and compassionate congregations—which is what I pray for FBC to be—don't have a problem working up a "prospect list." They don't find themselves wondering where the needy people are. God gives compassionate people eyes to see that they are all around. Moreover, compassion actually draws people out of hiding. Before long, you don't have to go looking for them because they come looking for you!

Your call to prayer—"Ask the Lord of the harvest to send out workers"—puts the rest of the disciples and me on notice that you are looking for people, for congregations, with a heart for people who are hurting. You are asking us to pray for the formation of a volunteer army of compassion that will fling itself into this sea of human need.

Lord, I want to live in the middle of this action. I want to be an answer to this prayer. I want the church I serve to be an answer to this prayer: a magnet for hurting, hopeful people who are being healed, right along with us, and transformed, right along with us, into wounded healers.

Raise my CQ—my compassion quotient. Raise the CQ of others in the church. Open doors of service and inspire us to be the healed people who spread your fame; once-blind people guiding others to the Sight-Giver and beggars telling other beggars where to find bread. And give us the capacity to do this down in the details of people's actual lives, where romantic notions of compassion must give way to the realities of people who aren't always likeable and problems that aren't always easily solved.

What Does It Cost to Care?

I still have vivid memories of a particular presentation I heard at a national small group conference I attended in Orlando in 1989. Dr, David Paap, Program Director for Stephen Ministries,[91] addressed the question, "What Does It Cost to Care?"[92]

He grabbed our attention at the outset with the story of "Peg": a recently divorced single parent, new to the city and new to Christian faith, whose needs were many and whose church, through benign neglect, ultimately failed her. The congregation simply didn't understand the true cost of caring, and their preoccupations with the needs of the organization trumped their concern for a woman whose needs were "as wide as they were deep." They received her warmly when she came to church, mistaking friendliness for true friendship. They responded to her desire to deepen her Christian life by giving her a volunteer position in the church kitchen for Wednesday night suppers. They tried to fix her up with a single man her age, oblivious to the unresolved grief she still experienced over her divorce. They had no plan for dealing with the special needs of single parents like her, and when her work schedule changed, they had no plan for serving her or anyone else whose nighttime work excluded them from the normal hours of church programming. Peg increasingly felt discouraged and alone. Telling herself that it might just take time to get closer to God and closer to people, she continued to attend church for two years, schedule permitting. When it became clear that patience had not resolved her dilemma, she quietly dropped out of church life altogether.

I've kept my notes on the specific guidance he provided that day for paying the price of true compassion, and I have referred to those notes frequently in leading the churches I've served.[93] But it's his title question that lingers most in my mind, knowing as I do how easy it is for me and those I influence to neglect this fundamental facet of Jesus' life. Jesus experienced something a good bit more than romantic sentiment when, according to Matthew 9:36, "he saw the crowds . . . and felt moved with compassion."

Jesus understood the cost of caring and readily paid it. He called people into relationship, accepting them as they were. He met them at their points of need, often seeing beneath the surface, as when he recognized the cot-conveyed paralytic's longing for forgiveness. He offered not just friendliness but true friendship, gathering them into a fellowship of camaraderie and joy.

Jesus saw those in the crowd neither as impediments to nor as implements of his operational agenda. Instead he saw them as people of worth and invested in them so that they could overcome their problems and reach their full potential. He introduced them to God and the coming kingdom and ennobled them with an invitation to participate in his life's work. Equipping and releasing them, he gave them freedom to test their wings and even to fail, always ready to bear with them patiently and help them "fail forward."[94]

Beyond this, Jesus was transparent with them, sharing from the heart and making himself vulnerable to them. Ultimately, he put his very life on the line for them, remaining loyal and devoted to them even when their loyalty to him collapsed in self-preserving fear. He died with their needs and the needs of a hurting world at the center of his concern.

This compassion of Jesus, a compassion that translates heartfelt sentiment into self-giving sacrifice, is the standard against which I measure my own. I remember the specific occasion during my junior year at Baylor when, having pondered this very scene in the Gospel of Matthew, I first prayed: "God, may Christ's kind of compassion take root in my life until my love for others matches his." This has remained a prayer refrain for me ever since.

In an interesting kind of way, I felt energized again when my devotional experiment with the red letters of Jesus brought me back to Matthew 9:35–38. The narrator's observation about Christ's compassion reminded me what matters most. It reminded me why I felt called into career ministry in the first place. I didn't say yes to career ministry because I wanted to stand at the helm of an impressive institution. I said yes to career ministry because I wanted to help people experience life at its best. John 10:10 is the theme verse of my life: "I have come that they might have life and that they might have it more abundantly." My sense of purpose is centered in the desire to help people discover and experience life at its best.

I will speak for myself. I find it all too easy for the demands of my day and the details of organizational leadership to take me a few degrees off course. Rarely does a kind of Dr. Jekyll and Mr. Hyde transformation occur, turning me into an ogre. Most often, it's just that responsibility gets in front of relationship and mere courtesy takes over for true compassion. I see less; I care less; I stumble past the opportunities of love.

In the course of this spiritual funk of mine, I couldn't rush God toward a resolution but I could do this: I could keep tuning my heart again and again to Christ's kind of compassion. I could keep looking for ways to love. As it had for years, Matthew 9:36 continued to serve as a touchstone, an almost daily source of inspiration and self-examination, whether I was navigating traffic or standing at the bedside of someone in the hospital. It made me want to treat store clerks and other service providers with respect. It made me want to listen with understanding to the person whose views on politics or the church were different from my own. It served as my number-one incentive for participating in community-based organizations, coming into relationship with people I would otherwise never have gotten to know. I couldn't conjure up God, but I could remind myself to keep people in front of programs. I could work on having more patience. I could look for opportunities to lighten people's loads and extend encouragement to them. I, in the manner of my Master, could embody the grace of God to the lovely and the irascible alike.

fourteen

Matthew 10:16

(16)"I am sending you out like sheep among wolves. Therefore be as shrewd as snakes and as innocent as doves."

Jesus, you tell me that I am a sheep in the midst of wolves. I am an innocent in the midst of predatory beasts. I am a naïve, gullible, trusting, in some ways defenseless person in the midst of wily, malevolent, self-serving schemers. I am an herbivore in the midst of carnivores. I am a messenger of peace in the midst of breeders of conflict. I bring a "yield-one's-life-to-God" message to social Darwinians, putting myself at the mercy of those who believe in survival of the fittest.

I enter a world where, by the world's standards, I am well down the food chain, easy prey for those who may decide to have me for lunch. You give me a new survivor's guide: Be shrewd as snakes and innocent as doves.

Jesus, you were the Exemplar of this way, the ultimate Machiavelli (with a loving twist!), always one step ahead of your enemies. Even in the end, when they thought they had finally bested you, it turns out you were using their ultimate weapon for your own purpose.

They killed you, thus becoming instruments in your climactic work of redemption. They sent you into the dungeon of death and, once there, you set us captives free.

Lord, this tension between the snake and the dove is one that I can manage only in your Spirit.[95] Your Spirit in me is the source not only of my speech, but of every quality that keeps me innocent and wise at the same time.

In my own strength, I fall off the rail on one side or the other—self-serving or overly trusting. Abide in me. I will abide in you.

The Word beyond the Word

Jesus' teaching sometimes only makes sense to someone with a porous worldview. Only someone who remains open to out-of-the-box insight can even begin to decipher a statement like, "Be shrewd as snakes and innocent as doves."

The original disciples of Jesus, those who in the previous Matthew entry prepared to head out two by two as advocates of Jesus' agenda, would never have followed Jesus in the first place had they not been open to a new voice saying surprising things. After all, Jesus regularly punctured holes in the tidy assumptions of their culture and its time-honored version of religion. Had they not been willing to have their worldview challenged, they never would have given Jesus the time of day.

"You have heard that it was said . . . but I say to you," Jesus said five times in the Sermon on the Mount, each time altering the moral bearings of the disciples and others while insisting that he had come not to abolish the law but to fulfill it.[96] "Be shrewd as snakes, innocent as doves," he now says, introducing yet another paradox into the vocabulary and practice of their faith.

There is a form of faith, a way some people choose, that glorifies the cold certainty of a closed mind. Locked into a well-defined framework of conviction, they ignore and even resist the inconvenient truths that life presents them. Joel Barker calls this the paradigm effect.[97] It enjoys the advantage of clarity and order. Unfortunately, it prevents a person from ongoing growth into the real world, a world vastly richer with truth, beauty, goodness, and love than any one system can contain.

Jesus showed little respect for humanly conceived systems. He called us to a person, not just to a perspective. He called us into relationship with the infinite God.

For those who are bent on the innocence of the dove to avail themselves of the wisdom of the snake, they must remain malleable, teachable, open to an expanded, even altered worldview. They must transcend the mere morality of their religious tradition and discover a canny morality that pleases God. They aren't likely to do this as long as they restrict themselves to tradition-reinforcing sources of authority.

Of the many gifts that came to me from my parents, one of those I appreciate the most is their openness to the extraordinary world. Our living room wall was lined with books on every conceivable subject (Long before the advent of the Internet, my dad prided himself on his ability to find on our shelf a reference related to any question a person might ask.). We built many of our vacations around excursions to historic sites and centers of art and culture. My parents encouraged my brothers and me to ask questions and research our way to answers. They modeled relationship-building with people of other cultures and faiths. They collaborated with us in our interests in science, math, history, art, spirituality, sports, Scouting, student government and music (even when it drew us into rock music, with drums, guitars, keyboards, and amplified rehearsals in the basement).

My parents were devoted followers of Jesus and committed leaders in the Baptist churches we belonged to wherever we moved; but they saw no contradiction between conviction and curiosity, between goodness and growth. They anchored us in faith and facilitated flights of discovery. They knew that by encouraging us to think for ourselves and explore, the risk existed that our journeys might lead us along paths other than those they would choose for us; but they deeply believed that the risk was worth it. They believed, in fact, that this risk was essential if we were to have a chance at experiencing and owning a rich life we could call our own.

Some might see this background as a liability rather than an asset, arguing that I could have avoided my crisis of faith had I gotten grounded in a longer, stronger set of core beliefs and steered clear of uncomfortable questions. I would insist on just the opposite. My problem wasn't openness of mind; it was outgrown assumptions, and this openness of mind made it easier for me to look and listen for God in both conventional and unconventional places. It increased the possibility that I might experience "the Word beyond the Word," that is, insight from God from some source beyond the Bible.

Theologians use the term "general revelation" to affirm God's unlimited capacity to make God's self known, whether it be through the person of Jesus, Scripture, nature, the unfolding course of human events, the inner witness of the Spirit, or some other source, likely or not. These sources of truth won't contradict each other if they truly point toward the One God. Quite the contrary, they can provide a corrective, a breakthrough of new awareness that protects us from the paradigm effect and its blind spots.

There are two wonderful and related stories in the book of Acts that actually show this principle at work: Acts 11:1–18 and 15:1–35. The early church, which initially was a Jewish subgroup that believed in Jesus as the fulfillment of their hopes for a messiah, was forced by experience to reconsider the exclusive Jewishness of God's saving plan. Gentiles were responding to the proclamation of good news in Christ, and the Holy Spirit was putting God's seal of approval on their conversions with dramatic demonstrations of power.[98]

Their astonishment that Gentile followers had received the same gift of the Holy Spirit that had come to Jewish Christians led them to embrace Gentiles within the family of faith[99] and then to relax ritual expectations of them.[100] Their openness to the Spirit liberated

them from the paradigm effect. It drove them to consider new possibilities and then return to the Scriptures to test the truth of their
discoveries.[101] They came to the conclusion that their new insight
and experience matched up with wisdom that had been in the Bible
all along.

According to the Bible, God is unlimited in the ways God can
make God's self known. God will even use an ass to speak to us![102]

Part of what I experienced during my time in the spiritual wilderness was a shaking loose from my own life version of the paradigm effect. My disorientation had to do, in part, with ways I had
to rethink, re-feel, and rearrange my life. At one level I knew this
to be true at the time; at another level it would only become clear
later. To the degree that I did know it to be true, I imagined that
God might need to get my attention in places and ways other than
where I normally looked for God. I suspected that God might need
to do this because these expected places for finding God had become
rutted with conventional thinking.

I couldn't have articulated it this clearly at the time. I simply
maintained the following pattern of behavior: I would keep studying
the Bible, anchoring myself in this essential reference point for faith;
but I wouldn't stop there. I would also continue to open myself to the
wisdom and light of God in the sacred and the secular, the explicitly
biblical and the other-than-biblical sources of light. I would avail
myself of God's beauty, goodness, and joy however God chose to
drop it in my lap. I would listen for God in likely *and* unlikely places.

Part III

Getting Stretched

You can't keep company with Jesus without having your assumptions, your attitudes, and your capacities stretched. The challenge is for faith to get stretched without snapping. The claims and commands of Christ put my credulity to the test, presenting a life worth wanting, but worth wondering about too.

fifteen

Matthew 11:28–30

(28)*"Come to me, all you who are weary and burdened, and I will give you rest. (29)Take my yoke upon you and learn from me, for I am gentle and humble in heart, and you will find rest for your souls. (30)For my yoke is easy and my burden is light."*

"Come to me"—this is your most personal invitation anywhere in Scripture. You call us, first, not to a task, but to a relationship—a relationship with you. You offer us rest.

You offer us rest at every level. *You offer physical rest,* a break in the action that allows us to take the loads off our backs—off our feet. *You offer mental rest,* a break from the mind-straining effort to figure things out, sort things through, plan, process, solve problems, wrestle with doubts, etc. *You offer emotional rest,* a break from fear, anxiety, guilt, anger, resentment, sadness, grief, depression, foreboding, despair. *You offer spiritual rest,* a homecoming for the soul. *You offer relational rest,* relief from the pushes and pulls of people.

Jesus, the rest you offer is a rest that can still occur in the midst of labor. You offer us the "easy yoke," the "light burden."

I am free. I am bound. You ask me to bind myself willingly to you as a co-laborer. You say that if I will keep company with you, walking and working and resting right alongside you, I will learn a new and healthier life balance.

There are times when my experience with the red letters feels like this. Just reading your words today and reflecting on what they mean for me makes me feel like I am falling back into a pool of clear, buoyant water. Now, as you take me by the hand, reading by reading, walk me into the new light of life. In the midst of life's daily demands, recreate me—let me be born anew.

Resting in God

In his classic, *Confessions*, St. Augustine wrote, "You have made us for yourself, O Lord, and our heart is restless until it rests in you."[103] This statement had the ring of profound truth for me from the first time I heard it, which accounts for why I love it so and also for why Matthew 11:28–30 is one of my favorite sayings of Jesus.

I first remember hearing his words at the end of Matthew 11 in the King James Version. His message became even more vivid for me when I read Eugene Peterson's paraphrase in *The Message:*

> Are you tired? Worn out? Burned out on religion? Come to me. Get away with me and you'll recover your life. I'll show you how to take a real rest. Walk with me and work with me—watch how I do it. Learn the unforced rhythms of grace. I won't lay anything heavy or ill-fitting on you. Keep company with me and you'll learn to live freely and lightly.[104]

As my journal entry shows, these words call up deep longing and awaken strong impressions about what Jesus is offering. Why did this prove so elusive an experience if Jesus wanted it and I wanted it, too?

Honesty forces me to acknowledge multiple explanations. For one thing, as much as I wanted rest in God, I wanted other things too, and these competed for my attention. I desired God but I desired achievement and life's pleasures as well.

At one level, it was as simple as this: it was hard to give God my undivided attention when every day had other things to get to—from staff meetings and writing deadlines to Chinese food and tennis. Let me be even more specific: Consider that I had a morning routine of contemplative prayer but I still caught myself, from time to time, turning from contemplation to the clock, making sure that my workout began with ESPN's *SportsCenter* at the top of the hour. The flaw in this tendency wasn't just that I shortchanged my time of spiritual solitude; it was also that it treated time with God as just one facet of a multifaceted life, when my honest belief was that God wanted to be in the middle of everything. I was still learning how to integrate God into all of the activities of my daily life and, more than that, to keep God at the center of my life as the Managing Director who separates the activity that matters from the activity that just clutters things up.

My divided attention came into play even when I was pursuing things out of the conviction that they gave God pleasure. Consider that I got a rush from setting and reaching goals. I got hooked on achievement very early in life—certainly by the time I learned to tie my shoes. I will even allow that it has served me well. It fueled me to make friends when I moved with my family from Oklahoma to New Jersey as a sixth-grader; it motivated me to kick up my effort another notch at Baylor University when high-school-level effort wasn't cutting it; and it made it possible for me to juggle the simultaneous challenges of pastoring, parenting, and Ph.D. work during seminary days. Whether leading a group of college students from the University of Tennessee on a mission trip to New York City or orchestrating a church-building campaign in Kansas City, the impulse to achieve inspired me to do things I never would have done otherwise.

My purposeful life served me well; but that did nothing to change the fact that it also thwarted my experience of the rest to which Jesus invited me. Purposeful pursuits, even when God-inspired, couldn't replace the experience of drawing down into the peace of God.

Were divided attention the full extent of my problem, it would have presented challenge enough—but there was more. For another thing, I wanted God but had to admit a degree of ambivalence. God wasn't all warmth and kindness; God was also righteous and demanding. God appealed to me but God unnerved me in ways, too.

German theologian Rudolph Otto[105] spoke of our experience of the awesome mystery of God as *"mysterium tremendum et fascinans,"* a Latin phrase that means "fearful and fascinating mystery." It perfectly matches this ambivalence. We are attracted to God while at the same time distanced in an awe-filled sense of our undeserving. Isaiah's encounter with God in Isaiah 6:1–8 captures the mystery, majesty and misery of it. Isaiah has a close encounter with God in all of God's splendor, and his awe-inspired wonder quickly gives way to abject horror. "Woe is me!" he cries. "I am ruined! For I am a man of unclean lips, and I live among a people of unclean lips, and my eyes have seen the King, the Lord Almighty."[106]

I could relate. The Bible teachers of my childhood made sure I knew about God's regal glory and my wretchedness. They taught me lessons about behaving myself, reinforcing them with stories from the Old Testament about the terrible things that happened to people who didn't do so. The stories set me on edge, given my instincts and behavior as a high-energy, boundary-pushing boy. I wasn't terribly bad; I worked at pleasing my parents, especially when it was convenient. However, I played with matches in the basement. I spit bubble gum in one of my brothers' hair. I stole my best friend's peso (and he was the pastor's son!). I fully respected the demands of my great and holy God, but for the life of me I could never get it completely right.

These childhood impressions survived my early experiences of grace, making me a follower of Jesus with a guilt complex. I was in my twenties before a fuller, richer perspective began to sink in. It didn't happen overnight, as if one cathartic experience of God's grace was all

I needed. It happened over time, as the good news of God's love for me kept coming wave upon wave: through my campus minister, Lonnie Hayter, and the stories he told of his own disarming experiences of God's love; through pastor John Claypool, who preached about the love of self for God's sake as the highest form of love, higher even than the love of God for God's sake; and through theologians and others who wrote about a pervasive YES! at the heart of the universe—God's Yes. I absorbed all of these lessons and stories and lived into the possibility they described. At the heart of them all was Jesus, the embodiment of love whom I believed to be the human face of God.

With Jesus as the human face of God, God becomes eminently approachable, an irresistible magnet for our affection and loyalty. It changes everything.

Still, even Jesus makes the daunting demands of discipleship perfectly clear. To follow him promises rest, yes; but it also promises self-sacrifice. He has an agenda for our lives connected with God's agenda for the world. As Max Lucado reminds us in his book, *Just Like Jesus*, Christ accepts us as we are, but he doesn't leave things there. He wants us to become just like him.[107]

For the most part, I was fine with all of this. I'd be lying, however, if I said I never had a concern about the direction of my life, completely yielded to God. I wanted God but had to admit a degree of ambivalence. To come into the orbit of God's rest was to place my life at God's disposal, whatever that might mean. My divided attention and my ambivalence compromised my ability to experience the rest that Jesus offers.

I will mention one more factor that worked against me: my excess adrenaline. From the earliest stages of my life, when my mom would hold down my knee to keep me from tapping my feet or cover my hand to keep me from drumming my fingers, I have been somewhat "wound up." Apparently, this energy radiates. I've heard my wife tell others that when our daughter and son were growing up, my mere entrance into the house would create waves of energy, transforming the tranquility of the home into a scene of temporary chaos, with our dog running in circles barking and our kids going wild.

I have an intrinsic restlessness, one that sometimes bubbles up and sometimes lurks just beneath the surface but that either way can feel like the hyperkinetic energy of a child past her bedtime, who is clearly exhausted and running on fumes. She can't see it; she is loathe to bring her waking life and her social life to a close. When I think of all the ways I keep going and going and going, I am amazed at my inability to stop until I have worn myself sick physically, emotionally and spiritually.

It hasn't helped through the years that this adrenaline-fueled life has made me productive and won me the affirmation of others. School teachers applauded my performance. Church members commented about everything I got done. Even when people worried out loud that I was doing too much, I often heard an approving subtext in their expressions of concern.

During my dark night of the soul, I had to come clean about all the ways I had neglected this rest which is at the heart of discipleship. I, the borderline hyperactive child who loved hugs but couldn't sit still long enough to enjoy them, had allowed the same pattern to color my relationship with my Maker.

It became a matter of sheer will to sit myself down and grow still and quiet. I had to go through a detox program of solitude to overcome my addiction to activity and external stimulation. Pulled in a thousand and one different directions, I had become "Legion" and needed Jesus to exorcize my demons so that I, like the Gerasene demoniac of old, could be seated and in my right mind.[108]

Two things worked to my advantage when it came to sitting myself down: a lifetime of self-discipline and studied exposure to the core disciplines of spiritual formation. As it relates to self-discipline, it's worth noting that though I have trouble curbing my energy, I do not suffer from attention deficit disorder. I have always had the ability to focus on whatever I'm doing and see it through to completion. Associated with this has been the ability to get started, which some would say is more difficult than seeing things through. My goal-oriented nature, sometimes a liability when it comes to inner ease, actually served me well when it came to acting on a decision to "stop, drop, and . . ."—rest. I had practiced self-discipline as a student and a professional. It had worked for me in athletics and personal fitness. I had no doubt that I could lean on it in these circumstances to refresh my practices of spirituality.

I say "refresh" my practices of spirituality because I was not a stranger to these activities. This served as my second advantage when it came to sitting myself down during my difficult passage through the spiritual dark. During high school days, I learned from a friend about having a "quiet time" in the morning, a time of Scripture reading and prayer that opened up my life to God at the beginning of the day. He got me into journal-keeping as well. During college days, I became acquainted with the resources of the Navigators, a Colorado-based organization that promotes Christian discipleship.[109] During the early years of pastoral ministry, professors at seminary and the writing of Richard Foster drew me to classical streams of spirituality, introducing me to the practical wisdom of Christian mentors, ancient and modern. Foster's book, *Celebration of Discipline*, became a companion guide nearly as valuable as my Bible. I leaned on his insights and instructions to take my faith formation to the next level, through:

- the inward disciplines of prayer, meditation, fasting and study;
- the outward disciplines of simplicity, solitude, submission and service; and
- the corporate disciplines of confession, worship, guidance and celebration.[110]

My devotional experience with the red letters of Matthew's gospel was an exercise of self-discipline to refresh my use of previously learned practices of spiritual formation. I hadn't abandoned these practices. They had just grown stale and I had allowed my habits of devotion to become sporadic. Sobered by God's silence, I kicked them back into gear, introducing what for me was a creative twist—the devotional focus, one by one, on the statements of Jesus.

I got up—usually before the sun came up. I sat down—in a quiet, comfortable place. I breathed deeply—relaxing my mind and body. I prayed—simply inviting God's presence, silent though God seemed. Then I turned to my Bible and read, opening my heart and my imagination to what Jesus would do and say next. My journal became the place where I wrote my responses to what I saw and heard.

The nice thing about this process was that once I experienced the quietness of spirit that the experiment spawned, it became compelling enough to keep bringing me back.

I had to continue relearning this way, ever the novice. What's more, I felt even more like a novice when it came to carrying this sense of rest into the remainder of the day. Having become acquainted with mentors, ancient and modern, who describe what it's like to sustain an inner experience of God's presence and peace no matter what may be going on in their outer world,[111] and having tasted this in appetizer portions in my life, I knew to want it and to believe that it was possible. My brushes with this—which I can't mark on the calendar of my personal history or describe in connection with specific events—had on every occasion come when I was settled into a pattern of solitude and morning prayer. My spiritual consciousness raised by establishing my awareness first thing in the morning, I had found myself more mindful of God and more grateful about my circumstances. I had felt more poised and more relaxed about moving between activity and inactivity, work and play, sociality and silence.

sixteen

Matthew 12:9–14

(9)Going on from that place, he went into their synagogue, (10)and a man with a shriveled hand was there. Looking for a reason to accuse Jesus, they asked him, "Is it lawful to heal on the Sabbath?"

(11)He said to them, **"If any of you has a sheep and it falls into a pit on the Sabbath, will you not take hold of it and lift it out?** (12)**How much more valuable is a man than a sheep! Therefore it is lawful to do good on the Sabbath."**

(13)Then he said to the man, **"Stretch out your hand."** So he stretched it out and it was completely restored, just as sound as the other. (14)But the Pharisees went out and plotted how they might kill Jesus.

It's the Sabbath, a day marked off by God for rest; a twenty-four hour period that, because of rules and regulations added over time, has become a long and complicated day of do's and don'ts. Your adversaries see an opportunity in the synagogue to test you, Jesus, anticipating that you will continue to condemn yourself by dismissing Sabbath restrictions.

They see a man with a withered hand and imagine—correctly, as it happens—that you will want to heal him. "Is it lawful to heal on the Sabbath?" they ask, and they plan to use your answer against you.

It's a dramatic moment, one fraught with tension and uncertainty. What will you say? What will you do? And what consequences will follow?

With your response—a question followed by an illustration—you basically say, "For God's sake, have a heart! Wake up and clear the cobwebs of legalistic confusion from your head! Step back from the elaborate web of logic that you have allowed to completely disorient you, and reclaim the wisdom of God in its simplicity! The law was created as a framework for the application of God's love and mercy. PEOPLE matter. Compassion matters.

"It is lawful to do good on the Sabbath."

You then turn your attention from your antagonists and every other onlooker and focus your resolute, compassionate eyes on the true object of your concern: the man with the withered hand. The air crackles with the static electricity of conflict.

"Stretch out your hand," you say. Move it in the direction of wholeness. Move it as far as you can make it reach, withered as it is, and I will do the rest.

This is the way of the disciplines of faith. There's something we can do, something within our reach. There are some things we cannot do, things beyond our reach, things that only you can do. You ask us to do what we can. You *command* us to do what we can.

You—and we—are surrounded by friends, advocates and naysayers. But your eyes remain fixed and undistracted. You draw an invisible circle around us and give us your undivided attention. You silently demand that we do the same.

"So he stretched it out and it was completely restored, just as sound as the other."

Lord, I am the man with the withered hand whose desire to be whole is strong enough to overcome all distractions. I am the broken man who this morning, as every morning, stretches forth my hand the little distance I can, hoping you will heal and restore me.

Lock the eyes of my heart on you, even as you lock the eyes of your heart on me. When I sit in devotion and when I rise into the action of the day, keep my eyes fixed on you. I will move as I can in your direction. Quiet the nay-saying voices that play in my head. Remove my uncertainty and doubt. Lengthen and strengthen me by the power that resides in you and that you alone can cause to course through me.

Faith and Doubt

When I was young, I thought of faith and doubt as opposites. I thought of them as mutually exclusive. To doubt, in my mind, was to exit God's country and cut myself adrift on a faithless ocean.

By the time of my journey through the spiritual wilderness, I no longer thought this way. I had become convinced that doubt takes shape within the province of faith. I had concluded that doubt doesn't exile us from our faith; it merely takes us to the edge of our faith where we experience our insecurity, our uncertainty, our suspicions. I thought of doubt as taking us to the question marks that form the boundary between what we know and don't know.

From this way of seeing things, doubt comes with finitude; at least it does for those who open themselves to life's imponderables. I do know some who seem to have no doubts. They have formed convictions to account for every aspect of their lives, their world, their relationship with God, their relationship with others.

I'm a little reluctant to encourage the cultivation of doubt; it's actually not a lot of fun. But we who suffer doubts can feel encouraged by the assurance that our doubts don't necessarily untether us and set us adrift in the emptiness of space. We need not waste time feeling guilty.

I didn't feel guilty about my doubts. I believed, in fact, that God could use my doubts as an opportunity for my growth. Through my doubts God could disquiet me so as to prompt a deeper exploration of faith and a closer walk with God. And because I believed there ultimately was no solution to doubt except the promise that we will one day know fully, even as we are fully known,[112] I was convinced that doubt could throw me back on God in utter dependence. I, like anyone who has ever suffered from doubt, was the man with the withered hand reaching out at Jesus' invitation, hoping against hope to be healed.

By the time I reached the story of the man with the withered hand, my faith and hope had gotten shaky. My experience of God's apparent absence continued to raise poignant questions about the sanity of my worldview. It led me to wonder whether there was such a thing as a personal God, whether Jesus was who he said he was, and whether prayer makes a difference. It unsettled virtually every aspect of biblical belief for me. It left me questioning my calling and my ultimate destiny.

At this tenuous time of my life, I still had to get up every day and go to work, which in my case meant leading a church that was at a tenuous time in its life too. The church was counting on me to pro-claim a message that was losing its grip on me. The gap between the Bible's version of "good news" and the "news" as I was reading it in the subtexts of my life made it increasingly difficult to carry out my duties. As preacher and teacher, I had a mandate to deliver messages from the Bible that encouraged people's faith. As first among equals in the leadership of a church in transition, I had a mandate to define the church's current reality, promote consensus about God's desired future for us, and inspire our wholehearted action in that direction. As pastoral care giver, I had a mandate to represent God's guidance and grace to people at their points of need.

Stewarding my role as pastor while dodging the dangers of hypoc-risy became a crucial exercise. My studies and experiences in pas-toral ministry convinced me that the church needed not only my confidence and clarity, but my true humanity, too. I felt obliged to work on being real without becoming a distraction; to measure out portions of my personal story while keeping the church's focus where it belonged. As a matter of faith—not the "complete confidence" or "utter certainty" of Hebrews 11:1, but the "I believe, help me in my unbelief" of Mark 9:24—I could teach the Scriptures, still declare the promises of God, and invite fellow strugglers[113] to join me on a journey toward the light.

There were daily temptations to sound more confident and certain than I was. True, I hadn't given up on God—not yet, at least—so I didn't need to feel like one of those charlatans who parade a false faith in front of gullible people. And true, I was fortunate to serve a congregation that allowed its pastor to be real and unfinished and subject to doubts. Nevertheless, because it seemed essential that I promote a can-do spirit, and because I knew that my mood and my message would influence this greatly, I erred—if at all—on the upbeat side of the equation. I took care not to wear my uncertainty on my sleeve.

My doubt and my need to manage it heightened the internal conflict of these days.

I clung to the hope that God was holding me in my uncertainty. I lived by the conviction that my security as a shaky believer had less to do with the faith I could muster on any given day than with the strength of God's promised love.

Here's how Jesus put it. "I give [my sheep] eternal life, and they shall never perish; no one can snatch them out of my hand. My Father, who has given them to me, is greater than all; no one can snatch them out of my Father's hand."[114]

One of my all-time favorite stories comes from the great black preacher, the Rev. Frederick G. Sampson, who spoke in chapel while I was at seminary. He illustrated this idea with an experience from his own parenting. One night he took his little boy outside to look at the stars. The boy was nervous because of the dark and made a request—"Daddy, hold my hand." Responding to the request, Rev.

Sampson held out his hand, and his son grabbed onto his index finger. A few moments and a few steps later, his son repeated his request—"Daddy, hold my hand!" A bit peeved, he responded, "Son, I AM holding your hand!" to which the son replied, "You're not holding my hand; I'm holding *yours!*"

The son, of course, was right, and he knew what a difference it made. Sampson immediately took his son's hand in his own. *Now,* if the son were to stumble, his father would have him in his grip. He could stumble without worrying that he would fall.

Biblical faith tells us that in our doubts we are being held by our heavenly Father, who knows our weakness. God promises to hold us and keep us, even when we walk out into the dark, even to the edge of the precipices where our doubts sometimes take us.

On the morning of the previous journal entry, when Jesus said, "Stretch out your hand," I was buoyed by the conviction that his strong grip on me mattered much more than my withered grip on him. I had little by way of faith or hope to give him, but what little I had I extended in his direction, counting on him to do the rest.

"Blessed are the poor in spirit, for theirs is the kingdom of heaven."[115]

seventeen

Matthew 13:1–9

(1)*That same day Jesus went out of the house and sat by the lake.*
(2)*Such large crowds gathered around him that he got into a boat
and sat in it, while all the people stood on the shore.* (3)*Then he told
them many things in parables, saying:* **"A farmer went out to sow
his seed.** (4)**As he was scattering the seed, some fell along the
path, and the birds came and ate it up.** (5)**Some fell on rocky
places, where it did not have much soil. It sprang up quickly,
because the soil was shallow.** (6)**But when the sun came up,
the plants were scorched, and they withered because they had
no root.** (7)**Other seed fell among thorns, which grew up and
choked the plants.** (8)**Still other seed fell on good soil, where it
produced a crop—a hundred, sixty or thirty times what was
sown.** (9)**He who has ears, let him hear."**

I am not the seed being transformed in this analogy. I am not the
seed bearing fruit. I am the soil in which the seed can take root. I am
the soil out of which the life in the seed can burst forth. I am the soil
out of which the fruitful potential of the Word—"the message of the
kingdom"[116]—can be realized.

You aren't so much concerned that *I* am fruitful as that your *Word* can become fruitful out of me. I like this arrangement. My responsibility isn't to be fruitful or make fruit. I am the soil. Soil isn't fruitful.

My responsibility is to provide a context, an environment, within which you can enact the miracle of life. I am the incubator of your kingdom love, the hothouse from which your kingdom way can spring forth with life. I am the small patch of earth from which you can multiply the effect of your mission, from which you can spread your influence on the world. As John Wimber, author and founder of the Vineyard Christian Fellowship, discovered meditating on Ephesians 2:10, you have good works to do through me, and they're your good works, not mine.[117] I can relax my effort to BE FRUITFUL and focus on being RESPONSIVE, WELCOMING, WILLING. I'll leave the fruitfulness to you and celebrate the fruitfulness of you and your Word.

The Still, Small Voice

I've talked about my frustrations waiting for God to "speak." The question remains: How exactly do we "hear" God? Or perhaps, in light of Jesus' parable of the soils, the question should be posed this way: How, beyond the written word, does God's "Word" get through to us and get planted in the soil of our life? How does God communicate God's presence and purpose?

My spiritual dilemma made this question in its multiple forms a pressing issue of major importance. I once thought I knew how God would get through to me. I wasn't so sure anymore. As I sorted things out again, the biblically tutored teacher in me scavenged for insight in my mental files, in resources on my shelves, and in memories from my experiences with God gone by. What I came up with sustained me through a long period of the dark and shaped my expectations as to how God might get through.

I knew, to begin with, that we reach for words from the realm of flesh and blood when explaining the Divine-human connection. At a loss for how to capture the experience of Divine Spirit meeting human spirit, we turn to talk like we find in the Bible:

- God walking in the garden in the cool of the day;[118]
- God's eyes ranging throughout the earth;[119]
- God's arm saving;[120]
- God's face shining upon us;[121]
- God's voice thundering[122] or whispering.[123]

We actually know that this language can't capture the true, full nature of a transcendent God. It can only offset that transcendence with a sense of God's immanence, God's nature as a personal, relational God.

We say that God is Spirit. We know that we are mortal. This difference between us creates a challenge when it comes to experiencing God's nearness and God's guidance. We can't see God with the naked eye; we can't hear God through the ears on our head; and we can't experience the touch of God's closeness on our skin the same way we experience the touch of family, friend or lover.

That's where our spirituality comes in. Spirituality, wherever we find it and whatever religious form it takes, begins with the conviction that God created us with spiritual sensibilities. That is, we can cultivate the capacity to discern the presence of God and interact with God in loving, fruitful ways.

This is what Jesus was talking about when the religious leader Nicodemus came to him at night and Jesus said, "No one can see the kingdom of God unless he is born again (or from above)."[124]

As I wrapped my mind around this again, it helped me to reach into the world of computers to clarify the point for myself. It is fairly well known that a Mac (the Macintosh, an Apple Corporation computer) and a PC (what once was called an IBM-compatible computer) use different computer language systems. This prevents Macs and PCs from communicating with each other, which presents problems of all kinds at home and work. Fortunately, some very bright people have come up with a way to bridge this gap. They have devised an interface, a common language system, that allows these two very different kinds of computers to interact.

What technical experts have done in the realm of computing is something like what biblical faith suggests that God has done in the spiritual realm. Biblical faith suggests that when creating us, God installed in human beings an operating system that enables us to pick up on God's signals and enjoy an intimate, personal relationship together. People of faith point to conscience, intuition and emotionally rich impressions of "the heart" (the seat of our emotions) as points of interface where God makes the connection between Spirit and flesh.

We reach for earthbound language to capture the nature of this, but that's only because these analogies come as close as we can to expressing the inexpressible. As spiritual creatures we see and are seen, we touch and are touched, we speak and we listen beyond what the five senses can register—though this isn't to say that there aren't times when the sense of God's nearness is so palpable that we literally hear God's voice or feel God's hand on our shoulder or see visible signs of God's presence. But even on these occasions we know we have experienced something that is only discernible to those "with eyes to see and ears to hear."[125]

I still have vivid memories of the story some friends of mine told me about their escape from violence while serving as missionaries in Eastern Europe. Ethnic violence erupted in their city and they— husband, wife, and two children—got caught in the crossfire while racing on foot to a site the U.S. Embassy had appointed for helicopter evacuation. As bullets flew, they crouched in the middle of the street, still in the line of fire, but paralyzed with fear. A man hurried over to them and got them on their feet. "Follow me!" he said. Scurrying along side streets, they followed him until they arrived at a quiet little square away from the violence. The four family members embraced each other and, as they did, they heard their escort say,

"You'll be safe now." They turned to say thanks but no one was there. "A person wouldn't have had time to disappear around a corner in the time it took us to turn," they say. While still trying to absorb what had happened, a friendly transport vehicle "happened" into the square, gathered them up, and drove them to the evacuation site where they flew to final safety, away from the reach of civil war. As people of faith they maintain the unshakable and awe-filled conviction that they had experienced God's tangible presence that day through an angel of mercy.

Now, let me get more personal with this. Through the years, I had become convinced that a God-given spiritual capacity made it possible for me to experience God in a variety of ways. An atheist would call this delusional or wishful thinking, but as a person of faith I would say that I had experienced God:

- through insights that arose out of the fog of my befuddled mind—like the inward moment of clarity that kept my family and me at Holmeswood Baptist Church instead of accepting an invitation to pastor another church in another state;

- through promptings that nudged me toward action—like the day I felt prompted to pray very specifically with an Ethiopian pre-med student that God would supply much-needed financial support and then walked out of my office with him and into conversation with a member of the church who, learning of the student's dilemma, volunteered on the spot to provide the support he needed;

- through a warm inner glow that made me feel surrounded by a Supreme Love—like an afternoon experience I had in the woods near a lake in Arkansas, when resting with my back against a log, I felt a shimmer of God's nearness in the light reflecting off ripples in the lake.

I had experienced God in material provisions just when I needed them—like when Priscilla and I received a check in the mail from someone who couldn't possibly have known how desperately we had been praying for precisely that amount. I had also experienced God in the words, deeds, and touch of others—like when Holmeswood Baptist Church deacon and friend Herm Ehrhard stood beside my hospital bed on the day I had my first reconstructive knee surgery and touched my shoulder as he prayed a kind and simple prayer for me.

My impressions of God's interacting with me hadn't all been affirming. Sometimes the sense of God's nearness, the "sound of God's voice" came in the form of conscience, confronting and accusing me. I sensed God displaying for me the gap between the life I was leading and the life that was wanting to live through me. I felt God holding up a mirror to me, forcing me to see myself under the glare of a truth-seeking divine light.

Most days, God broke through to me in the subtle ways I've just mentioned. These served as my staircase toward heaven and the means by which I experienced God coming down the staircase toward me.

On special occasions I experienced more. I have already mentioned that as a sixteen-year-old, I decided on the career path of ministry because of an audible voice in my head saying, "Greg, be a preacher." At another turning point years later, I had a breakthrough of emotional healing while sitting at an outdoor table in Pasadena, California. With journal and pen in hand, I had the sense that God had broken through and that I had become a scribe to record what God had to say. The message that flowed through my pen and into my heart had a ring of truth about it that lay well beyond the default mode of my sensibilities at that time. I had been struggling with feelings of unworthiness, a recurring theme in my life. Here's some of how an intruding inner voice responded:

I love you. Unlike any other, I have created you, and I delight in the unique, wonderful person you are. I know your shortcomings; I know your sins. No deed has escaped my eyes. No word has slipped past my ears. No thoughts, no imaginings have gone unnoticed. But I forgive you those things. I love you still. Nothing you have done to distort the unique creation you are, nothing you have done to twist and tear at your true self, can keep me from recognizing you and longing for you and loving you and wanting to awaken and unleash you for all you're worth . . .

You have been damaged in life, even as you have been your own reckless driver. . . . But grace—my grace—has been with you every step of the way . . .

I have plans for you; that should be clear to you by now; but they are plans that have nothing to do with proving yourself. Come into my realm of renewal and joy and life and love . . .

Listen . . . Listen! Listen, and I will speak. Listen, and clarity will come. Listen—moment by moment, hour by hour, day by day—and my will for you will unfold. You don't have to be afraid of anything: of life, of death, of making a mistake, of regrets, of imperfection. Let me direct; let me take care of seeing to the balance of your need. I will be easier as your Master than you are on yourself.

And I will offer you something otherwise unavailable to you: life power: the courage of love; the lightness of grace.

That day I felt touched by grace. I felt my worth through what felt like Holy words planted in my heart.

Through the years, nature also provided me with experiences of what felt like the presence of God. I have fond memories of a solitary walk along the hillside and into a quiet forest of the Cotswolds in England in February 1998 when I had what I considered a theophany. My five senses came alive to an unusual degree and I felt God's presence in the breeze that rustled the leaves and the sound of a babbling brook. A song rose up in me, "Run River, Run,"[126] and then another, more conventionally spiritual one, "I've Got a River of Life (flowing out of me),"[127] and I had the sense that God was somehow singing those songs in me. I experienced what felt like God's nearness, God's joy, God's love.

These amplified impressions of God's nearness had come few and far between for me, but they continued to warm me in that wintry time when I only had my memories to sustain my faith. Recalling these moments didn't restore me spiritually to the full warmth of day, but it did keep a lamplight burning until the sun could rise again. I felt deeply grateful for every sign and memory of God's interest in my life.

In the pursuit of a relationship with God, I remained quite conscious of the fact that it didn't just depend on me. I knew that for the Divine-human connection to occur, God had to take the initiative. This wasn't to say that there weren't things I could do to facilitate it. Meditation, prayer, solitude, service, and spiritual reading—by these means and others I put myself in a position to experience God's presence and God's grace.

Nonetheless, I remained convinced that God was the one who would choose how and when to come. My awareness of this intensified during the long, dry spell during which my longing for Divine direction and my sense of God's silence fed on each other and became almost overwhelming.

If you've experienced a lifetime of this communication system working a particular way, it becomes quite unnerving when it no longer works the same way. My pattern of expectations had become formulaic. Those months confronted me with renewed awareness that the God of biblical faith operates under no obligation to come at our beck and call. God's love for us, however great it may be, doesn't erase God's freedom.

eighteen

Matthew 13:44–46

(44)*"The kingdom of heaven is like treasure hidden in a field. When a man found it, he hid it again, and then in his joy went and sold all he had and bought that field.*

(45)*"Again, the kingdom of heaven is like a merchant looking for fine pearls.* (46)*When he found one of great value, he went away and sold everything he had and bought it."*

You compare the kingdom to hidden treasure, something of extraordinary value whose location, whose very existence, is unknown until a person stumbles upon it. You compare the kingdom to a pearl of unparalleled value, worth selling everything to obtain. Your kingdom is a treasure. Indeed, this life in Christ, this new way of being, this existence in full awareness of and surrender to the life and love and bounty and power and authority of God, is incalculably rich and exhilarating.

It's hidden. Jesus, you yourself seem to be conscious of the fact that this kingdom existence, this richly fulfilling way of life, actually eludes most of those you tell about it. Like someone pointing to something in the distance but failing to get another person to lock onto it—"Don't you see it? It's right there, right where you're looking!"—you know that only some of us—babes, open to wonder; babes, not yet sealed away in our beliefs, our paradigms, our mind-closing, will-resistant ways—only some of us will "get it."

But those of us who do get it will be blown away by it. We will know immediately that we have stumbled upon (actually, we have been graciously led to) something priceless, something worth more than everything we've got. Those of us who get it will be filled with joy. We know it can be ours.

It's worth noting that our first instinct isn't to share it; it is to secure it for ourselves. We don't want to steal it—we want it fair and square—so first we must purchase the land in which it lies undiscovered. To do so costs us our entire estate, everything we own. No matter; we know that what we'll have in the bargain far exceeds that price. Others may think we're crazy but we know better! The same is true of the pearl. It costs everything but the cost is worth it.

Selling out to you, Jesus, is what it means to lay claim to the kingdom. Selling out to you means recognizing that my riches, my relationships, my work, my plans—everything I possess and hold dear—is meager stuff compared to the incomparable riches of the life you hold out to me. Lord, I willingly claim this life. I exchange for it everything I have.

Believing Is Seeing

Nearly twenty years ago I happened across an article in *Newsweek* by Dr. Wayne Dyer in which he reversed the order of the well-known cliché, "Seeing is believing."[128] According to common wisdom, "the proof is in the pudding" and "actions speak louder than words." In other words, we need evidence to support a person's claim.

Dyer suggested a different way of looking at things. He pointed to the ways our pre-conceptions will either open us up to or close us off from realities right before our eyes. He encouraged an attitude of positive, possibility thinking as the more creative way to live. "Believing is seeing," he wrote, and life unfolds best for those who believe the best and act accordingly.

The Gospel of John gives us a story in support of this unconventional wisdom. It tells us the story of Jesus' disciple, Thomas, who wanted to see for himself whether news of Jesus' resurrection was true. Thomas hadn't been present at Jesus' first resurrection appearance to the disciples. When told about it, he declared: "Unless I see the nail marks in his hands and put my finger where the nails were, and put my hand into his side, I will not believe it."[129]

In other words, he was saying, "I want proof. Seeing is believing."

Thomas got his wish but, when he did, he also got the challenge of his life. One week after Jesus' first appearance to the disciples, he returned and stood among them. After a general greeting, he turned his gaze on Thomas and extended his nail-scarred hands to him. "Go ahead, Thomas, have at it. Probe my hands. Reach out and stick your fingers into my side." Then he added, *"Stop doubting and believe."*[130]

Thomas immediately dropped to his knees in praise, no further proof needed. "My Lord and my God!" he exclaimed.

Jesus seemed unimpressed. "Because you have seen me, you have believed; *blessed are those who have not seen and yet have believed."*[131] Jesus confirms the reversal of conventional thinking. There is a sense in which "believing is seeing," not the other way around.

For centuries of seekers who couldn't be there when Jesus made his resurrection appearances, our faith depends on our giving credence to the testimony of those who WERE there. Our ability to BELIEVE without seeing is what allows us to SEE in the deeper sense of that word, to discover the hidden treasure that is life in Christ. Faith precedes sight.

This doesn't make faith any easier, unfortunately. In fact, during my spiritual wilderness experience, I wrestled with the implications of this, given my frustrations experiencing God.

I found my head spinning. Seeing is believing. Believing is seeing.

Not seeing is not believing. Not believing is not seeing. None of these statements said anything about actual reality at the other end of my perceptions, though the first of these statements seemed closest to placing the burden of proof where it belonged. In other words, I was replaying the role of Thomas.

But is it really unfair to ask, from time to time, how our experience of faith matches up with the promises of faith? "Test me," the Bible reports God as saying. "I will bless you," God says. Do we have to apologize for periodic inquiries into God's actual performance?

I know that there's a fundamental, seemingly unsolvable dilemma here. Our ability even to "see," that is, to test, perceive, and evaluate, is a factor of faith, since we are flesh and God is Spirit. I want empirical evidence to support the verdict that there's really a God at the other end of my prayers. I mostly have to rely on impressions and "coincidences," any of which could be explained away without recourse to faith. I'm left with a stand-off between the believer and the skeptic in me.

Perception: We will see what we want to see, what we decide to see. We won't see what we decide not to see. Does this mean that reality itself makes no independent claims on us, that there is no center of Truth that is the same for all people, everywhere, for all time? Surely we're not left with a Peter Pan world in which "reality" is whatever you want it to be!

At least empiricism has this going for it: It posits an observable reality independent of what we want and don't want, and it supplies tools for examining this reality.

What it can't do is the one thing I wanted more than anything during my time in the spiritual dark: a living relationship with God. Empiricism remains hopelessly detached. It can hypothesize and theorize and engage in experiments to prove or falsify presuppositions. It can analyze the data and dissect the moving parts, but it can't make things live or create a loving connection.

Truth be told, I really wanted both. I'm not saying that this was appropriate; I'm just being honest about what I wanted. I wanted empirical reasons that reinforced my love relationship with God. I wanted to see and believe. I wanted to believe and see. I didn't want to experience God intermittently; I wanted to enjoy a palpable, intimate, ongoing relationship. Absent this, it was understandable that doubt crept in and that explanations other than orthodox Christianity commended themselves.

Frankly, I don't think you have to buy the argument that Jesus was either a lunatic, a liar, or Lord.[132] There are other alternatives. Even wildly insane people can still scratch the surface of truth, and demagogues can tell the truth even when they think they're lying. The Don Quixotes of the world can inspire us with noble dreams despite their senility. The great and the small all have angles of insight and fragments of experience from which to patch together a vision of time and eternity as sincere as it is tentative and— to one degree or another—flawed.

This isn't to say that all faiths are equal. There must be a reality independent of our thoughts, emotions, and wants; and some versions of the truth inevitably get closer to reality than others. Who's to say that Jesus doesn't give us something imperfect, but closer to the truth than other versions of reality? Who's to say that Jesus wasn't brilliant, sane, and sincere, but still somewhat off?

The insistence of a resurrection becomes a major factor, a decisive point of contention in this overall question. It provided a resting place for my faith during my dark night of the soul. Christians point to Jesus as the definitive breakthrough of God into human reality, the Truth Teller without equal. His resurrection, if it actually occurred, authenticates his claims above all others. I continued to believe it did occur, and I was not without strong supporting evidence for this remarkable conclusion. There was the empty tomb. There were the hundreds of eye witnesses to his post-death appearances. There was the radical reversal of the disciples' confidence and their tenacity as proclaimers of the resurrection.

Some have suggested that Jesus' body was stolen by the disciples, who then manufactured the story that he had risen from the dead; but is it really conceivable that people perpetuating a hoax would be willing to die to protect that lie? Others have suggested that he didn't really die, but merely swooned; but is it really conceivable that someone could survive what Jesus suffered on Friday and inspire confidence on Sunday that he was the death-conquering Lord of life?[133]

I had justifiable reasons for my belief in Jesus' resurrection, which in turn solidified my conviction that Jesus was and is who the Bible portrays him to be: the human face of God and the Lord of life. But having said this, I had to return to the acknowledgement that none of us can arrive at faith by way of empiricism. The rational, analytical, left brain[134] will never uncover anything more than the residue of Jesus' presence here. It will be able to find evidence that he was here; but at best, all this will do is create a circumstantial case for his existence. It can do no better. After all, it remains, by its very nature, detached and earthbound. It lacks the Geiger counter of love. It remains a stranger to affection. It "feels" only what it can touch; not what "touches" it at the deeper levels of reality.

In the course of wrestling with God's illusiveness, I acknowledged again that I would never "know" God by left-brain means, any more than a scientist can dissect his way into a heart-to-heart relationship with the woman he loves. A scalpel can take him to each heart, but all it will leave him are the bloody pieces. It will also leave him and the woman of his dreams—dead.

Even if God were tangible, I would remain a stranger to God if my left brain were all I had. For lack of a sixth sense, I would have to think of myself as a blind man who "sees" God, a deaf man who "hears" God with the heart, or a quadriplegic who can "feel" God's presence and "rest" in God's "arms."

I reminded myself to trust what my heart told me. Or, as faith would rephrase it: I reminded myself to trust what God, through the stories and words of Jesus, was telling my heart. I kept telling my lonely soul to trust the "Aha!" and "Ahhh" . . . of love.

nineteen

Matthew 14:22–27

(22)Immediately Jesus made the disciples get into the boat and go on ahead of him to the other side, while he dismissed the crowd. (23)After he had dismissed them, he went up on a mountainside by himself to pray. When evening came, he was there alone, (24)but the boat was already a considerable distance from land, buffeted by the waves because the wind was against it.

(25)During the fourth watch of the night Jesus went out to them, walking on the lake. (26)When the disciples saw him walking on the lake, they were terrified. "It's a ghost," they said, and cried out in fear.

(27)But Jesus immediately said to them: **"Take courage! It is I. Don't be afraid."**

"It is I." This is the centerpiece of your statement. This is the reason to banish fear and put courage in its place. "It is I"—meaning, not a ghost, not a spooky, malevolent presence, not a foreboding power come to do you harm; but good-will-friend, Son-of-God Jesus. "It is I"—meaning, "You're safe now; nothing can harm you."

I think of the Scottish pastor's tale from his childhood, walking home at night through a dangerous ravine. He hears footsteps behind him and, terrified, he presses his little body against the rock effacement. The sound of the steps grows stronger as someone nears; then a voice comes out of the darkness, "John, it's me"—the most welcome voice in the world: the voice of his father. He rushes into his father's arms and clings for joy and relief to his legs.[135]

"It is I." The terrified disciples hear your reassuring voice, and terror turns to relief and joy. You don't really even need to add, "Don't be afraid." Your presence—or rather, the realization of your presence—erases fear and fills them with courage again.

I know the truth of this. When fear gets the upper hand, it's a good bet I'm struggling at the oars of my life with the sense that I'm all alone, that I'm going to sink or swim by my own strength. I know how easily this happens and how terrifying it can feel. I know what it's like to become increasingly worn out and overwhelmed by challenges and to begin to see something ominous in every shadow. And I know how transformative it feels when you, the risen Christ, walk across the waves that are taking me under and identify yourself as present and accounted for and Master of everything you survey.

My level of fear is directly related to the degree to which I think I'm on my own. My level of courage is directly related to the degree to which I'm navigating the waters with the strong sense that you are by my side.

Come, Jesus, come.

Serendipity

A wilderness experience of faith isn't all darkness and desperation. There is light in the dark black night.

There certainly was for me. I came to relish my morning excursions into the life and words of Jesus, expectant that he and those around him would "speak" to me. I was seldom disappointed.

I experienced the previous entry very much this way. With my prayerful imagination fully engaged, I struggled at the oars with the other disciples. I experienced sheer terror when a phantom-like figure approached on the water. I experienced palpable relief when I heard the phantom speak and realized it was Jesus.

Understand, please, that this doesn't mean the heavens opened up for me each morning or that the presenting problem of God's elusiveness resolved itself in a bright flash of light and love. My appeals for clarity of direction continued unsatisfied; my longing for close company with God remained an ache in my chest, a hope against hope.

Still, hints of the Divine met me in virtually every anecdote, and I experienced the joy of one of God's better gifts: the gift of imagination. How do you explain the catalytic effect of entering with mind and heart into the story of Jesus other than to say that something comes alive in the encounter? It's almost as if a spiritual chemical reaction occurs, releasing energy and insight, conviction and renewal.

Were I given to romantic impressions (and I sometimes am) I would say that as the seeking heart sets its eyes on the waiting word, God's Spirit touches the place of meeting and says, "Let there be light!" Only something like this satisfies my sense of the electrical current of creativity that I experienced many a morning.

There were mornings when I would take a first look at the next red letters of Jesus and think, "There's not going to be much to chew on here," only to find myself drawn more and more deeply into the meaning and significance of what I was seeing and hearing. None of my experiences illustrates this for me more effectively than the morning I came to Matthew 8:28–34, the story of Jesus' encounter with two Gerasene demoniacs. That morning's story had a single red-letter word in it: "Go." I remember seeing it and laughing inwardly at the very idea of coaxing an hour's worth of devotion out of it. Nevertheless, that's exactly what happened. The story opened itself up to me and Jesus' single-word command to the demons shook the ground beneath me. That morning he not only restored the sanity of two crazed psychopaths; he cast out a few inner demons in my own unsettled soul, leaving me seated and a little more "in my right mind."

I am grateful to Ignatius of Loyola and his *Spiritual Exercises*[136] for insights into this kind of process. He was the one who encouraged me to engage my five senses in the contemplative reading of Scripture. The more patiently and mindfully I allowed myself to step into each scene, the more vivid the experience became and the richer the insights became into my life.

Richard Foster's chapter on meditation in *Celebration of Discipline* put me onto this aspect of Ignatius' work in the first place. In that chapter, Foster points out that when meditating on Scripture, we don't seek to analyze; we seek to internalize and personalize. For this to happen, we must resist the temptation to skim over the surface; "we must be willing to go down into the recreating silences, into the inner world of contemplation."[137] Through Christian meditation we "descend with the mind into the heart, there to meet Jesus, face to face."[138]

I took Foster's guidance to heart, as well as that of Ignatius, and through the stories of Matthew, the Jesus of Scripture touched me, reassured me, and evoked my praise. He confronted me, challenged me, and laid claims on my life.

Notice what was occurring through this process. Rather than my trying to read Jesus' life and make sense of his life in light of *my* world and *my* worldview, Jesus was getting to read my life and make sense of my life in light of *his* world and *his* worldview. His agenda preempted mine.

This was actually a saving grace for me. The life concerns that drove me to the red letters in the first place had disoriented me. My world felt unstable; my perspectives unclear. I really wanted to see the world through his eyes and recalibrate my life in closer keeping with his. Though separated from me by a great gulf of time, the stories of Matthew put Jesus before me as a loving and penetrating light.

When Jesus responded to John the Baptist, who couldn't understand why Jesus needed baptizing, he was also responding to me and my currently pressing demand for explanations. When inviting fishermen to become fishers of men, he was reminding me (and thereby encouraging me) that my life mission would always be integrally connected to the way he had wired me. His stories of healing were many. In some of his healings, his gaze and his grace fell on me as the beneficiary of his power; he saw my particular needs that day and addressed them. In others of his healings, his gaze and his grace fell elsewhere, which drew my eyes to the needs of others and prompted me to consider how, that very day, I could convey some of Jesus' grace in my circles of concern.

My prayer for the gift of God's presence was as yet unanswered. The lesser, but serendipitous—that is, lovely and surprising—gift of a spiritually awakened imagination came instead.

twenty

Matthew 14:28–33

(28) *"Lord, if it's you," Peter replied, "tell me to come to you on the water."*

(29) **"Come,"** *he said.*

Then Peter got down out of the boat, walked on the water and came toward Jesus. (30) *But when he saw the wind, he was afraid and, beginning to sink, cried out, "Lord, save me!"*

(31) *Immediately Jesus reached out his hand and caught him.* **"You of little faith,"** *he said,* **"why did you doubt?"**

(32) *And when they climbed into the boat, the wind died down.* (33) *Then those who were in the boat worshiped him, saying, "Truly you are the Son of God."*

Peter gets out of the boat, and, amazingly, he can walk on water! How absolutely astounding! With steps of faith he gains your supernatural capacity! He does what's humanly impossible! He defies the laws of physics!

When we take the step of faith toward you, Jesus, it's us plus you—an all-conquering combination.

But we must beware. We've got to keep our eyes fixed on you. The minute we turn our thoughts to the obstacles and our human limitations, we're sunk.

That's what happens to Peter. When he takes his eyes off of you, he goes down.

You step in immediately, take Peter's hand, and pull him up. Then you gently chide him. I don't think you want Peter or any other would-be water-walkers to learn the wrong lesson. Peter's mistake wasn't getting out of the boat. His mistake was taking his eyes off of you.

It's all too easy for us to take a risk of faith and come to the wrong conclusion about the complications that follow. It's all too easy to wish we'd never risked in the first place. You want us to remember what it felt like to go for broke and transcend our limits. You want us to feel your joy. You want us to get back up and go at it again.

Stretching and the Silence of God

A prayerful reading of the story of Peter walking on water confronted me with another explanation for the seeming silence of God. It was possible that I couldn't and wouldn't hear God until I was willing to "step out of the boat," that is, until I confronted the side of me that prefers to play it safe and moved beyond my comfort zone as a person of faith.

Some people, because of nature or nurture, are wired as risk-takers. My native risk-taking instincts don't come close to matching theirs. Some of them get a rush from stretching their physical limits and living at the dangerous edge between life and death. I think of Evel Knievel and any number of athletes who race cars, scale mountains, or slalom down steep slopes. I think of Marine volunteers and firefighters and police officers. Others express their risk-taking instincts as entrepreneurs, staking their financial future on a business idea that may or may not work.

When this risk-taking instinct gets put in the service of God, interesting things happen:

- Comfortably situated on his family's estate, Abraham exchanges mansions for tents and heads out with his household, not knowing where their travels will take them.[139]

- Painfully aware of his liabilities—eighty years old, a speech impediment, and a criminal record, among other things— Moses heads back to where there's still a warrant for his arrest and rallies a nation of captives around the idea of freedom.[140]

- Well along his way toward becoming a preeminent leader of one religious movement, Saul of Tarsus, a.k.a. the apostle Paul, flips his loyalties and devotes the rest of his life to a faith he once despised.[141]

The Bible's stories of risk-taking faith have always inspired me. They have moved others as well, like:

- Mother Teresa of Calcutta, who felt called out of the security of a Calcutta convent to help the poor while living among them.

- Martin Luther King, Jr., who put his life on the line to overturn centuries of racial injustice while relying on the non-violent principles of Jesus.

- Truett Cathy, the founder of Chick-fil-A, Inc., who built his business refusing to believe that it spelled entrepreneurial disaster to honor the biblical concept of the Sabbath by closing his restaurants on Sundays.

At one level, all of these examples of the risk-taking spirit can be distilled into the Nike slogan, "Just Do It!" For me, at the time of the previous reading in Matthew, the "Just Do It" incitement to faith-filled action felt like the inspiration I needed as I led First

Baptist Church, Shreveport. The church had been in decline for forty years when I got there; it continued to struggle after I arrived. At my prompting, the church engaged the services of an outstanding church consultant, George Bullard,[142] to help us look at our current circumstances and discern a more promising and God-given future story.

By its very nature, this process invited us to own our strengths, our passions, and even our limitations while dreaming inside and outside the box about our future. Members who clamored for change loved the potential of this process and engaged it supportively. Members who preferred stability participated with some reluctance, as cooperative as they could be while standing guard over programs, practices and places they held dear.

Meanwhile, decisions had to be made on a weekly basis that would influence the direction of the church, like how much to tweak worship services, what to do about a staff opening, or whether to give preference to a new ministry or an old ministry when finalizing the church budget. As a change-leader I had to constantly decide when to apply the accelerator and when to apply the brakes.

I had to keep managing my own motives and feelings while these things were happening. The innovator in me wanted to champion the interests of those clamoring for change; the comforter in me wanted to protect those who had things to lose were change to come. I even had to acknowledge my personal ambivalence, knowing that both the explorer and the homesteader lived in me.

Peter's walking-on-water experience created an uncomfortable moment for the homesteader in me. I had to ask myself: How could I expect to experience God's presence and power if I was tucked away in safe harbor while God was out on the open sea beckoning me to join him there? The Bible has many great stories of men and women pressing beyond their personal limits because their faith propelled them.[143] The story of Peter walking on water was one of the best. I sensed in me a struggle between playing it safe and daring deed. One part of me wanted to shrink back in fear and stick with the comfortable and familiar. Another part of me wanted to take a flying leap beyond my limits, pioneer uncharted territory, do the invigorating, difficult thing.

I felt like it was a safe bet (ironic turn of phrase) that God wanted me to embrace life's adventure and that I would find God most palpably present out at the edge, where I had to count on Divine grace and strength. It brought to mind the quote, "Attempt something so big for God that, without God, it is bound to fail."[144]

Going with this wisdom got complicated by a truth about the way I'm wired: I'm not by nature a "Just Do It" person. I'm an idea man first and an action man second. I'm more of a designer than a builder. My pleasure with a project reaches its apex while it's still on the drawing board. Because I'm a people person, this designer preference predisposes me to "talking about things" rather than just "getting on with it." I love sharing my enthusiasm with others. I also want to know what they think and how they feel. My interest in consensus trumps my interest in construction.

This isn't to say that I have none of the "Just Do It" spirit in me. When I reflect back over my life, I'm pleasantly surprised at the number of ways I have acted on impulses toward faith and adventure: Choosing Priscilla as my lifetime partner; going for a Ph.D.; taking a detour from seminary to do a one-year internship as College Minister at First Baptist Church, Knoxville, Tennessee; jumping at the opportunity to get First Baptist involved in homebuilding in the inner city of Shreveport; getting off the pastoral rail and risking a non-profit existence in 2001.

I, like so many of us, am a walking polarity. There's a part of me that ponders; there's another part of me that plunges in. This is all well and good in one sense; I am who I am, and I can play to my strengths. There is another sense, however, in which all tendencies create vulnerabilities. In my case, the drawing board and the discussion room could become buffers muffling a Voice I said I wanted to hear.

God, as Jesus embodies God, isn't in the practice of catering to us when we're playing it safe, avoiding risk, attempting to preserve our carefully fashioned existence. During my dark night of the soul I found myself in a battle between faith and fear, discomfited by the sense that God was beckoning me beyond my present boundaries. There was a leaping I needed to do. There were risks I needed to take.

If only I could know which way I needed to leap.

twenty-one

Matthew 15:29–38

(29)Jesus left there and went along the Sea of Galilee. Then he went up on a mountainside and sat down. (30)Great crowds came to him, bringing the lame, the blind, the crippled, the mute and many others, and laid them at his feet; and he healed them. (31)The people were amazed when they saw the mute speaking, the crippled made well, the lame walking and the blind seeing. And they praised the God of Israel.

(32)Jesus called his disciples to him and said, **"I have compassion for these people; they have already been with me three days and have nothing to eat. I do not want to send them away hungry, or they may collapse on the way."**

(33)His disciples answered, "Where could we get enough bread in this remote place to feed such a crowd?"

*(34)***"How many loaves do you have?"** *Jesus asked.*

"Seven," they replied, "and a few small fish."

(35)He told the crowd to sit down on the ground. (36)Then he took the seven loaves and the fish, and when he had given thanks, he broke

them and gave them to the disciples, and they in turn to the people. (37)They all ate and were satisfied. Afterward the disciples picked up seven basketfuls of broken pieces that were left over. (38)The number of those who ate was four thousand, besides women and children.

I am struck, first of all, by the fact that I am your ongoing presence in the world. I, who have the luxury of eating and fasting when I choose, carry in my heart—if your risen Presence, your Spirit, dwells in me—your compassion for the hungry: those who "fast" because they have no choice.

Second: Even granting that your compassion arouses me, I confront my limits to address the hunger. The need seems to exceed my capacity. That's how the disciples felt when you proposed feeding the crowd (They felt this way even after participating in a previous feeding of an even larger crowd with less bread and fewer fish!). They felt overwhelmed. So do I.

You ask a question in response to the disciples' incredulity, their readiness to throw up their hands in defeat: "How many loaves do you have?" Answer: "Seven loaves . . . plus," they add, as if to accent the preposterous nature of your request, "a few little fishes."

Did it really matter? No. When the feeding is finished, seven basketfuls remain. You, Jesus, are the author of a "new math." Our limited capacity plus your limitless capacity add up to more than enough.

We live in a city where people will go hungry tonight. We live in a world where tens of thousands die each day for lack of nourishment. You dare us to address the need in the spirit of compassion and with confidence in God's bounty.

Here, then, is the message for me today: Don't just stand there; do something! Display the glory of God in a miracle of compassion that exceeds human capacity. Meet survival needs and then address the hunger of the heart that feeding the body awakens.

Compassionate Service

Disagreement exists among Christians over which comes first: evangelism or social service. One group believes that Christians exist as a people of faith to share Christ's good news of salvation with those who haven't heard it. They don't oppose social service; they just don't see it as Christianity's principal business. In fact, they note that social service can become a substitute for evangelism. They warn that Christians can spend their energy meeting people's physical, emotional and economic needs and never actually talk with them about Jesus.

The other group focuses on the social agenda of Jesus and insists on this as a pattern for the Christian community. If Christians truly love people the way Jesus loved people, they will meet them at their points of need with the practical power of God. They will feed the hungry, clothe the naked, tend to the needs of the sick, visit those behind bars, and welcome displaced strangers into their company.[145] This group finds inspiration for compassionate service in passages like the two feedings of the multitudes in Matthew.

Personally, I don't see why the issue gets set up as an either/or dilemma. It strikes me that meeting people at their point of physical hunger and thirst and meeting people at their point of spiritual hunger and thirst belong together.

Gary Haugen, an attorney and follower of Christ who founded International Justice Mission to address global human rights abuse, cuts to the chase when he says, "God has a passion for the world and for justice . . . How do those suffering in the world believe us when we say, 'God is good'? We are God's only plan. The body of Christ shows up, and it becomes possible to believe."[146]

Haugen actually made this comment during a presentation at the 2008 Willow Creek Association Leadership Summit. I served as host pastor of one of the satellite sites for this conference and did so right in the midst of my dark night of the soul. He and the other presenters at the conference couldn't have come my way at a more opportune time. They served as indisputable examples of what can happen when everyday people get a compassionate idea in their head and decide to do something about it to the glory of God. They demonstrated the power and genius of giving one's life away for Christ's sake and for the good of the world.

A trip to Rwanda as part of a United Nations investigating team opened Haugen's eyes to the effects of genocide. An experience in South Africa opened his eyes to apartheid and the more hopeful effects of courageous leadership. His experiences inspired him to create a global justice movement to fight slavery, sex trade, police brutality, and other forms of oppression.[147]

Wendy Kopp, another speaker at the summit, told the story behind her founding Teach for America, a national teachers movement that places top college graduates in the toughest contexts for two years to put at-risk kids on a better educational and life trajectory. While a student at Princeton, she roomed with a brilliant but struggling young woman from Brooklyn whose public school education hadn't prepared her to compete. The experience confronted Wendy with how profoundly the accident of birth impacts a person's prospects. She decided to do something about it.[148]

I was equally moved by the example of Catherine Rohr, a twenty-five-year-old investment broker who walked away from a $200,000 per year job to start a prison entrepreneurship program in the Texas penal system. Invited to visit a prison during a weekend trip to Texas, Catherine saw a side of prison life she hadn't expected. Rather than a place filled with wild, caged animals, she found deeply human, moldable men thirsty for change. She also saw entrepreneurial potential in the illegal activity that put many of these men behind bars. What would happen, she asked herself, if we equipped these men with legitimate business skills?[149]

The stories of Gary Haugen, Wendy Kopp and Catherine Rohr inspired me, and they matched up beautifully with an example of Christian imagination that became a more personal part of my life during this same time. In August 2005, Hurricane Katrina struck the Gulf Coast, scattering the people of New Orleans and other communities to cities like ours. At the invitation of a local leader, Millard and Linda Fuller came to Shreveport with an eye toward capitalizing on the urgent need for new housing.

The Fullers, of course, were founders of Habitat for Humanity, an organization inspired by Jesus' vision of God's kingdom on earth and dedicated to eliminating substandard housing around the world. Having just formed a new organization with the same mission, Fuller Center for Housing,[150] they agreed to work with us in the inner city of Shreveport to replace dilapidated, shotgun housing with safe, affordable homes for locals and displaced families from South Louisiana.

Our church got in at the outset of this initiative, and I count the opportunity to collaborate with and then befriend Millard Fuller before his death as one of my greatest privileges. Habitat for Humanity and Fuller Center embody the answer to the false dichotomy between evangelism and compassionate service. Rooted in a Sermon-on-the-Mount worldview, they have remained explicitly and unapologetically Christian; you can't participate without getting a strong dose of Jesus. At the same time, they have social transformation clearly in their sights—eliminating substandard housing, lifting people out of poverty, altering the terms of home ownership, transforming neighborhoods, building the interpersonal fabric of community.

This matches what Jesus did. He remained steadfastly committed to the creation of a society that understood the holistic nature of salvation and peace. To create a dichotomy between evangelism and social service is more Greek than Hebrew. Hebrew faith has always appreciated that you can't separate the physical, intellectual, social, spiritual, and environmental dimensions of existence into separate compartments. Every aspect flows into the other.

That's why the authors of James and 1 John can expose the phony nature of a so-called love that sees the need of another and responds with nothing more than a benediction.[151] It's why Jesus, in a way that should shock evangelicals more than it does, ties our ultimate destiny to our treatment of the hungry, the thirsty, strangers, the threadbare, the sick, and the imprisoned.[152]

It's also why both versions of Jesus' launching the public phase of his life show his intensely human interest in the joys and sorrows of daily life. The Gospel of Luke depicts Jesus in the synagogue on the Sabbath reading from Isaiah 61:1–2 and announcing that the time for the fulfillment of its promise of justice and healing has arrived.[153] The Gospel of John depicts Jesus at a wedding, taking steps to assure the uninterrupted joy of the occasion.[154]

The "good news"—a translation of the Greek word, $\varepsilon\dot{\upsilon}\alpha\gamma\gamma\dot{\varepsilon}\lambda\iota o\nu$, from which we get our word "evangelism"—the good news of Jesus Christ is time and eternity all woven together into the possibility of a new humanity, a new creation, a new heaven, and a new earth.

At a very personal level, the stories of Jesus, whose compassion transformed people physically and spiritually, aroused in me a desire to recognize need and do something about it. I had no intentions of turning my spiritual wilderness experience into a slog through self-obsession. I wanted the compassion of Christ, even if only experienced second-hand through the stories of Matthew, to keep liberating me from self and for others. As a congregational leader, I also wanted this compassion to inspire the local church I served in a continuous recommitment to the true and holistic mission of the Church universal.

The compassion of Christ meets us where we are and compels a renewal of our own compassion and a restoration of our confidence that power beyond our own will multiply the effect of our service if we will but put our compassion into play.

Jesus may not ask us single-handedly to solve problems like world hunger, but he does in some way ask us to get out of the boat and join him. He does in some way challenge us to step out beyond our strength and exercise compassion with him, trusting the power and genius of what happens next.

Part IV

Mountains
and
Molehills

How do the big and little issues of daily life play against the unfolding drama of Jesus' life? Based on my experience, this is what I would say: It doesn't matter whether we're looking up at mountains—daunted by the obstacles in our way—or looking down from the mountains—inspired by Godlike perspective; the life and words of Jesus cast a whole new light on the world and our place in it.

twenty-two

Matthew 16:21–23

(21)From that time on Jesus began to explain to his disciples that he must go to Jerusalem and suffer many things at the hands of the elders, chief priests and teachers of the law, and that he must be killed and on the third day be raised to life.

(22)Peter took him aside and began to rebuke him. "Never, Lord!" he said. "This shall never happen to you!"

*(23)Jesus turned and said to Peter, **"Get behind me, Satan! You are a stumbling block to me; you do not have in mind the things of God, but the things of men."***

It would come as no consolation for Peter, but we could say to him: "Don't take it personally. Jesus isn't condemning you; he's condemning Satan, who is trying to get at him through you. You are nothing more than a well-meaning, unwitting conduit."

This happens all the time in our love for others. It begins with our thinking we know what's best for them. It expresses itself in our pressuring them toward the course we prefer. This incident should serve to humble us about our ability to know what's best for others. Beyond the parenting of children, when we have a responsibility to protect and guide, we must respect the right, the need, for others to discern the path God has for them. We can consult and question, but ultimately we must defer to their judgment and show our love and friendship by means of good will and personal support. "I may not personally agree with or understand your decision, but I respect your right to make it, and I will be here for you, come what may."

Lord, I take two lessons from this:

- I must grow in my ability to know and do your will, resolutely.

- I must respect others as they discern and follow your will for them.

Grant me insight to know, willingness of spirit to do, and resoluteness of purpose to fulfill your will for my life. Grant me the grace to yield this same right to others.

Personality and Faith

I think I speak for a host of others when I say that I have a special place in my heart for Jesus' disciple Peter. He carried his convictions on his sleeve. He said out loud what those around him thought but wouldn't say. A man of enthusiasm, he could take flight toward heavenly inspirations in one moment and come crashing to earth the very next. Peter's personality distinguishes him among the disciples and endears him to all.

Peter's quirkiness has a way of reminding me just how much personality influences our relationship with God. Doesn't it make sense that how we're wired will color the way we experience God and express our faith?

In the earliest stages of spiritual development, it's inevitable that we will mimic the spirituality of others. In fact, it's good that we have mentors in faith as long as we live. But at points along the way, we discover that what works for one doesn't necessarily work for another.

I remember, for instance, a discipleship group during college days at Baylor that met at 6:00 A.M. on Tuesdays. One of the participants, Dan, had good intentions of making the arrangement work for him, but struggled to get to the group on time or even to show up. He was a late-night person; for him, 6:00 A.M. felt like an *un*godly hour. The group's facilitator expressed disappointment when, a few weeks into the meetings, Dan's lateness had once again proved disruptive. Dan responded by blurting out, "This group just isn't on my priority list!" I'm fairly sure it was his last time to attend.

What works for some doesn't necessarily work for everyone.

I've got to take seriously the way I'm wired. For instance, I'm an Extravert (E) rather than an Introvert (I).[155] I can allow for how I gain stimulation toward spiritual development in group contexts and why the spiritual disciplines of solitude and silence come harder for me.

I'm an iNtuitive (N) rather than a Sensate (S) person. The world of big ideas and future possibilities comes naturally to me and helps explain why I love to ponder the great themes of faith. It also explains why I value the way my wife, a Sensate, tethers me to the here and now and helps me experience the spiritual dimension of my five senses. I owe my love of the outdoors and many of my outdoor experiences of Transcendence to the influence Priscilla has had on my life.

I'm a Thinker (T) and a Feeler (F), balanced between my detached, analytical side and my empathetic, relational side. The polarities of these two sides of my spiritual life have created some interesting tensions through the years as I have tried to discern God's guidance as an organizational leader. The change-leader in me, with its focus on objectives and tasks, bumps up against the tender-hearted shepherd in me, with its focus on how people feel. When the pursuit of objectives causes people distress, which it inevitably does, I get caught between my need to keep going and my need to be nice. Hearing God through the din of these two voices hasn't always been easy.

Finally, I'm a Judging (J) type more than a Perceiving (P) type, which is a way of saying that I like order, aim and completion, whereas others are more into spontaneity, flexibility and playfulness. This makes it easier for me to develop spiritual disciplines. It makes it more difficult for me to balance my life between work and rest, seriousness and playfulness.

I've got to take seriously how I'm wired.

I've also got to allow for how things evolve. Psychologist Carl Jung had a lot to say about the ways under-expressed dimensions of personality come into play in the second half of our lives. I've found this to be true of the spontaneous, less-organized side of my personality.

Quite frankly, it came to play an increasingly significant role in my attitude about pastoral work. I had always considered myself a strong J—very organized, methodical, committed to finishing things I started. But more recently something in me had become increasingly resistant to structure. There came a time, I can't remember now when it was, when this relentless organizing and acting became tiresome to me. I still had lists but I became much less driven by them. I found myself ignoring my lists and going with the flow as each day presented itself.

I do know that some of this had to do with an awareness of how much of my life I had lived without living it because I was always pushing so hard into the future. When I was in my early forties, I had a dream one night that jolted me out of my sleep. In the dream I was in a physician's office sitting on an examining table. The doctor came in with bad news: I had a terminal condition and only days to live. In the dream, I remember thinking, *What a bummer! Here I am, only now learning to live in the present moment, and it's all over! I will basically not have had a life because I've spent the only life I had one step removed from it, caught up in goals, plans and strategic thinking.*

I woke with a start and sat up in the dark, my heart racing. In those next waking moments, grateful that it was "just a dream," I had an epiphany. I didn't want to waste my todays living in tomorrow. I didn't want the responsible adult in me holding back the child in me that wanted to come out and play.

In the interplay of my lead characteristics and my under-expressed characteristics, the balance of power shifted.

What did this have to do with my spirituality? Well, everything. I became less structured in the routines of morning devotion. I became more mindful of my five senses as portals for experiencing God and enjoying God's world. I began to listen to the child within and its capacity for expressiveness and wonder. The doing side of my life finally met its match in the being side.

The irony is that during my dark night many of these lessons came unlearned, and life became a series of daily skirmishes between the child in me at play in the fields of the Lord and the fretful adult in me hustling to secure a place under the sun.

Not only did I need to take seriously the way I'm wired, I also needed to pay attention to the way my selfhood was evolving over time.

Then, too, I had to acknowledge how my make-up, my wiring, limited me. The givens of my life pointed not only to my native strengths but also to my inherent weaknesses, the realities of my life that come with finitude.

For instance, there are devotees of spirituality who can spend extended periods of time in isolation. Wired as Introverts, they grasp the ways and means of solitude intuitively and develop rich inner lives. Consider further that the Thinking types among these Introverts have an even stronger, native capacity to center themselves, even when surrounded by the pressure of others. These capacities come in handy when it comes to cultivating a God-guided life.

I, on the other hand, am an Extravert, and the affectional/feeling side of my life trumps the thinking side of my life when pressed to choose between the two. Centering proves more difficult for me because the voices of others play in my head and make it more difficult for me to sort out whose wants are speaking—God's, mine or those of others. Centering also proves more difficult for me because of a gravitational pull toward rather than away from society. I am less naturally given to solitude and silence than the introvert.

This doesn't mean that I can't offset these tendencies in meaningful ways. I think, for instance, of the ways I have exercised my organized side to structure habits of devotion and solitude. This book itself is testimony to habits of contemplation and mindful prayer that have become lifelines for me in the midst of life's demands and details. These habits have given me a practical way to move into the re-creating silence, where my heart can cry out to God and wait for God to break through in me.

At the same time, I must acknowledge my default ways. I will never be a Simon Stylites, the early Christian hermit who spent decades in the desert, sitting on a pillar in isolation and prayer. I will always feel the tug of others' moods and opinions and find myself battling between empathy and detachment when centering down and getting a sense of guidance. I will spend a lifetime engaging my five senses in an exploration and enjoyment of the world, but I will ever remain an intuitive whose native land is the realm of ideas, ideals and dreams.

There is yet one other aspect of personality and faith I want to note, with some attention to how it played out during this unique time in my life. Father Murray Clayton, my dear friend and spiritual director during my time in Shreveport, introduced me to the enneagram, a personality-based guide with roots in Sufi wisdom and applications in the Christian spiritual life.[156] Unlike some personality programs with their almost exclusive focus on the positive ("I'm okay, you're okay"), the enneagram balances a celebration of who we are with an honest assessment of the vulnerabilities that come with each type. It identifies nine different styles and explores what makes them tick, including each style's virtues and vices, aspirations and fears.

I particularly remember locating myself somewhere between the two types whose primary fears were failure and need. It's interesting to see how these tendencies have played themselves out through the years and how they impacted my life during this period in the spiritual wilderness. My fear of failure mounted to the point of occasional panic. My fear of need made me reluctant to talk with anyone about it.

My moments of panic came when I was alone. They came during those times in my overbooked life when I wasn't preparing material on a deadline, leading a meeting, or having an appointment. They surfaced in the early morning, when I had time to think, or in the evening, when I headed home at the end of an exhausting day.

First would come the fear of failure, prophesying a looming disaster. Then would come the fear of need, telling me not to bother anyone about how I felt, telling me that I should be able to handle it and warning me not to whine. I battled my fears through prayer and self-talk and—despite my fear of need—through heart-to-hearts with Priscilla and a few other friends. At one point during my Shreveport years, I even contracted with an older colleague in another city to talk on the phone regularly and deal with the fear and fatigue that were weighing me down.

In several journal entries my fear of failure stepped front and center. I specifically recall the day I arrived at the story of Peter walking on water. I had to allow for how my fear of failure had compromised my decisiveness as a leader, how it had led to partial measures and lack of clarity in communication. As the senior pastor of a church where every decision seemed to make some group mad and hasten another set of departures, I had to fight twin tendencies: the tendency to strike compromises that made no one truly happy and the tendency to look back with misgivings after decisions were made. The clarity and confidence of my calls to action were clouded by my effort to placate those who hadn't gotten their way.

I had the conviction in spiritual terms that the combination of my adaptive-dealing temperament and my fears made it hard sometimes for God to get my attention over the clamoring and competing voices of church people that played in my head. Was God truly indifferent to my appeals for guidance or were other voices drowning out God's reply?

When it comes to the impact of my personality on my experience in the cloud-covered spiritual valley, I'm sure I haven't plumbed all the depths, even now. Nevertheless, I know that my personality came into play in empowering and limiting ways. It served as the filter through which my experience of God would happen, if it were to happen at all.

twenty-three

Matthew 16:24–27

(24)Then Jesus said to his disciples, "If anyone would come after me, he must deny himself and take up his cross and follow me. (25)For whoever wants to save his life will lose it, but whoever loses his life for me will find it. (26)What good will it be for a man if he gains the whole world, yet forfeits his soul? Or what can a man give in exchange for his soul? (27)For the Son of Man is going to come in his Father's glory with his angels, and then he will reward each person according to what he has done."

You lay down a challenge to would-be disciples. We can't think that following you has to do with just:

- being your closest companions (BFJ's—"Best Friends of Jesus");

- having front row seats for your miracles and your messages;

- enjoying your delegated rights, privileges and powers.

These things do come with the package—but so do hardship and suffering. To live, we must die. To find ourselves, we must give our lives away.

True life is cruciform. True love is cruciform. And joy isn't just at the end of suffering; we find it in suffering itself. This isn't masochism. Joy comes from seeing the good that God has brought in the midst of it.[157] It comes from experiencing an intensified sense of fellowship with God.[158]

Jesus, you focus on the destiny of the soul, and you tell me that I can gain everything I think I want, up to and including the whole world, and lose my soul in the bargain. In other words, I need to look with sobriety at the persistent longings toward which I bend my life and prayers. Noted pastor and author Harry Emerson Fosdick was right; we tend to get what we truly want. The universe yields to our deepest desires, for better and for worse.[159]

The Journey inward and the Journey beyond Self

There's a danger in the spiritual journey, the danger that the journey will become self-centered navel gazing. I'll confess it: During my spiritual crisis I frequently fixated on my thoughts, my feelings, my desires and dreads, my words and deeds. My selfhood kept jumping into the picture. There were times, I now realize, when I was holding up a mirror rather than a magnifying glass in my search for God.

If you identify with this, you can take some consolation in the fact that one of the great books of the Bible, the book of Psalms, has a good bit of mirror gazing:

- "Be merciful to me, Lord; for I am faint; O Lord, heal me, for my bones are in agony. My soul is in anguish. How long, O Lord, how long?"[160]

- "Keep me as the apple of your eye; hide me in the shadow of your wings from the wicked who assail me, from my mortal enemies who surround me."[161]

- "When I kept silent about my sin, my bones wasted away through my groaning all day long. For day and night your hand was heavy upon me; my strength was sapped as in the heat of summer."[162]

More than one of the Psalms has a self-centered quality to it. Confused by the gap between the way life actually works and the way it's supposed to work, or distressed, discouraged, and defeated, the psalmists pour out their pain.

Don't misunderstand me. From a biblical perspective, it's perfectly okay to let God know what you think, feel or want. The writers of the psalms and prophets like Jeremiah, for instance, had high levels of self-awareness and showed no reluctance to share this quality with God. But here's the deal: They were "God-ward" in their conversations, and their cries most often ended in praise. There was something a good bit more than a soliloquy going on.

As far as I'm concerned, the most depressing stretch of the Bible comes in Ecclesiastes, where someone who calls himself "the Teacher" takes off on an extended excursion of self-obsessed introspection and ends up saying, "Meaningless! Meaningless! Utterly meaningless! Everything is meaningless."[163]

The self-centered nature of his contemplation reveals itself in statements like these:

- "I thought to myself . . ."[164]
- "I tried to cheer myself . . ."[165]
- "So I reflected on all this and concluded . . ."[166]

His self-guided tour into the mysteries of time, toil, education, achievement, and materialistic pleasure leave him exhausted and forlorn. He experiences the futility of self-obsession.

Christian discipleship has two answers to this danger. First, it offers Christ as our escort into the inner terrain. Second, it suggests that we find self by losing self.

As to the first, in Christian meditation we don't go alone with our mind into our heart; we have Christ himself as our escort. We keep our eyes on him as he walks us into the truth of who we are, where we've been, and who we can become. His Lordship humbles us. His grace reassures us. He alleviates the dangers of self-justifying delusion on the one hand and self-condemning despair on the other. He continually reminds us that God is at the center of the universe, thus helping us not to take ourselves too seriously.

Christian discipleship's second answer to the danger of self-obsession is the cross: the invitation to find self by losing self. The ultimate paradox of life is that we find our lives not by fixating on self but by focusing away from self on God and others. That's why Jesus, the Master Mentor, invites us to follow him by saying, "If any man will come after me, let him deny himself, and take up his cross, and follow me. For whoever will save his life shall lose it: and whoever will lose his life for my sake shall find it."[167]

Jesus, in the red letters, kept prodding me beyond myself. Doing this became a saving grace.

It helped that I had had an early experience in soul-liberating freedom from self-obsession. During the three summers following my final two years of high school and first year at college, I worked as a YMCA day-camp counselor. From the time I arrived at work each morning until the time I got back in my car at the end of the day, the first through third graders in my charge had my undivided attention. I didn't have the luxury of self-concern because they demanded every ounce of my energy.

It didn't take me long to realize that I actually felt better about life when serving these kids than I did when taking my emotional temperature all the time. Living for others made me feel more vigorous and alive. I had living proof about the counter-intuitive wisdom of the cross as a way of life.

During my dark night of the soul, I kept returning to this young-adult experience as a reminder that God was as likely to come to me in the midst of self-giving service as in the course of my transparent cries of the heart. I didn't have to fear my honest confessions; but I dared not linger there too long.

twenty-four

Matthew 17:1–8

(1)After six days Jesus took with him Peter, James and John the brother of James, and led them up a high mountain by themselves. (2)There he was transfigured before them. His face shone like the sun, and his clothes became as white as the light. (3)Just then there appeared before them Moses and Elijah, talking with Jesus.

(4)Peter said to Jesus, "Lord, it is good for us to be here. If you wish, I will put up three shelters—one for you, one for Moses and one for Elijah."

(5)While he was still speaking, a bright cloud enveloped them, and a voice from the cloud said, "This is my Son, whom I love; with him I am well pleased. Listen to him!"

(6)When the disciples heard this, they fell facedown to the ground, terrified. (7)But Jesus came and touched them. **"Get up,"** he said. **"Don't be afraid."** (8)When they looked up, they saw no one except Jesus.

We long for a meeting of heaven and earth. When the meeting comes, it overwhelms us. God isn't the Wizard of Oz, a fear-evoking fraud who turns out to be a little old man pulling levers behind a curtain. Pull back the curtain on God and Heaven breaks through with thunder and lightning—a voice that booms and a light that blinds. Encounter with the Holy Power above all power is AWEFUL, in the truest sense of that word—"full of awe"; tremendous and terrifying, all at the same time.

Note how suddenly a disciple's enthusiasm and confidence gets shattered in the encounter. At first, Peter devises plans for a permanent mountain residence. Upon hearing God's voice, he and the others crumble to the ground and hide their faces in horrific fear. Their confidence melts. They quiver in the face of Divine Majesty.

When I plead for your Presence, I'd best understand what I'm asking for. You come not as Tame Shepherd, tending to my requests, but as Transcendent Lord of heaven and earth, Master and Power to an infinite degree. You come as Overwhelming Glory, Basso Profundo, Soul-Shattering, Soul-Searching Lightning and Holiness, and I am speechless in the realization that you ARE Consuming Fire, the Great I AM.

Your first actions and words come as a great welcome, Jesus. You move to us in concern. You touch us with compassion. You speak to us with reassurance. "Arise, do not be afraid." You, the human face of God, make it safe for me to long for your appearance. I can see you and not die.[168] I can see you, and live. In fact, seeing you, I—for the first time—DO live.

God Is Great; God Is Good

Perhaps I should have been more terrified than I was when I launched my journey into the red letters of Jesus, but I had come to see Love in the magnificent eyes of the Holy One. Jesus himself had helped me understand that God was *for* me, not *against* me. Jesus himself had come as God in human flesh to clarify this, once and for all.

Desire, Not Dread

John 3:16 didn't become the most beloved and well-known verse in the Bible by accident. In this verse, Jesus tells us that "God so loved the world that he gave his one and only Son, that whoever believes in him shall not perish but have eternal life." Love drives God's appearing.

The follow-up words of John 3:17 bring further reassurance. "For God did not send his Son into the world to condemn the world, but to save the world through him." Jesus came not to condemn, but to save.

I meet people on a regular basis who have turned their backs on biblical faith because of traumatic experiences with fear- and guilt-fixated Christians. Of all the reasons for rejecting God, this may be the most unfortunate since it allows misguided representatives of Christ to prevent others from giving the real Jesus a chance. For whatever other problems I was having with God during my experience in the dry land of God's silence, I rested easy about the implications of a fresh encounter with God.

Perhaps I shouldn't have; my confidence about my convictions had been compromised. I could very easily have fallen prey to disquieting uncertainty about what kind of God I would have to deal with if that God ever stepped out of the dark. Instead, I maintained confidence that God, as Jesus portrayed God, was the One for whom I was waiting. I wanted renewed relationship. I longed for it, giving little thought to how terrifying it might prove. I believed what Jesus said; God would come to me not to condemn, but to save. "God is love," the author of 1 John writes. "Whoever lives in love lives in God, and God in him. In this way, love is made complete among us so that we will have confidence on the day of judgment."[169]

Desire and Respect

I felt confident to desire rather than dread an encounter with God; but having established this, I must now say more, because the story of Jesus' transfiguration reminded me to maintain the fruitful tension between gratitude for God's love and respect for God's Lordship. Yes, as the author of 1 John reminds us, "perfect love drives out fear"[170]—to experience God's love in Christ is to break free from the fear of divine judgment. But God, who offers intimacy of relationship through Jesus, remains the Great God of the Universe. God doesn't sacrifice God's holiness—God's transcendent Otherness, God's Mystery—when wrapping us in the arms of Infinite Love.

J. B. Phillips's book, *Your God Is Too Small*, has become a modern classic with its critique of popular images of God, images that don't do God justice and don't command our highest admiration and respect.[171] He debunks such notions of God as "Resident Policeman," "Parental Hangover," "Grand Old Man," "Meek-and-Mild," "Heavenly Bosom," "God-in-a-Box," and "Pale Galilean." In their place he introduces readers to the actual God of the Bible, the God above and beyond us and in and for us, the God of Grandeur and Grace whom we come to know best in the person of Jesus.

Can anything less than this kind of God satisfy the longings of our hearts? Unless God transcends the complications of the world, unless God has a point of view that exceeds all others, unless God reigns as nothing less than the Lord of all that is, we seek and worship in vain.

Trusting God's Love, Respecting God's Lordship

By implication, then, there is no contradiction between trusting God's love and respecting God's Lordship. But if this is true, then we can't pretend to know in advance what might happen when a meeting of heaven and earth takes place. To say that God is love doesn't mean that God can't confront as well as comfort or that God can't unsettle us with agendas not our own. Remember what the Voice from heaven said at the end of the experience of transfiguration? "This is my Son, whom I love; with him I am well pleased. *Listen to him!*"

Anyone who thinks they want to embark on a journey toward God should take stock before beginning the journey to make sure they're open to the bracing as well as the beautiful aspects of an encounter. If we're truly listening, we must ready ourselves for anything we might hear and any way the Risen One might shape and direct us.

I like the way the Pulitzer Prize-winning author Annie Dillard puts it:

> On the whole, I do not find Christians, outside the catacombs, sufficiently sensible of the conditions. Does anyone have the foggiest idea what sort of power we so blithely invoke? Or, as I suspect, does no one believe a word of it? The churches are children playing on the floor with their chemistry sets, mixing up a batch of TNT to kill a Sunday morning. It is madness to wear ladies' straw hats and velvet hats to church; we should all be wearing crash helmets. Ushers should issue life preservers and signal flares; they should lash us to our pews. For the sleeping god may wake some day and take offense, or the waking god may draw us out to where we can never return.[172]

God Is Great; God Is Good

God is Great; God is Good. God is Love; God is Demand. To love God as God is revealed in the Bible is to hold these two sides of faith together. If we can manage this, it actually becomes conceivable, at last, to reclaim the much misunderstood saying, "The fear of the Lord is the beginning of wisdom."[173]

This "fear"—more accurately translated, "sober, awe-filled respect"—reflects a full appreciation for the transcendent holiness, power and glory of God. As the apostle Paul told one of his audiences, "The God who made the world and everything in it is the Lord of heaven and earth . . . In him we live and move and have our being."[174]

But notice that "sober, awe-filled respect" is only the *beginning* of wisdom. Once we've learned this lesson there's more, much more. Yes, to expose ourselves *to* the Light of God is to expose ourselves *in* the Light of God; but it is to do so in a way that liberates us in love. Biblical faith affirms that God in God's holiness is driven by love. God is driven not to tear us down but to build us up; not to devastate us but to recreate us; not to steal our lives from us but to give our lives back to us—in a way that leads us to realize that we're actually experiencing life, transcendent, capital L "Life"—for the first time.

In the crucible of my unrequited longing for God, I was banking on this to be true.

twenty-five

Matthew 17:14–20

(14)When they came to the crowd, a man approached Jesus and knelt before him. (15)"Lord, have mercy on my son," he said. "He has seizures and is suffering greatly. He often falls into the fire or into the water. (16)I brought him to your disciples, but they could not heal him."

(17)**"O unbelieving and perverse generation,"** Jesus replied, **"how long shall I stay with you? How long shall I put up with you? Bring the boy here to me."** (18)Jesus rebuked the demon, and it came out of the boy, and he was healed from that moment.

(19)Then the disciples came to Jesus in private and asked, "Why couldn't we drive it out?"

(20)He replied, **"Because you have so little faith. I tell you the truth, if you have faith as small as a mustard seed, you can say to this mountain, 'Move from here to there' and it will move. Nothing will be impossible for you."**

You tell us that faith is the key to working miracles and that the problem is our lack of it. You tell us that we have power and authority at our fingertips to command mountains to move, so much so that a mere mustard seed of faith will get the job done!

How do I deal with this—as a person and as a pastor? How do I step beyond the puny expressions of my palliative compassion and become a true source of divine healing?

You are insisting that my moral choices, my daily routines, my conversations, the thoughts that roll around in my head, the feelings and desires that arise and subside in me, my physical condition, the circumstances and trends of the church, this city, our nation and other nations, our culture and other cultures all reflect, at their deepest level, the current state of a teeming spiritual "population," and you are telling me and my fellow disciples that you have granted us power and authority to have a hand in aligning these forces with your purposeful will. You are saying that the full force of your creative Divine power can flow through us.

If this is true, then I am a racecar running like a scooter. I am dynamite acting like a little Fourth of July firecracker. I am the Power of Heaven acting like a clump of earth. Overwhelmed by superhuman challenges, I have superhuman strength at my disposal.

Open my eyes that I may see the spiritual dimension of all that's going on, and train me to become increasingly agile and effective at mastering this co-creative work. I can't hope to take this step of faith without a deeply serious engagement in relationship with you, one that causes me to unplug from fog-inducing immersion in my secular milieu so as to begin to see you and the spiritual realm more clearly through the haze of humanity.

Let's begin right now.

Shouting into the Wind

At this point in my wilderness journey the verdict actually was still out for me as to whether biblical faith was merited. I know this sounds odd, given the strength of my conviction in the previous journal entry, but such was the nature of my "bi-polarity" during those days. The story of Jesus had me in its grip, but I couldn't shake a nagging doubt. I took Jesus to heart when he challenged the disciples' faith. Still, troubling questions lingered.

A voice in my head asked, *Is the good news too good to be true?* Or is it, as Frederick Buechner suggests in *Telling the Truth: The Gospel as Comedy, Tragedy, and Fairy Tale*, too good *not* to be true?[175] Am I justified to believe in a God who intervenes in the course of human events? Does God care about the major movements of our time and the mundane matters of our daily lives? Do our prayers make a difference? And when things go as we have prayed they would, is this evidence that God has acted, or is it simply the result of the natural laws of cause and effect?

I teetered between credulity and incredulity. One side of me wanted to experiment with mustard-seed faith; another side of me stood ready to jettison the grander notions of a personal, providential God. I found myself at one and the same time believing *and not* believing, praying *and questioning* the value of prayer.

From childhood I had accepted the biblical worldview and the challenge of God that I pray in faith, believing. I had accepted the idea that there was a personal God at the other end of my communication who heard and responded to the cries of my heart. I had repeatedly acted on the assumption that I must pray, believing,[176] and that when I did, I could move mountains.[177]

The journal entry related to Jesus' statement about faith that moves mountains reveals my continuing desire to believe. But my two years in the spiritual wilderness brought to a head my suspicion that one must give into delusion to believe this way. Disappointment waiting for God reached the point at which prayer felt like shouting into the wind.

Why bother? What difference does it make?

These weren't rhetorical questions for me, and I suspect they're not rhetorical questions for most people. I'm guessing that every-one who has ever lived has wanted to have reason to believe in the responsive, intervening love of God. I'm guessing everyone has wanted cause to ask, seek, and knock, believing.[178] I'm guess-ing everyone has even wanted, at one time or another, to believe in miracles—God's decisive, supernatural action to turn circumstances in a favorable direction.

According to the Bible, God hears the cry of captive people and sets them free,[179] God makes a passageway through the water,[180] God singlehandedly stops enemy armies,[181] God heals diseases and stills storms and raises the dead.[182] According to the Bible, God loves us, hears us, responds to us, and lights a path for us, whether it is the pil-lar of fire by night[183] or the whisper in the wind by day.[184]

Most of us must admit to limited evidence that this really is the way the world works. I regularly talk with sincere people of faith who can't recall any incontrovertible experience of the miraculous, any so-called answer to prayer that defies natural explanation. Many of us struggle to identify any results from divine-human conversation that simply had to be an in-breaking of an interested, personal Father.

I have already shared anecdotes from my life that felt like break-throughs of the Divine, and these have had a profound effect on my faith. But I have to admit that these experiences wouldn't stand up in a court of law. I can't produce evidence that would force a skeptic to admit that the biblical worldview holds true.

So I find myself identifying with the disciples in the aftermath of the healing of the boy with uncontrollable seizures. "So little faith," Jesus answers them when they ask why they couldn't heal him.[185] Interestingly enough, the father's well-known plea for more faith comes on this same occasion. The Gospel of Mark records that the father, challenged to believe in Jesus' healing power, cries, "I believe; help me in my unbelief!"[186]

Uncertainty sneaks into my prayers, and I have a list of ready expla-nations in case nothing happens in response to my requests. Let's say

I pray for a patient to get well, but her condition actually worsens. I'm prepared to suggest that God may have put her on a path toward wellness other than the one I had in mind, or that the wellness God has in mind is spiritual rather than physical. I might say that I had prayed without true understanding, imposing an agenda on God inconsistent with God's actual interests. With any of these explanations I have an out that masks my misgivings. I must lean on God's grace to complete what I lack in faith. Otherwise my prayers don't stand a chance.

Here's the deal: despite my misgivings during my dark night of the soul, I still operated on the assumption that God would produce evidence that God was alive and well and active on behalf of those who seek God. I still led the church I pastored to "attempt something so big for God that, without God, it will fail."[187] I still wanted to believe in a mountain-moving God and the power of a prayer partnership with this God.

I also confess that I thought it reasonable to walk away from the claims of faith if a lifetime of prayer went unanswered . . .

. . . Except for this: The Bible pulled out the ultimate trump card, bearing witness to—and calling for—a faith that believes in the face of all evidence to the contrary. Hebrews 11, for instance, presents an honor roll of faithful women and men and observes, "All these people were still living by faith when they died. They did not receive the things promised; they only saw them and welcomed them from a distance."[188] Biblical faith dares us to cling to the view of a powerful, personal, providential God even if circumstances seem for the moment to defy the empirical test.

Wow. Isn't that a bit audacious? Doesn't that beg credulity? Can't that be considered psychotic?

We have been asked by God to lay a wager on divine faithfulness. We have been challenged to live as people of faith, believing and praying, whatever the conspicuous outcomes of our prayers.

Jesus' challenge dared me to stretch my faith. The disciples' perplexity more closely matched my present experience.

twenty-six

Matthew 18:18–20

(18)"I tell you the truth, whatever you bind on earth will be bound in heaven, and whatever you loose on earth will be loosed in heaven.

(19)*"Again, I tell you that if two of you on earth agree about anything you ask for, it will be done for you by my Father in heaven. (20)For where two or three come together in my name, there am I with them."*

Unbottle us, Lord, as people of command power; we fail on this score more than on the side of presumption. Discipline us as well, so that our power and authority move in a Divine-human synergy that transforms lives.

It strikes me that one of the discernment questions to ask in preparation for the prayers that bind and loose is this: "Am I willing to act decisively in cooperation with my prayer?" For instance, I may pray, "Transform the inner-city neighborhood of Allendale." Question: Am I willing to roll up my sleeves and work toward that end? If not, what am I saying about my prayers? My sense is that we must invest ourselves in our praying or else our prayers are wishful thinking, mere applause from the balcony.

Your announcement about the power and authority you have placed in our hands sounds almost like a commanding officer preparing troops for armed conflict; only in our case, we're waging peace, not war. You put us on the front line to love people and battle the destructive forces that thwart them. Considered in this light, praying isn't arm-chair army work; it's soldiering in the trenches; it's spiritual combat on the battlefield. What we're binding and loosing are principalities and powers.[189] In prayer, we're armed with the nuclear power of heaven and weapons of transformation. Innocent people surround the targets of the guided missiles that are our prayers.

We have scary power, given what you are telling us here; but we don't—we dare not—keep it under wraps because it's scary. We let you train us to aim it in the right spirit and the right way.

Lord, teach us to pray!

The Problem of Prayer

I couldn't get away from Jesus' persistent invitation to pray, believing. Here it came again, promising a power in prayer partnership that could dramatically alter conditions in the world. It was almost as if God wanted to hammer me with reminders to live by faith, not sight.

I could recall a litany of biblical promises in this regard:

- "Delight yourself in the Lord, and he will give you the desires of your heart."[190]

- "If you seek me, you will find me, when you search for me with all your heart."[191]

- "Ask and it will be given to you; seek and you will find; knock and the door will be opened to you. For everyone who asks receives; he who seeks finds; and to him who knocks, the door will be opened."[192]

- "If you, then, though you are evil, know how to give good gifts to your children, how much more will your Father in heaven give good gifts to those who ask him!"[193]

In the Bible, God repeatedly promises responsiveness, and Jesus does the same. We are challenged to call on God, to ask, seek, knock. We are challenged to ask in faith[194] and to ask in Jesus' name.[195] We are challenged to persist.[196]

Throughout the Bible and across the centuries of believing people, petitionary prayer has been seen as a powerful means of grace. Behind it is the idea that God sees us in our need, hears us when we cry,[197] and loves us with a responsive Father's built-in bias for action.[198] In fact, Jesus tells us that the all-seeing, all-knowing, omnipresent God already knows what we need before we ask.[199] Not only does God know what we need; God cares. God cares about even the smallest details of our lives.[200] God certainly cares about the basic necessities of life, and so Jesus tells us we need not worry about what we shall eat, drink or wear.[201]

According to biblical faith, heaven bends its attention and its energy in the direction of our prayers, so much so that miracles can happen. We are encouraged to believe that God will, at times, defy the very laws of nature—as we understand them—in response to urgent, believing prayer.[202] In fact, the Bible provides stories from beginning to end in testimony to this possibility.

Prayer changes things. Prayer changes everything.

Clearly, the Bible reverberates with the call to boldness in prayer and the promise that it makes a difference. But at the risk of sounding like a broken record, don't these strong words about prayer heighten the uneasiness we feel when our experience fails to match up with the Bible's claims?

What accounts for the ragged record of prayer-filled request and response? Has sin gotten in the way?[203] Is the problem a lack of faith?[204] Do I need more persistence?[205] Is it, instead, that we are asking or have asked amiss?[206]

I am told that the prayers of a righteous man are powerful and effective.[207] Is this the difference maker? Is there something in me that thwarts prayer's power?

Wrestling with the biblical text during my faith struggle, I had to allow for other possibilities too:

- The possibility that there are things going on in the purposes of God beyond what we can know now;

- The possibility that there may be a grace in unanswered prayer (Oscar Wilde once said, "When the gods wish to punish us, they answer our prayers."[208]);

- The possibility that God only intervenes sporadically, as God deems appropriate;

- The possibility that prayer really doesn't work as the Bible says it does. Either it once did, under special circumstances in the course of salvation history, but no longer does; or, it never did, and what we call answered prayer is really nothing more than the quirks of natural history interpreted as miracles through the eyes of believing faith.

The whole idea of "seeing is believing/believing is seeing" that I have already written about throws a wrinkle in the conversation that can't be resolved through pure logic or empiricism. We are left with what Peter Berger called "the heretical imperative" ("heretical" coming from a Greek word which in its root form means "choice").[209] According to Berger, we face the inescapability of choosing a way of faith in a world of competing truth claims.

We must choose to believe or not believe and then live accordingly.

We can't ignore the example of people like Shadrach, Meshach, and Abednego and Habakkuk and Peter and John who refuse to yield their faith, even in the face of all evidence to the contrary:

- "If we are thrown into the blazing furnace, the God we serve is able to save us from it, and he will rescue us from your hand, O King. But even if he does not, we want you to know, O King, that we will not serve your gods or worship the image of gold you have set up."[210]

- "Though the fig tree does not bud and there are no grapes on the vines, though the olive crop fails and the fields produce no food, though there are no sheep in the pen and no cattle in the stalls, yet will I rejoice in the Lord, I will be joyful in God my Savior. The Sovereign Lord is my strength."[211]

- In response to threats of punishment from the Sanhedrin unless they cease and desist as proclaimers of Christ, Peter and John show the same defiant confidence: "Judge for yourselves whether it is right in God's sight to obey you rather than God. For we cannot help speaking about what we have seen and heard."[212]

Jesus himself becomes our prime exemplar. He prays for deliverance from a gruesome fate, but yields to the Father's will.[213] Then, in the last agonizing hours of his life he cries out in distress, out of a sense of God-forsakenness;[214] yet he refuses to yield his faith. "Father, into your hands I commit my spirit," he says, just before taking his last breath.[215]

Here, then, is the challenge that comes with the promises of Scripture: the challenge to believe and to act accordingly. It's the challenge to believe in God as one who cares about the intimate details of our lives, everyone else's life, and the mind-bogglingly complex world God nourishes and sustains. It's the challenge to believe in answered prayer, the possibility of miracles, and even God's ability to do the impossible.[216]

A caveat seems in order at this point. To believe this way doesn't mean to believe that the promises of the Bible come as a guarantee. Some people, despite prayers, still die. Poor people still go hungry. Threadbare people go improperly clothed. Thirsty people die for lack of potable water. The human prayer/divine response equation doesn't work as simply as any would like it to, and circumstances arise—problems persist—that severely test credulity.

However, in my tenuous grasp on faith during those days in the dark, I dared not stop praying. Who could know what a difference it might make? At the same time, I had to battle to let go of worry, despite Jesus' urging that I do so.[217] I carried Philippians 4:6–7 like prescription medicine wherever I went—"Be anxious for nothing, but by prayer and petition, with thanksgiving, let your requests be made known to God; and the peace of God which passes understanding will guard your hearts and minds in Christ Jesus." I also leaned on the encouragement of texts that assured me of God's strength to come out ahead on the other side of life's storms.[218]

In the end, I couldn't help bringing the mountains and molehills of my concern to God. Feeling very much like a child, I was unable to resist asking God, "Will you, please, move a mountain for me?"

twenty-seven

Matthew 19:27–30

(27)Peter answered him, "We have left everything to follow you! What then will there be for us?"

(28)Jesus said to them, **"I tell you the truth, at the renewal of all things, when the Son of Man sits on his glorious throne, you who have followed me will also sit on twelve thrones, judging the twelve tribes of Israel.** *(29)* **And everyone who has left houses or brothers or sisters or father or mother or children or fields for my sake will receive a hundred times as much and will inherit eternal life.** *(30)* **But many who are first will be last, and many who are last will be first."**

Peter's question—"We have left everything to follow you! What then will there be for us?"—goes down for me as one of the most vulnerable and poignant in all of Scripture. He and the other disciples have wagered their whole lives, and everything they have on you. Has this sellout been in vain? In the final analysis will they find that heaven eludes them, too?

Jesus, you provide immediate reassurance. You calm the disciples' anxious hearts. Pointing to the end of time and the final judgment, you tell the twelve that they will have thrones on either side of you. Furthermore, having forsaken even the comforts of family to follow you, they will find their family expanded a hundred-fold, and they will enjoy an inheritance that outstrips anything they can imagine. As children of God, they will inherit eternal life.

Master, there have been times when I've wondered if I am running the race in vain. There have been times even recently when I have questioned the sanity of my service, my faith, and the choices I've made to follow you. There have been times, in other words, when I have regretted my life. Where has my life gotten me? What has it gotten me? What do I have to show for it?

Answer: Your life has not been in vain. Hang in there!

Christians: Can't Live with Them; Can't Live without Them

Let me make a confession in light of Jesus' promise of a great, happy family for those who sell out to him. I'm not proud of what I'm about to confess, and my biblical-theological training and my experience as a pastoral counselor tells me better, but here it goes anyway: I'm not always crazy about Christian community.

There are times when the sweet joy of Christian friendship and fellowship touches me so deeply that it brings me to tears; but just as often I experience Christians in community as fickle, disappointing, and even dangerous. Navigating the ups and downs of human relationships, even (and sometimes especially) Christian relationships, can be a tiring, tedious and occasionally treacherous challenge.

There are friends, colleagues, acquaintances, strangers and enemies—overt and covert. There are allies and confidants. There is healthy interpersonal communication, and there is passive-aggressiveness, gossip, unresolved anger, divisiveness, and all of the other healthy and unhealthy stuff that goes on in our interactions in the world at large.

I could write this off by saying, "What do you expect? We're only human." However, I can't shake the conviction that life among followers of Jesus promises something better. We believe that God's Spirit lives in us and among us, and according to the apostle Paul, "the fruit of the Spirit is love, joy, peace, patience, kindness, goodness, faithfulness, gentleness and self-control."[219] It's understandable that we would fall short of this ideal as unfinished followers; but too often I have the sense that we've settled for being "saved" and let ourselves off the hook about anything more.

When we settle, it's not safe to be together. One of the most disturbing things I've ever heard about Christian community is that "the Church is the only army that shoots its wounded." Ouch!

No wonder we sometimes hide from one another. In a setting designed to invite transparency and mutual understanding, we too often guard ourselves against knowing one another and being known. I am not immune from this myself. I have developed a mask for when I need it that is so sophisticated that I can kid even myself into believing it; a mask so convincing that I am in some ways a stranger to myself. Intimacy is no less a problem for me than it is for anyone else. I can make people feel close while guarding my true, deepest self.

I read what German pastor, theologian, and martyr Dietrich Bonhoeffer wrote in his wise little book, *Life Together* and know to my discomfort that it is true:

> Let him who cannot be alone beware of community . . . Let him who is not in community beware of being alone . . . Each by itself has profound pitfalls and perils. One who wants fellowship without solitude plunges into the void of words and feelings, and one who seeks solitude without fellowship perishes in the abyss of vanity, self-infatuation and despair.[220]

Here's the deal: Christian community holds an irresistible appeal for me, and at the same time it scares me. I long to be known, understood, cared for, valued, encouraged, welcomed and accepted unconditionally. I want to belong, to be included, to participate in common purpose. At the same time, I fear being fully known, exposed, and rejected. I also hate the limits imposed on my freedom that come with belonging. I want my autonomy. I want my way. I want to keep my options open. I dare say that most of us who live in western civilization these days could make a similar confession.

As the article "We, the Lonely People"[221] put it so beautifully years ago, I want community, but I want my freedom more. My feelings about Christian community parallel the old misogynist statement by a man about women: "Christians: can't live with 'em; can't live without 'em."

During my walk through the loneliness of the spiritual desert, something inside me told me that my ultimate wholeness would demand that I learn to trust my way more completely into Christian community. My fear of community held me back and kept me at arm's length (my own arms length) away. I knew how to be friendly and cordial. I even knew how to manufacture a level of intimacy. Sometimes it felt like false intimacy.

As a pastor, the issue got complicated by the expectations of others and my own efforts at image management. It's harder in some ways for us to be real than others. Given the expectations of others, the price of transparency can be steep. Many pastors conclude that they can't have true friends among the members of the churches they pastor. The experience-tempered among us live with a sober realization that our place in community is partly personal, partly positional.

As the previous Bonhoeffer statement suggests, neither solitude nor community is sufficient unto itself. I, for instance, had to deal with how my extraversion and my people-pleasing, adaptive-dealing could turn me into what everyone else thought, felt, or wanted to the exclusion of what the inner voice thought, felt, or wanted. The cacophony of everyone else's expectations, hopes and fears, real and imagined, could silence my own self-awareness and the voice of God.

At the same time, I knew that Christian community was an essential divine tool if God were to guide me. I could not do this journey alone. Nor, in terms of the ultimate promise of a great family feast at the end of history, did I want to.

During my dark night of the soul, I experienced this tension in a profound kind of way. It actually became a major element in my reassessment of calling. Honesty forced me to acknowledge how my guarded attitude toward community and relationship-building limited my capacity to facilitate the *esprit de corps* and unity of the people of the church whom I pastored.

Confessions of an Ambivalent Member of the Christian Family

Interestingly enough, it took a repeat reading of Jesus' promise of a great, happy family to reawaken me to how much this promise means to me. It took a second dose of Jesus' reassurance to rekindle my hope. Given my fear of and yearning for belonging and friendship and true community, given my underlying loneliness, and given how easily I teared up when watching movies about forgiveness and reconciliation or seeing wounded friends embrace again, it surprised me that my heart didn't swell instantaneously at the promise of a large, loving family and pure acceptance.

On second reading, it did. I could see that Jesus was offering a real *Cheers*[222] destiny; true community, a place where "everybody knows your name." Family. Home. Knowing and being known. Loving and being loved. Accepting and being accepted. Valuing and being valued. He was promising a relational context where the delight I feel about others is matched by the delight others feel about me—not just when I'm new, but in an enriched way over time.

My extraordinary mental block, the one that kept me from connecting with, being moved by, and writing in my journal about the matter the first go round, reflected the defensive barrier I had put up. My deepest longing—acceptance—was offset and trumped by my greatest fear—rejection. I was able to let down my defenses a bit that second morning and, as I did, something interesting happened: I began seeing the faces of people I love—in the church and beyond—and I felt deep gratitude for them. It was as if they had been offered to me as a promissory note, a foretaste of the ultimate possibilities of love.

I knew that I was surrounded by others who had the same visceral hopes and fears about relationship that I did. It explained why we were sometimes so thin-skinned, so sensitive to apparent slights, so busy accepting and rejecting each other, and so prone to lock onto other excuses for conflict and side-taking.

I don't know anyone who at one level or another can't benefit from a dose of the reassurance Jesus offers in Matthew 19:28–30. All of us have our guard up at one level or another and need a Voice to slip past the weary watchman of our wary souls and hand-deliver a message of love—not just Divine love, but community love; not just God's unconditional acceptance, but the promise of a family—a great, extended household—of enduring and mutual affection and delight.

I needed that message then, for sure.

twenty-eight

Matthew 20:20–21

(20)Then the mother of Zebedee's sons came to Jesus with her sons and, kneeling down, asked a favor of him.

*(21)**"What is it you want?"** he asked.*

James' and John's mother—"the mother of Zebedee's sons"—comes to you with a request. We can look ahead to see what that request and your response are going to be; but for now, we only have this woman asking for a favor, and we have your open, but non-committal reaction: "What do you want?"

Okay, I'm the one with a want, coming to you to ask for it. I'm the one coming to you because I believe in your power and authority to make it happen. I'm the one settled in confidence about your capacity to grant my request who now wants to win your willingness, knowing that you can do whatever you decide to do.

"What do you want?"

What do I want? And what do my true desires reveal about me? What do I want? And do I really know what I'm asking? What do I want? And how do my wants match what you want for me?

Are my wants self-serving? Am I fixed on what's in it for me, like this mother, who responds to your question by seeking favors for her two sons? Though this isn't entirely true of me, you're about to unmask me to the degree that it is and set me straight.

For now, your open-ended question gives me the opening I need to examine my mind, my heart, and my wants to see what's really there. Your question gives me a chance to refine my wants and consider carefully what my request will be.

The Prayer of Examen

At times I have envied those who live with almost supernatural certainty. They seem to have clarity about everything. God seems to explain their circumstances to them without equivocation. Falling into a situation like the one I experienced, they would know immediately why it was happening and waste no time before consoling themselves or confronting themselves, as the situation might suggest.

A lifetime of experience with God made me prefer modesty when it came to explaining God and the circumstances of life. I had come to have a deep respect for the vast distance between God's perspective in God's infinite glory and our groping for perspective from our vantage point as finite, imperfect human beings. The gap between God's "from-above" viewpoint and our "from-below" viewpoint leaves us at times—left me at least—perplexed and reaching for explanations.

Yes, I remained convinced, God could break through with clarity—revelation is the ultimate answer to our finitude, the means of assurance that we know what's going on—but I was suspicious that the certainty with which some people experienced everything that befell them had less to do with a special gift they enjoyed as receptacles of God's revelation than it did with a personality, temperament, or dogmatism that made them rush to reasons in the course of their black-and-white lives.

Some of us cringe at complexity. But sometimes, like it or not, life is complex, and to rush toward simple answers is to lose the opportunity of a deeper walk with God. My brush with darkness drew me into a searching consideration of the many reasons God might have fallen silent. It led me, in other words, into what has been called the *prayer of examen*.

In the prayer of examen we invite God to walk with us into an honest self-assessment that clarifies and cleanses. We open our lives to the burning and/or illuminating light of God's insight and holiness. Here's how David puts it at the end of the remarkable Psalm 139:

Search me, O God, and know my heart;
test me and know my anxious
thoughts.
See if there is any offensive way in me,
and lead me in the way everlasting.[223]

In my dark night of the soul there was something ironic about my pursuit of revelatory insight, because, even here, my seeking met silence. "Why," I would ask, "am I experiencing your silence, God?" and all I could do was guess.

I did have the advantage of biblical wisdom and the very words of Jesus to suggest a range of possibilities. Looking back over my prayer notes each day during this experience, I recognize the extent to which Matthew's account of the life of Jesus prodded me and probed the inner recesses of my life. I wasn't just reading Jesus' life; he was reading mine.

I came to appreciate at an all-new level how the timeless wisdom of Scripture could be an authentic expression of God's living presence at that time; a genuine means by which God could walk with me in the valley of self-searching prayer. I might have preferred one simple explanation for God's silence, but I had to allow for the possibility that multiple factors had converged to create a sound-proof wall between the two of us:

- God could be seasoning me.

- God could be stretching me.

- God could be cleansing me.

- God could be healing me of brokenness.

- God could be patiently preparing me for a breakthrough of insight and direction.

I mention God's patience intentionally because I came to suspect, in my more honest moments, that God could be facing the greater test of patience during the suspended animation of those days. Under the bright light of the Scripture I could see the strength of my hopes and fears and preconceived notions. I could own up to my agendas and allow, at least in principle, that what I wanted mattered a lot less than what God wanted.

However, knowing something in principle and getting it right in practice are two different things . . .

Part V

Downward

Spiral

Sometimes things have to get worse before they get better. This certainly proved true for Jesus. It proved true for me, too. The downward spiral of my faith bumped up against the climactic crisis of Jesus' life, and had a telling effect.

twenty-nine

Matthew 21:18–22

(18)Early in the morning, as he was on his way back to the city, he was hungry. (19)Seeing a fig tree by the road, he went up to it but found nothing on it except leaves. Then he said to it, **"May you never bear fruit again!"** *Immediately the tree withered.*

(20)When the disciples saw this, they were amazed. "How did the fig tree wither so quickly?" they asked.

(21)Jesus replied, **"I tell you the truth, if you have faith and do not doubt, not only can you do what was done to the fig tree, but also you can say to this mountain, 'Go, throw yourself into the sea,' and it will be done.** *(22)***If you believe, you will receive whatever you ask for in prayer."**

You see a fig tree, and being hungry, go to it for fruit to eat. Seeing only leaves, you curse the fig tree, and it withers immediately. My first reaction is shock. I don't think of you as having it out for trees, even shabby performers.

But then, I realize you have a lot on your mind. You've stood at a distance and wept over Jerusalem, the capital city of Israel, grieving over how out of alignment the culture has become. You're approaching the high water mark of your conflict with religious leaders; each day the tension has heightened even more. You no doubt anticipate where this fateful week is heading.

It's fair to say you have a lot on your mind when you curse the fig tree. But I'm suddenly realizing that this means more than I first intended. I was finding excuses for you, given what looks like an overreaction. Now it dawns on me that "having a lot on your mind" could actually be a way of saying that your curse has a profoundly symbolic significance. Your curse, though it certainly is bad news for the fig tree, is really aimed at the whole sorry mess that has been made of your original hopes for Israel. In keeping with the grand tradition of Hebrew prophets, who comfort the afflicted and afflict the comfortable, you denounce what you see. Much of it looks like God's in name only. Rotten to the core, this culture and its leaders have been tried in your eyes and found wanting. In their utter spiritual impotence, they stand condemned. The withering has begun from the inside out. Their demise is only a matter of time.

The application of this to my life and the church's life is significant and unnerving. I'd be lying if I said that my current struggles and the church's current struggles don't make me feel a bit like Ebenezer Scrooge at the end of his frightening glimpse into his future. Pleading with the silent, shadowy, and merciless Ghost of Christmas Future, he asks, "Are these the shadows of the things that Will be, or are they the shadows of things that May be, only?"[224] I tremble at the prospects of condemnation; I cling to hope that the future isn't sealed.

I don't want to dodge the implications of your cursing for me. I can't honestly say I feel deeply effective or qualified, and I don't experience this as a lack of faith as much as an honest assessment of strengths and limitations. Furthermore, months of spiritual discipline, intended to put me in your presence, where you can speak and

I can hear, yields nothing in terms of guidance. On the critical, core issue of the moment, you remain silent.

But, wait a minute. Is the problem for me fruit*lessness*, or is it the need to more deeply reflect on fruit*fulness*? There's a sense in which you could be saying, "I have placed billboards all along the highway of your life, if only you had been willing to see them. My message has been, 'GO WITH WHERE THE FRUIT LEADS YOU.'"

Where do I see fruitfulness, and what does that suggest about the direction life wants to take me? This, after all, is one of God's best clues as to vocation, vocation meaning "the direction of God's calling." What do you do best and enjoy most? Where, when, and how are you most fruitful?

I have this uneasy sense that am still leading an "ugly duckling" life, and I am hoping that you can match me up with my true vocation. I want to discover the "swan" life, the beauty and fruitfulness that come when I am living in synergy with the purposes for which I was created.

Seasoning and the Silence of God

I have already established that living in my vocational "sweet spot"[225]—that place where 1) my gifts, 2) my passions, and 3) God's purposes intersect—has been one of the central interests of my life.[226] Making lots of money doesn't motivate me. The idea of building an empire leaves me cold. What *does* set my heart on fire is the idea that I could experience the synergy of my God-given strengths in the service of God's purposes for the world.

Given how much this matters to me, you would think that I would have gotten in sync in these terms years ago. Instead, I have struggled off and on throughout my adult life, never feeling completely at home in my "vocational skin."

I have accepted that in the real world, every job includes unpleasant as well as pleasant tasks; but I have refused to accept the fate of one man I know who said, "I spend 90 percent of my time doing things I don't want to do in order to get to the 10 percent I truly love." To me, this sounds like a recipe for misery. It puts me in mind of the observation bestselling authors and business consultants Marcus Buckingham and Donald Clifton make in their book, *Now, Discover Your Strengths*:

> Most of us have little sense of our talents and strengths, much less the ability to build our lives around them. Instead, guided by our parents, by our teachers, by our managers, and by psychology's fascination with pathology, we become experts in our weaknesses and spend our lives trying to repair these flaws, while our strengths lie dormant and neglected.[227]

At the heart of my internal conflict during my dark night of the soul was the conviction that the time had come to settle this matter, to get on with life in better alignment with the way God wired me. I had the sense that God was doing some decisive work in this regard. I also had the sense that God couldn't do it quickly. God had to take me through a disorienting and reorienting process of self-discovery. God had to prepare me to settle into divinely inspired purposes for the next stage of my life.

Unpleasant though God's elusiveness might be, it could relate to a silent, patient work God was doing in the moonlit night. It might not be time yet for God to speak. There might be some seasoning that needed to take place first, a kind of preparation for hearing God's word.

Author and educator Parker Palmer uses the metaphors of autumn and winter to describe these more difficult seasoning experiences of faith.[228] The bright colors of autumn gift us with a beauty that is tinged with the sense of impending loss, the knowledge that the days are growing shorter and "summer's abundance [is decaying] toward winter's death." And yet a seeding of new life occurs as summer's growth falls to the ground and gets scattered by the wind. Palmer reminds us to trust the seeding of new life that occurs in the "autumnal events" of our lives—"the decline of meaning, the decay of relationships, the death of a work." These losses, real or pending, will eventually reveal themselves as precursors to new seasons of life that wouldn't have occurred had a kind of dying not released us from the life we were leading.

Palmer presses further to extol the stark beauty, the deep rest, and the utter clarity of winter, in nature and life. "Despite all appearances," he writes, "nature is not dead in winter—it has gone underground to renew itself and prepare for spring." And stripped of the outward profusion of life, our bare lives become clearer to us in a way similar to a walk in the woods among trees stripped of their leaves.

I resonate deeply with these images. My descent into a long season of the silence of God felt like the coming of autumn. Eventually, it felt like the dead of winter. I lost even the vestiges of passion that had inspired me toward ministry as a 16 year old. I trudged through my duties, clinging with sheer discipline to the work habits I had incorporated into my life as a young man.

I had begun my vocational journey with high hopes and confidence—God was going to use me on a grand scale to turn people God's way! Despite sobering lessons in the years that followed, I had always been able to rekindle a sense of vision and passion with the help of a national ministry conference or a vacation with Priscilla and the kids. Time—and, I believed, the Spirit—continued to chip the sharp edges of ego and grandiosity off of my vocational aspirations, but a fire of purpose endured. It seemed that all I needed was a time of physical, spiritual, mental, social, and emotional renewal—what leadership expert Stephen Covey calls "sharpening the saw."[229]

I had the feeling this time that I needed something more and different. The spirit of high adventure gave way, and all that remained was a stoic determination to stay at the helm until divine orders were amended—or (as I could still allow) I had been infused with a supernatural resurgence of enthusiasm.

As already mentioned, there were times when I even regretted my life. Putting this out in the open feels a little like a baseball player's breach of the taboo against talking to a pitcher in the late innings of a no-hitter. Merely mentioning regret seems like giving it ground to send its roots into the soul. I kept cautioning myself not to think that way, even though I felt like I was on the downhill side of a life that hadn't lived up to its potential. I was dying inside. Winter had come.

When summer gives way to autumn and autumn gives way to winter, it's nice to have someone like Parker Palmer put the experience in more promising perspective. His words did that for me.

There is a dying that leads to life. There is a seeing in the dark. We may prefer the brightness and bounty of spring and summer; yet without these opposite elements in the seasons of life, we cannot have them.

I look back now at my dark night of the soul and can see the necessary dying that was going on then, the clarity that came hard, and the seeding of new life that was going on in the winter depths.

thirty

Matthew 22:1–10

(1)Jesus spoke to them again in parables, saying: (2)**"The kingdom of heaven is like a king who prepared a wedding banquet for his son.** (3)**He sent his servants to those who had been invited to the banquet to tell them to come, but they refused to come.**

(4)**"Then he sent some more servants and said, 'Tell those who have been invited that I have prepared my dinner: My oxen and fattened cattle have been butchered, and everything is ready. Come to the wedding banquet.'**

(5)**"But they paid no attention and went off—one to his field, another to his business.** (6)**The rest seized his servants, mistreated them and killed them.** (7)**The king was enraged. He sent his army and destroyed those murderers and burned their city.**

(8)**"Then he said to his servants, 'The wedding banquet is ready, but those I invited did not deserve to come.** (9)**Go to the street corners and invite to the banquet anyone you find.'** (10)**So the servants went out into the streets and gathered all** *the people they could find, both good and bad, and the wedding hall was filled with guests."*

This is a parable of the kingdom of heaven. Across time, you, king of heaven, have invited us into a life with you that can be compared to a royal wedding with all of its pomp, ceremony and extravagant joy.

Our response to you is preposterous. We have spurned your extraordinary offer. We have made ourselves strangers and even enemies of your love.

This morning I find myself most aware of how I "go my way," like the banquet invitees who couldn't be bothered. They had people to see, places to go, things to do. I do, too, which creates a gravitational pull toward the material world of work and recreation and away from the re-creating experience of a life centered in you.

This is ironic in one way: I am a professional follower, a full-time religious person who makes the church run. Yet like the religious leaders to whom you first tell this parable, I can engage my professional life but miss the essential opportunity I invite others to enjoy.

I'm not opposed to you but I do neglect you. I allow other interests to supersede my interest in you. I satisfy myself with pathetic alternatives to spiritual intimacy—a little prayer, a little Bible reading, a little writing in my journal, and I'm on my way—with a tendency toward an earnest, tiring work from which I can't excuse myself.

The good news for me is that it's not too late to accept your invitation to enter into the feast of heaven; to delight in life with you. Lord, let me recognize your invitation for what it is. Let me sing with excitement and joy that I have been included. Let me rush to your palace with pride and anticipation. Let a festive spirit rise within me. Let my joy in you transcend all other joy.

The Speed of Life

Most of those who refused Jesus' invitation into the joy of the kingdom were simply too busy to give the invitation serious consideration. Hurry had them in its spell.

Psychiatrist Carl Jüng once said, "Hurry is not of the devil; it is the devil."[230] I have to agree. There's something deeply and disturbingly spiritual about the "blinding speed" that passes as normal in contemporary American culture. Disturbingly spiritual? Yes. We're not dealing with something benign or merely complicating here. We're dealing with something that takes its cue from our restless souls and that has a destiny-distorting life of its own.

Hurry causes us to skim over the surface of life. Focused on what's next, we rush past what's now. Obsessed with where we're going, we lose sight of where we are.

Hurry may seem innocent—but it's not. Hurry sucks the life out of us. It makes us shallow, dependent on sound bites and conventional thinking. It makes us sloppy, prone toward shoddy work and clutter. It makes us negligent, oblivious to what's going on around us and forgetful of the things that matter most to us and others.

Hurry causes accidents and arguments. It raises blood pressure and lowers self-restraint. It numbs the five senses and dulls our capacity for love.

In our hurry we say things we don't mean, we do things we regret, and we rush past the beauty, goodness, and affection that could have been ours had we only made the time. Jesus reminds us of this, too: In our hurry we can miss the great celebrations of life; we can even miss the ultimate prize—the feast of fellowship with God.

Given my sense of God's absence during the months that I prayed through Matthew, and given my own tendencies toward hurry, Jesus' parable of the wedding feast made me want to slow down. I had to ask myself: How might I be missing God because I had crowded God out, hoping to catch a gulp of God on the fly?

The discipline of morning devotion became my first line of attack against this tendency. Before scurrying into other agendas and filling my day with noise, I gave God my waking thoughts and cleared space into which God might come.

I had done this on a fairly regular basis since late high school days. My red-letter experiment served as the particular structure for morning devotion during a stretch of my time in the spiritual wilderness. It was important that I had this structure, because I didn't feel equally inspired every morning. Left to the ebb and flow of mood and schedule, I might have abandoned the experiment at several points along the way.

Theologian and author Richard Foster, writing about the spiritual discipline of meditation, provides helpful advice for incorporating this pattern into our lives.[231] He reminds us that devotion has less to do with our effort to interpret Scripture, analyze life, and talk to God than it does with waiting and listening with willingness of heart. There's a sense, then, in which meditation is simply *a vital stillness in the presence of God.*

Starting the day this way can have a transformative effect on the rest of our waking hours. Practicing patience of heart in the quiet of a private place sets a tone that can impact the way we drive, the attitude with which we wait in lines, the pace of our eating, and the time and attention we give to others, the lovely and irritating alike. It can enliven our awareness of the world around us, increasing our capacity for wonder, gratitude, and love.

Pastor and bestselling author John Ortberg calls this way of life "slowing."[232] Noting that "Jesus was often busy, but never hurried,"[233] he encourages radical action. "If we are to follow Jesus, we must ruthlessly eliminate hurry from our lives—because, by definition, we can't move faster than the one we are following."[234]

By the time I arrived at Jesus' parable of the wedding feast, I knew that hurry had had a cumulative effect on my life. It had hyped me into an unsustainable existence. It had run me until the tread had come off my tires. It had worn me out. I heard myself saying to my confidants, "I'm sensing a pull in a new vocational direction, but I'm not sure whether it's God or fatigue talking!"

My entry on the parable of the wedding feast coincides with conversations I had with key leaders of the church about blocking off an extended time for reflection and renewal. I will forever feel grateful to these wise leaders who supported my request and facilitated a sabbatical in the spring of 2009. That time proved decisive in ways I'll say more about later.

In the rhythms of life we do well to make time for "solitude" breaks, not only daily, but seasonally. Periodically, we need to take a day, a week, and—if we can manage it—even longer to clear our heads and hearts. In a spirit of retreat, these times allow us to rest and recalibrate. I love the way Carl Sandburg put it: "It is necessary for a man to go away by himself and experience loneliness, to sit on a rock in the forest and to ask himself, 'Who am I, and where have I been, and where am I going?'"[235]

I won't presume to speak for everyone, but something about the ever-accelerating pace of modern life seems insane to me, and I don't like the way I succumb to its speed addiction. I want to keep learning how to operate at a truer, healthier speed—the speed of Life.

thirty-one

Matthew 22:34–40

(34)Hearing that Jesus had silenced the Sadducees the Pharisees got together. (35)One of them, an expert in the law, tested him with this question:

(36)"Teacher, which is the greatest commandment in the Law?"
(37)Jesus replied: "'Love the Lord your God with all your heart and with all your soul and with all your mind.' (38)This is the first and greatest commandment. (39)And the second is like it: 'Love your neighbor as yourself.' (40)All the Law and the Prophets hang on these two commandments."

The irony in this exchange between you and the Pharisee-lawyer is that in cooking up a question to stump you, your adversaries landed on THE topic you knew best, the topic that drove your life, your ministry, and your message. More ironic still, they landed on the issue that defined their failure, the crux of your dispute with them.

You knew that when life is reduced to its essence, it's all about relationship, it's all about love. You expressed this (in action, first and last, and also in word); you pleaded for this; and you condemned these religious leaders for their utter contempt for the spirit of love at the heart of the law. In the end, you gave your life as the ultimate expression of this.

I remember a story my dad liked to tell of a colleague of his in the AT&T system who was so brilliant that there was scarcely a subject he knew nothing about—and he seemed to know about most things in great detail, much to the dismay of his associates. His co-workers had a plan: They would conspire to bone up on a topic that they would know better than he. They searched for a subject as obscure as possible and finally landed on "underwater welding." Laying their hands on the definitive textbook on the subject, they studied it from first page to last. Then they brought the subject up the next time they were all together. They expected their brilliant friend to be mystified and impressed. In a tone of surprise, he asked, "Where did you learn all that stuff about underwater welding?" They named the book, to which their colleague replied, "I sometimes work under a pseudonym. I wrote that book!"

Jesus, you wrote the book on love, and everything there is to know about it can be found in you. Everything can be found by loving you and loving as you do.

Flirting with Atheism, Part I

Are you ready for a little literary whiplash? If you're reading through this book in sequence, you have just read my entry from the morning I reflected on one of the defining statements of Jesus' life, the Great Commandment—"Love the Lord your God with all your heart and with all your soul and with all your mind. Love your neighbor as yourself." My entry ends with a warm-hearted tribute to Jesus and the affirmation that everything there is to know about love can be found in him.

On the heels of such an entry, it may seem like a total disconnect to deal with the tug I felt toward atheism during my extended journey across the dry landscape of God's silence. Is it actually possible to celebrate the uncanny wisdom of Jesus in one breath and reject his claims the next?

It is. The juxtaposition of two wildly different worlds—the world of Matthew's gospel and the world as I was experiencing it—grew increasingly difficult to bear. My faith ran hot and cold. I engaged in an ongoing tug of war between the version of truth I wanted to trust and the version of truth I feared. Had I been kidding myself all along about the reality of God?

On the morning of my amazement at Jesus' insight into love, a skeptical little thought crept into my mind again, only this time with greater insistence than ever. The thought was this: Jesus could have been brilliant and partly right, nothing more. We can embrace his ethics of neighborly love without worshiping him as God in human flesh. In fact, we can benefit from his wisdom and still reject belief in a personal God.

How had it come to this? At a certain level, it was because I was losing my grip on long-held faith assumptions. My prolonged experience of God's absence and a lifetime of wrestling with the way the world seems to work had turned me into a diagnostician of the soul, trying to come up with new explanations for my dis-ease.

In fact, I could hear a voice in my head that sounded a bit like a physician bringing bad news. "I know you don't want to contemplate a world without a loving God who holds you and protects you and guides you and sustains you and blesses you, but that's what you're going to have to do now. I'm sorry, but that's just the way things are."

"Imagine there's no heaven," John Lennon had suggested. Based on the evidence I had in hand from the archive of my own life, I found myself trying his suggestion on for size.

Christian apologist Josh McDowell's idea of "evidence that demands a verdict"[236] is actually a two-edged sword. If you're going to put together a case for God based on facts, you also have to allow for the possibility that the facts point in the opposite direction. A well-known litany of facts can be put together to do just that:

- suffering in the world;

- injustice;

- unanswered prayer;

- gaps between biblical promises and life experience;

- naturalistic explanations for the world as we know it;

- cause and effect in our daily lives (Consider, for instance this observation: "The harder I work, the luckier I get.").

Contemplation of a world without God isn't just an academic exercise, of course. It's a deeply personal, existentially profound experience. For me it was a radical departure of faith. I would have to dismantle and reconstruct my life, my work, and my relationships in their totality. It would change everything.

Furthermore, and most profoundly, it would force me to deal with fears related to my ultimate destiny, fears related to eternity, fears related to how everything would end for me. How do you make a wager against God when the wager is your very soul? I've never been a gambler (not since losing at strip poker during a boys' birthday sleepover in fifth grade!); I certainly find it almost inconceivable to gamble my soul away. The stakes couldn't be higher when it comes to faith in God. The safe bet is to believe in God and hope for the best.

That doesn't mean it's irresponsible to contemplate the alternative. I felt honor-bound to engage in a mental-emotional-volitional exercise related to a godless world, or at least a world in which God doesn't play an active role. I didn't want to build my life on a false foundation, and I had accumulated a substantial amount of circumstantial evidence that I was doing just that.

Having been immersed (literally and figuratively) in the evangelical world, I know how blasphemous this sounds. I also know how prevalent this possibility is in the hidden recesses of many an evangelical heart and how frequently it expresses itself in practical atheism. We worship in an "I-can-do-all-things-through-Christ"[237] sanctuary and then walk out its doors into a "God-helps-those-who-help-themselves" world. God, for too many of us, is a "God of the gaps," relevant only at the edges of our lives that can't otherwise be explained or managed. I laugh when I hear people demonizing Darwinian science while practicing social Darwinism in their daily lives.

Let me suggest that we all come out of hiding and get real. At a bare minimum, let's quit kidding ourselves or protesting that we have more certainty than we do.

There is a way of locking out life's questions that can become pathological, the creation of a psychological defense system rooted in visceral fear. Occasionally I'll hear someone shut down discussion by saying, "The Bible says it; I believe it; that settles it!" When I hear this, I can't help but think of the line from *Hamlet:* "The lady dost protest too much, methinks."[238] Blustering certainty sounds more like insecurity to me.

The truth of the matter for me, on the other hand, is that my excursions into atheism didn't convince me of its merits. One matter alone was enough to turn me back: I couldn't make sense of the world without some kind of Intelligent Designer.

During my studies in scientific atheism I gained new appreciation for the plausibility of their worldview. I had to grant the statistical possibility that in a universe as vast as ours one planet among a billion billion planets could end up as the earth has through purely natural processes of evolution. But it still begs credulity to think that the intricacy and delicate balance of the world arose to its present form as a matter of natural selection, nothing more. Furthermore, not even the most ardent atheists have an explanation for the origin of the world. How do you get from nothing to something apart from some transcendent Being?[239]

Atheism in its purist form didn't win the contest for my mind; but what it did do was tempt me toward a retreat from biblical faith and its version of the way the world operates. In this alternate universe God functions through natural patterns of cause and effect and must be viewed primarily as an impersonal force. I am pretty much on my own.

In this universe we learn through trial and error and wisdom traditions (which themselves developed out of a cultural version of natural selection) how best to get along in the world. God leaves us pretty much on our own to work things out, to get things right or wrong.

There's no intimacy with God in this alternate universe, and those who say otherwise are simply projecting their longings onto the backdrop of the universe; that is, they are seeing what they want to see, turning the actual world into a theater of their imaginations.[240] They are psychotic, in the sense that they have broken with reality and become wrapped up in a delusional world. They're Elwood P. Dowell, Jimmy Stewart's character in the 1950 film adaptation of the play *Harvey*, carrying on a conversation with an "imaginary," six-foot-tall rabbit.[241]

None of this is designed to make one happy. This is, in fact, a much less attractive world and it leaves us vulnerable in the face of life's contingencies. I also have to agree with noted philosopher and atheist Daniel Dennett that there is very little difference between this version of God and having no god at all.[242]

Would that God might make it easier to hang onto conventional faith. A little consistency would help. Instead, circumstances work one way and then another. In my season of uncertainty, for instance, I watched one child come back from the brink and another die. We had prayed for both.

The almost laughable thing about my excursions into this alternate universe is that each time I landed on its shore I found myself talking to God. I simply couldn't get God, in personal-relational terms, out of my system.

Despite being a trained theologian who has studied this matter extensively, I don't have a tidy intellectual solution for the problem that is God. Trying to predict God's involvement in our lives makes weather forecasting look like child's play by comparison.[243] It's not for nothing that we affirm God's supremacy, God's autonomy, God's sovereignty.

In the end, the defining answer God gave Moses when Moses wanted to know who he was talking to says it all: "I AM who I am."[244] God is the Great I AM whose thoughts are higher than our thoughts and whose ways are higher than our ways.[245]

Not that this means we can know nothing about God. Through the red letters of Matthew, I clung to Jesus with continued conviction that in him God had made God's self known. I might not be able to plumb the depths of the mystery of God, but in Jesus I could see into the mystery and know the essential truth: namely, that God, the Great I AM, is Love.[246]

Let me say one thing more, lest my viewpoint be confused with the viewpoint of those who arrive at this conclusion and quit asking questions. I am of the opinion that churches and other holding environments of faith need not censor our hard questions. God's mystery continues to beguile and distress us and provoke a *seeking* faith, and when we come to the apparent disconnects between the claims of biblical faith and the evidence we have in hand, we can press into the perplexity with confidence that there are explanations, though we can't fully comprehend them yet.[247]

As I would soon discover, however, pressing into the perplexity wasn't going to get me out of the dark. Fortunately—and in a way I couldn't see yet—my red-letter journey through Matthew had already placed me on a pathway out, and its winding turns would lead me into the light in a poignant, transformative way.

thirty-two

Matthew 25:14–30

(14)"Again, it will be like a man going on a journey, who called his servants and entrusted his property to them. (15)To one he gave five talents of money, to another two talents, and to another one talent, each according to his ability. Then he went on his journey. (16)The man who had received the five talents went at once and put his money to work and gained five more. (17)So also, the one with the two talents gained two more. (18)But the man who had received the one talent went off, dug a hole in the ground and hid his master's money.

(19)"After a long time the master of those servants returned and settled accounts with them. (20)The man who had received the five talents brought the other five. 'Master,' he said, 'you entrusted me with five talents. See, I have gained five more.'

(21)"His master replied, 'Well done, good and faithful servant! You have been faithful with a few things; I will put you in charge of many things. Come and share your master's happiness!'

(22)"The man with the two talents also came. 'Master,' he said, 'you entrusted me with two talents; see, I have gained two more.'

(23)"His master replied, 'Well done, good and faithful servant! You have been faithful with a few things; I will put you in charge of many things. Come and share your master's happiness!'

(24)"Then the man who had received the one talent came. 'Master,' he said, 'I knew that you are a hard man, harvesting where you have not sown and gathering where you have not scattered seed. (25)So I was afraid and went out and hid your talent in the ground. See, here is what belongs to you.'

(26)"His master replied, 'You wicked, lazy servant! So you knew that I harvest where I have not sown and gather where I have not scattered seed? (27)Well then, you should have put my money on deposit with the bankers, so that when I returned I would have received it back with interest.

(28)"'Take the talent from him and give it to the one who has the ten talents. (29)For everyone who has will be given more, and he will have an abundance. Whoever does not have, even what he has will be taken from him. (30)And throw that worthless servant outside, into the darkness, where there will be weeping and gnashing of teeth.'"

Do I just need to take the plunge and live like the five- or two-talent servant, or do I need to accept that my talents are misplaced?

I am coming to the conclusion that the latter is true. Several indicators point to this.

I have done many things to "build" and "act" and "risk," without the success I anticipated. Let's see, what examples come to mind first? Thirty years of pastoring, faithful preaching and teaching; program and ministry creation to develop Christian disciples and release them as people of influence into the world; involvement as a leader at the city, state, and national level; defining moments of leading congregations to take a leap of faith—one year's 30 percent jump in giving, two capital projects, sponsorship of a refugee family from Southeast Asia, home construction in the inner city.

My "failures," if you can call them that, have had as much to do with my limitations and those of others around me as anything else—like seeing the big picture and understanding the objective, but needing tactical support to get there. I've looked to and leaned on the tactical gifts of others, sometimes to good effect; but on the whole, the effect seems inadequate.

I'm uncomfortable even presenting this litany about my life and ministry; it feels whiny and self-justifying. But that misses the point of the exercise. I'm not trying to justify myself; I'm just trying to explain why my circumstances have me baffled and defeated. I'm just trying to state what seems like a fact to me: that there are plenty of examples of my working hard and staying adventuresome and caring about the right things—of operating in the spirit of the first two servants in the story rather than the third. This, quite frankly, accounts for my frustration with you. I feel like you have given me a road map to fruitfulness that doesn't get me there. I feel like you have left me without your promised blessing, the promise that you would reward my faithfulness by multiplying its effect. It's almost as if you've hung me out to dry.

I want to add another character to your parable: the servant who traded with the talents he was given and who, despite his faithfulness, lost some or all of it or ended up about where he began. He didn't cave in to fear. He kept getting up in the morning with fresh resolve. He felt fear and pushed past his fear, and he kept fighting his laziness and the spirit of procrastination, all to no end.

I'd like to hear what the lord in your parable would have to say to this character!

Jesus, I know I'm far from perfect, but I am befuddled and frustrated by the gap between the life you have promised and the life I have experienced in my walk of faith. Either I'm totally not getting it, or your way is hogwash, or you have iced me out—an exception to Grace.

I simply can't bring myself to give up. I long for congruence between the life I have been created to live and the life I'm actually leading! I want to "let my life speak"[248] in the Divine sense of living in the sweet spot of your calling FRUITFULLY, JOYFULLY, CONFIDENTLY!

Flirting with Atheism, Part II

In the crisis of faith that comes when God falls silent, it's tempting to reconsider the very foundation of faith. No longer now is the voice in the head tempting one to defy God; the voice in the head is tempting one to give up on God altogether.

That's what happened to me. Looking back, I can see the frustration that drove me. At those times I was a mechanic of the spiritual life looking under the hood and failing miserably to figure out what was going wrong; so much so that I finally reached the point of exasperation and walked away in disgust. I was the angry lover who, put out with the one I love, allowed the conflict to escalate to the point of a total split.

There were times, in other words, when anger rather than intellect provoked me to say that I was ready to discard the whole idea of God, to turn my back on faith. Here's a sampling of my journal entries:

- "*Screw it! What I'd like to do right now is turn my back not only on the church but on you—what little of you there seems to be in the world I inhabit . . .*"

- "*Imagine there's no heaven. If there's no heaven . . . My occupation is a joke. I live under no obligation to fulfill a destiny or answer a calling. I can quit praying. I can come to terms with a heartless universe. I can eat, drink, and do whatever my residual loves and values and interests suggest; my loyalties included. I can expose the hypocrisies of organized religion and set myself free from it."*

- *"Here's the truth about the current state of my faith: My heart is telling me that the biblical worldview is little more than interesting fiction . . . 'You.' I've spent a lifetime turned toward a 'you' that won't respond to my questions or my pleas for relationship. I'm up to my elbows in 'Tar-Baby,'[249] having mistaken something inanimate for a Living Soul."*

- *"You're on your own, Baby!"*

- *"This year, for the first time, I have considered turning my back on you and the New Testament myth of sin and salvation and life and hope. My disappointment and borderline despair have brought me to the point of saying it's all a crock . . ."*

Exasperation had a lot to do with my contemplations of a world without God. Interestingly enough, at one of my points of exasperation I happened to view an old episode of the television series *The West Wing* that captured the dramatic intensity of my feelings.[250] In "Two Cathedrals," the pressures of leadership and life have pushed President Jed Bartlet to the breaking point. He must cope with a crisis in Haiti; an unprecedented tropical storm headed toward Washington, D.C.; the pending announcement that he has multiple sclerosis, a condition he has willfully concealed from the public; and the *coup de grace*—the senseless death of a his personal secretary and longtime confidante, Mrs. Landingham.

At the end of Mrs. Landingham's funeral in the National Cathedral, President Bartlet asks that Secret Service agents seal the cathedral, leaving him alone for a few minutes. Once he hears the cathedral doors clang shut, he turns his face toward heaven and lets God have it, calling God a "son-of-a-bitch" and a "feckless thug." Lambasting God for God's stern and mystifying judgments, he resorts to Latin, in keeping with his Roman Catholic upbringing. "Gratias tibi ago, domine . . . 'I give thanks to you, O Lord. Am I really to believe that these are the acts of a loving God? A just God? A wise God? To hell with your punishments. I was your servant here on Earth. And I spread your word and I did your work. To hell with your punishments. To hell with you!'"

In a final act of anger and defiance, Bartlet lights a cigarette, takes a drag, and throws the cigarette onto the marble floor at the center of an inlayed cross, stamping it out with his shoe. Then he walks down the center aisle and out the door.

In his director's commentary on this episode, Tommy Schlamme describes Bartlet's outburst in the cathedral as "the act of a child's rage." After watching the episode and hearing Schlamme's observation, here's what I wrote in my journal: "Lord, mine is a child's rage. Mine is a child's anger. Mine is a cry for your Presence, your Pardon, and your Power!"

This outburst of the angry child doesn't really amount to atheism. What it amounts to is a dismissal of God out of fear that God has dismissed us. Anxiety rather than atheism lies at its heart.

We faith-filled people often act atheistic in our anxiety and nervous activity. We're schizophrenic: one minute spouting our confidence in God, the next minute experiencing disappointment and rushing into frenetic action to control outcomes as if they were all up to us. We know the Serenity Prayer,[251] but we are loathe to live it. We don't know the difference between the things we *can* change and the things we *can't*, so we err on the side of trying to change everything ourselves. We lack confidence in God.

Much of my atheism was the frustrated activist still trying too hard to control outcomes, unable to accept that I don't really know what I'm doing.

Another thing: Being the big-picture person I am, I have a hard time carrying on down in the subplots of daily life if I don't know how they connect with and facilitate the larger story. Some of my consternation during my dark night of the soul reflected my inability to relax into the daily details of a chapter-turning time in my life, accepting that I couldn't yet discern the meaning of the current chapter or the shape of the chapter to come. I had to re-learn the wisdom of poet Madeleine L'Engle's observation in "Act III, Scene ii":

To grow up
is to find
the small part you are playing
in this extraordinary drama
written by
someone else.[252]

Here then was my atheism: It was the atheism of a frustrated control freak who was ready to reject a God I couldn't manipulate. It was the atheism of an impatient problem-solver who, failing to come up with a solution, considered giving up.

M. Scott Peck, in his classic book, *The Road Less Traveled*, confronts this tendency and illustrates how it works with a story of his own mechanical breakthrough. The offhanded remark of a handyman neighbor caused him to reconsider what he had always thought of as his handyman disability. "You just don't take the time," his neighbor told him.

Trying the idea on for size when the next opportunity presented itself, Peck discovered that by "taking the time" he was able to solve a problem one of his clients was having with her parking brake. He immediately understood the larger implication of this lesson. He understood that the issue of patience impacts our ability to solve not only the little problems of everyday life but also the bigger problems of our intellectual, social, and spiritual lives.[253]

Hurry was a problem for me. Impatience was a problem. Willful restlessness of spirit was a problem.

I didn't like the baffling nature of God's ways, but I didn't have to give into frustration over this fact. I didn't have to stomp my feet or throw a temper tantrum. I didn't have to engage in brinkmanship to get the responses from God that I wanted.

I am grateful, though, that God didn't reject me, even when my frustration made me feel like rejecting God.

thirty-three

Matthew 26:26–29

(26)*While they were eating, Jesus took bread, gave thanks and broke it, and gave it to his disciples, saying,* **"Take and eat; this is my body."**

(27)*Then he took the cup, gave thanks and offered it to them, saying,* **"Drink from it, all of you.** (28)**This is my blood of the covenant, which is poured out for many for the forgiveness of sins.** (29)**I tell you, I will not drink of this fruit of the vine from now on until that day when I drink it anew with you in my Father's kingdom."**

You ask me—you instruct me—to take bread that you've blessed and broken. You ask me to take a cup of wine over which you've given thanks. You ask me to accept your terrible self-giving as the beneficiary of a new promise, a promise that supplants the covenant promise at Mount Sinai.

Will I do it? Will I "drink the Kool-Aid," as the saying goes—an allusion to the suicidal decision of Jim Jones' followers in Jonestown? Will I buy into your death talk? Will I accept it as a sacrament, a signing-off with saving effect?

Yes—and doing so, I know myself to need what you offer. I know myself to need a better solution to my brokenness, my sin, than what the old covenant provided. I hate that I do. You offer the bread and the cup and in doing so say, "I will pay the price of your sin, once and for all. I will take your brokenness, your confusion, your dis-ease—all of it—and absorb it and thus transform it."

I will join you, Jesus, in fellowship with your suffering, in conformity with your death.[254] I am so sorry for my part! But if it *has* come to this, I will not refuse your peace offering, your Passover blood, your atoning sacrifice. In fact, I am stunned by your demeanor and the tone of voice with which you hold out these elements to me—in community. There is a generosity and good will in your voice and a kindness and compassion in your eyes. You are so willing!

Sin and the Silence of God

From childhood forward I have thought of sin as the first and most likely reason for God's silence. As the prophet Isaiah puts it, "Surely the arm of the Lord is not too short to save, nor his ear too dull to hear. But your iniquities have separated you from your God; your sins have hidden his face from you so that he will not hear."[255]

I would note, parenthetically, that at its heart separation is not about the ways our sin leads God to cut God's self off from us; it's about how we cut ourselves off from God, how sin dulls us spiritually so that "seeing, we don't see" and "hearing, we don't hear."[256] A kind of spiritual paradigm effect develops.

Furthermore, we go into hiding in the aftermath of sin. In our shame, we don't really want to see God for fear of God's frown.

I had no trouble enumerating ways I had fallen short of the Bible's high standards for life, reasons any one of which could explain what felt like God's indifference to my darkness. At the same time, I could also marshal biblical reminders of forgiveness and grace, reasons to believe that sin hadn't really created a lingering obstacle to relationship with God. At points throughout my period of spiritual darkness I wrestled with the matter of sin and engaged in spiritual exercises to cleanse my heart in prayerful confession and contrition.

I went to Psalm 51 more than any other passage of Scripture as a guide for my confession. "Have mercy on me, O God, according to your unfailing love," the psalm begins, and word-for-word I would pray it. "For I know my transgressions, and my sin is always before me," it continues. These words would prompt me to be as honest and specific as I knew to be. "Against you, you only, have I sinned and done what is evil in your sight." At this point, I couldn't help myself; I acknowledged not only how my sin had offended God, but also how it had betrayed and damaged others. And then I would allow the psalmist's desire to express my own: "Wash me, and I will be whiter than snow . . . Create in me a pure heart, O God, and renew a steadfast spirit within me . . . Restore to me the joy of your salvation and grant me a willing spirit, to sustain me." I wanted not only forgiveness; I wanted cleansing; I wanted transformation.

It was important to me not only to confess, in a spirit of true contrition, but also to claim the promise that comes in the Bible for those who do come clean. I never concluded one of these sessions without saying from memory the words of 1 John 1:9: "If we confess our sins, God is faithful and just and will forgive us our sins and cleanse us from all unrighteousness." By faith, I would write "Forgiven" across the mental record of my wrongs.

A question naturally follows: What could possibly have been so bad as to make me think it would derail my life and career? At the risk of disappointing anyone looking for something juicy, let me confess that I didn't need to murder anyone, steal anyone's property, or commit adultery to suffer under the accusations of conscience. From childhood forward, I had taken seriously my tutoring in the Sermon on the Mount. Jesus put the emphasis there on the condition of the heart. Misplaced anger mattered to him as much as murder.[257] The wandering eye condemned a person as much as "a roll in the hay."[258]

The daily little dramas of promise-making and promise-keeping revealed the character of the soul.[259]

My thoughts, words, and actions—trivial in some people's estimate—eroded the inner landscape of my life, sometimes coming in gulley washers of misunderstanding and misplaced anger—in these cases I had fence-mending to do; sometimes coming as the drip, drip, drip of things like prurient thought, flippant speech or procrastination.

I felt undeserving—at times prompted by specific things I had thought, said, or done; at times prompted by my pre-established patterns of spiritual discipline. Confession, I was convinced, belonged in the rhythms of my spirituality, right alongside celebration, prayer and service. Either way, there was never anything routine about this. I felt my imperfection sincerely and sometimes acutely; wanting to see God as desperately as I did, I sought whatever was within my power to facilitate purity of heart. Jesus, after all, had said, "Blessed are the pure in heart, for they will see God."[260]

Frankly, the tendency of many of us—I think I have many soul mates in this regard—is to trivialize the true nature of sin. Ever ready to stone others and ourselves over a short list of socially designated sins, we fail to see how our fundamental fears and self-centeredness stunt our relationship with God and blind us to the needs and interests of others and to our actual place in the bigger world.

At this point in my dark night of the soul, here was the sin I came to see as my number one roadblock to relationship with God: pride. I had to confront how hubris had overtaken humility when it came to dealing with my limits. I had gotten angry with God about a lot of things, and one of those things was vocation. I felt more disappointment than satisfaction about the investment of my life. I felt like God owed me an explanation and clarity of direction.

But part of the galling truth in my inability to realize all of my early adult dreams was that finitude stopped me. That is, I bumped up against my givens and the limits they imposed on my ability to achieve all I thought I should.

What I interpreted as the silence of God was, in part, the fact that God had already addressed the truth of who I am, and all my pleading for help to rise above my givens, my limits, was childish grandiosity. God was speaking through the givens of my life. He had, in fact, been speaking through the givens of my life for years, and my ego had prevented me from facing the facts.

It's not a sin to have limits as a leader. It's not a sin . . .

- . . . to do better at strategic thinking than with tactical details;

- . . . to adapt and adjust when placed in the middle of conflicting interests;

- . . . to lead with the heart over the head, when push comes to shove.

None of these characteristics is sinful; they just are. But as givens, they impact where and how I can succeed, and where and how I will fail. Some of my praying amounted to the request that God would make me something I was not, like he turned quivering Gideon into a valiant warrior.[261] James 4:1–3 talks about the ineffectiveness of misguided prayer. Some of my praying amounted to just this kind of thing. No wonder this praying met silence.

Pride prevented me from accepting the graciousness of my givens. It kept me pleading with God for what God had no intentions to give. This was the real sin in my story, a sin very different from what I feared as an explanation for God's silence. I had to confess it and receive God's pardon.

I would come to learn more about the implications of this in due time. For the moment, Jesus' invitation to accept the provisions of his flesh and blood eased me out of my indignation and reminded me to get over my disappointments with life. His invitation simplified things for me. All I needed to do for the moment was accept his invitation and stick with him to the end.

thirty-four

Matthew 26:31–35

(31)*Then Jesus told them,* **"This very night you will all fall away on account of me, for it is written:**

> **"'I will strike the shepherd,**
> **and the sheep of the flock will be scattered.'**

> (32)*But after I have risen, I will go ahead of you into Galilee."*

(33)*Peter replied, "Even if all fall away on account of you, I never will."*

(34)**"I tell you the truth,"** *Jesus answered,* **"this very night, before the rooster crows, you will disown me three times."**

(35)*But Peter declared, "Even if I have to die with you, I will never disown you." And all the other disciples said the same.*

This morning I am brought up short by the faithless alternative that runs through my mind. I have actually contemplated wrapping the darkness around me and falling back into the abyss of your absence. I find myself near the point of expecting that if I fall back I will simply confirm that you have already walked away.

You are having none of it. You confront me with my denial. You called me, and I followed—as a child of faith and more. Your calling brought me into ministry, through years of intensive preparation and even more years of congregational shepherding.

What will I do now?

You will die with us—with me—as deserters. You will take even this onto the load of brokenness and darkness that you will carry to the cross. You will do this and *not* desert us: "But after I am risen again, I will go before you into Galilee."

You will hang in there with us, even though we don't hang in there with you. I take some small comfort in this. I would much prefer a better outcome all around, but I can't shake the notion, entirely, that your grace will get the last word, even for me. This is the frayed thread of faith that holds my heavy, limp hope as it dangles over the void.

Dismantling and Re-constructing Faith

Peter and the other disciples would learn some hard lessons over the course of that crucifixion weekend. They would learn the limits of their loyalty and the flaws of their faith. They would learn to what extent their expectations did not match Jesus' intentions.

Before the weekend ended they would have to rethink God. Circumstances, and God's gracious work through those circumstances, would dismantle their faith and begin the process of reconstruction.

A two-fold cross and resurrection took place between Friday and Sunday. Jesus died and rose again and so, in another sense, did the disciples. Jesus' death crucified their faith, and when he rose again, their faith—in a transformed way—was resurrected, too.

I can relate. My travails in the spiritual wilderness sucked the oxygen out of my belief system. My way of experiencing and following God groaned under the weight of reality. God's mystifying action (or should I say inaction?) left me disillusioned and dismayed. Who had deserted whom, I asked myself? Where did the betrayal truly lie?

A lifetime of disappointments culminated in this moment. It wasn't just two years of silence that got to me; it was five decades and more of the clash between a biblical worldview and life in a modern/post-modern world.

This wasn't just personal, either. I empathized with disillusioned sufferers around the world and over time. I sometimes felt like I was playing the ultimate version of "Where's Waldo?" [262] when looking for God in Nazi Germany or Darfur or in the aftermath of hurricanes and tragic accidents.

Where was God's power? Where was God's providence? Where was God's mercy? Right in front of me, only not in the way I wanted them. Jesus' compliance upon arrest unnerved the disciples and sent them running. "Do something!" they must have thought; and when he seemed to do nothing, they lost heart and left. "Do something!" I myself had cried more than once. When he seemed to do nothing I, too, lost heart and was ready to run.

With the benefit of my awareness of the end of Jesus' story, I could now see that Jesus' willingness to suffer didn't represent a failure of his promise; it posed a challenge for me to re-center my worldview, to re-work my understanding of biblical faith, to grow beyond my magical thinking about the providence of God. It dawned on me—not for the first time, but certainly at a deeper level, a level more saturated with hard-earned experience—that God's most profound power comes as strength in weakness and life through death.

I kept wanting God's supernatural interventions, God's way *around* suffering. God, in Christ, confronted me again with God's way *through* suffering. I kept wanting easy answers and life's versions of thirty-minute sitcom resolutions to the dilemmas and difficulties of a fractured, fractious world. God, in Christ, confronted me with the counterintuitive way of the cross.

We weren't dealing with easy fixes here. The wave of a wand wouldn't do it.

The apostle Paul offered the personal application of this universal truth in a statement I had memorized years before: "No trial, testing, or temptation has overtaken you but such as is common to humanity. And God is faithful, who will not allow you to be tested beyond what you can bear. When you are tested, God will also provide a way out *so that you may be able to endure it.*"[263] When the plea for a resolution of difficulties doesn't result in sudden relief, God invites us to place our hand in God's hand and keep walking through the dark. Faith calls for perseverance—and trust.

On the level of our personal lives, we can't possibly know all of the tangled threads that God must deal with to loosen us from the problems that tie us in knots. On the larger stage of history, we can't begin to imagine all that comes with halting the momentum of violence, resolving the wildness of nature, and setting the world right.

My faith is less infantile now. I am less likely to hope that God will suddenly take me out of difficult circumstances at the snap of a finger or that God will produce the changed circumstances I want in the world without my personal involvement with others in the rough-and-tumble realities that bring about that change. I also understand that much of this patient work extends across generations of time.

I still believe that God, from time to time, engages in miraculous interventions; but I have deepened in appreciation for the way God, more often, works in the undertow of history to stir things up and turn things around. For every parting of the Red Sea we can point to a thousand Desmond Tutus devoting their lives to the pursuit of justice.

Through it all we can see evidence that Martin Luther King Jr. was right: "The arc of the moral universe is long, but it bends towards justice."[264] Evil collapses in on itself, and God's way does prevail in the long run. All of this is evidence of a God whose genius, finesse and patience exceeds anything I can imagine. While fully honoring free will and the normal rules of nature, God still manages to bring things along in the direction of divine purpose, grace and love.

My faith remains simple enough to believe that this holds true not only for the great saga of history, but also for the personal little dramas of our uncertain lives.

thirty-five

Matthew 26:36–38

(36)*Then Jesus went with his disciples to a place called Gethsemane, and he said to them,* **"Sit here while I go over there and pray."** (37)*He took Peter and the two sons of Zebedee along with him, and he began to be sorrowful and troubled.* (38)*Then he said to them,* **"My soul is overwhelmed with sorrow to the point of death. Stay here and keep watch with me."**

Right now, as you prepare for the climactic struggle of your soul, you simply ask that we wait here with you. You ask that we wait and watch. We cannot bear your cross for you. We cannot "remove the cup" of suffering from you. What we can do—the one and only thing we can do—is tarry here and watch with you. Our presence with you in your distress, our support of you by staying awake and providing a perimeter of care and protection, our love expressed in a partnership of prayer—this we can do, and you ask it of us.

The poet Rainer Maria Rilke offered this definition of love: "Love . . . consists in this, that two solitudes protect and border and salute each other."[265] This is the love you ask of us in your dark hour.

Throughout life, love and friendship ask this of us, and though never to the extent we experience here, it matters that we understand our role and find the strength to play it. Presence is what these moments call for, compassionate presence. To manage this, we must manage our referred stress, our almost irresistible urge for fight or flight.

How loyal will I be? How strong will my love prove? How far am I willing to go and how long into the stress of the night? And how much restraint will I show? How faithfully will I remain with you at the boundary between what's mine and what must be yours alone to do?

Hanging in There with Jesus

In an earlier reflection piece, I introduced Edwin Friedman's idea of "non-anxious presence."[266] Nonanxious presence is a way of living that stays relationally connected to others without internalizing their anxiety. The trick, according to Friedman, is to remain calm and present, centering ourselves apart from people's emotional state while hanging in there with them.

That's exactly what the journey of the cross requires of us. It calls for us to hang in there with Jesus, loving him intimately while letting him bear the almost unbearable weight of his destiny.

We don't do this by some trick of imagination, remaining within earshot of Jesus' agony while pretending to be somewhere else like, say, a sun-drenched beach in the Bahamas. We do this by means of compassionate self-restraint. In keeping with the meaning of the Greek word behind our word "sympathy" (sym—"together"; pathos—"suffering"), non-anxious presence asks that we *suffer with* Jesus, that we feel his pain, while resisting the temptation to take that pain away.

I can't count the number of times I have had conversations with friends and family of people in pain who can't bear to stand by as their loved ones suffer. "What can I do? What can I say?" they'll ask.

Sometimes, indeed, there are simple, practical things they can do to lighten a loved one's load; but jumping into their difficulties with advice or interference simply complicates things.

When I suggest prayer and presence as love's most powerful expression of support, people generally respond by saying, "Surely there's more!" They overestimate the helpfulness of direct intervention. They underestimate the power of simply *being there*.

We can ask ourselves this question: In our times of stress and crisis, what do we best remember about the people who walked with us through our experience? Do we best remember their problem-solving efforts and words of wisdom, or do we best remember their simple kindnesses and the warmth of their presence?

Out of an irresistible urge to do something, we interfere, we give unwanted advice; in general, we make nuisances of ourselves. We usually don't even realize it because the victims of our "help" are too polite to tell us.

At the opposite extreme, we sometimes find another's suffering unbearable. It unnerves us. It awakens our own worst fears. It confronts us with feelings of sadness and vulnerability. It makes us want to run. Not knowing what to say or do, we back away, leaving the people who matter to us feeling abandoned and unloved.

In their best-selling book, *Boundaries*, Drs. Henry Cloud and John Townsend confront our tendencies to over function and under function, establishing simple principles for walking in relationship with love and mutual respect.[267] Getting clear about interpersonal boundaries puts us in a better position to exercise healthy love in times of stress. This is precisely what Rainer Maria Rilke had in mind with his definition of love, mentioned in the previous journal entry: "Love . . . consists in this, that two solitudes protect and border and salute each other."

Garden of Gethsemane love places us as close to the suffering of another as is humanly possible. It draws our hearts into their pain. At the same time, it leaves a space between us—the space within which they must experience their own anguish and find their own way.

To the degree that we have cultivated the gift of empathy, we know how fitting it is that the word has its roots in the word *suffering*. Not only do we suffer in our sense of connection; we suffer in the self-restraint that love demands.

I don't know if I have ever experienced the truth of this more deeply than when I found myself with Jesus in the climactic stages of these red-letter devotionals. He had yanked me out of self-pity with his reminders of what would befall him. He had invited me to join him on a journey to the cross. Now he welcomed me into the company of his closest companions, only a few steps away from his private battle of the soul.

He wanted me with him, heart and soul—but we both knew the line past which I could not go. I could not take his pain away. He had to suffer that *for me*.

Part VI

Dying
for
Life

Be careful what you ask for. If you're dying for life, then death may be exactly what you get. But if the dying is a dying with Christ, there will be more to the story than first appearances suggest. That's what I discovered—or should I say *re*-discovered—when I hitched my life-in-crisis to Jesus and went the distance with him.

thirty-six

Matthew 26:39, 42

(39)*Going a little farther, he fell with his face to the ground and prayed,* **"My Father, if it is possible, may this cup be taken from me. Yet not as I will, but as you will."** . . .

(42)*He went away a second time and prayed,* **"My Father, if it is not possible for this cup to be taken away unless I drink it, may your will be done."**

History hinges on this moment. Heavenly Father, you, who in this drama choose to suffer the gruesome dying of your Son,[268] could have come up with a Plan B in response to your Son's appeal. Jesus, you the Son, could have abandoned the mission. You could have chosen disregard and disobedience. History hinges—our destiny and the fate of the world turns—on the fact that you didn't. Despite a pressure under which anyone else would have collapsed, you proved loyal and true. Even now, you relinquish your will to the Father's. Even here, you rest in the inscrutable wisdom of God.

This is your obedience, your path . . . toward the salvation of the world. I would accent this first and foremost, lest in making personal applications, I miss the central matter. O Lord, bless you, lying there flat on the ground in your grief! Bless you, face in hands in *extremis!* Bless you that you endured, that you refused to give up on God, that you found your way to acceptance, that your willingness eclipsed your willfulness! And thank you, Father, that you reward willingness with inner peace! Thank you that the prayer of relinquishment, though it doesn't create a bypass around suffering, does provide "a way of escape" through it[269]—an inner ease, like the calm in the eye of a Category 5 hurricane, as your Son carries his mission through to its completion!

Now, for personal application: Lord, teach me this willingness of spirit, this creative way through suffering, this trust and obedience, come what may. May *your* way become *my* way.

I will define my current crisis of vocation and my inner conflict between hope and fear in this way. Lord, hold my hand and guide me through to the vibrant rest of relinquishment. Teach me the joy of trustful obedience. Train me in the easy yoke,[270] that way of living beyond strain and inner struggle. Draw me into the simplicity of loving and following you.

Willfulness *versus* Willingness

I can't say for sure where I first learned the practical distinction between willfulness and willingness, but psychiatrist and contemplative theologian Gerald May's *Will and Spirit*[271] provided the lesson I remember best. His book awakened the desire in me to cultivate a spirit of receptivity, so that God, rather than I, could lead my life. I find this one of the most difficult things to do, with resistance points every step of the way. Willfulness, I have discovered, can even hide in the sheep's clothing of a willingness I say I want.

During this chapter of my life, here was my challenge in a nutshell: The difficulty of truly hearing God increased as my longing to hear God increased. Why? It was because the strength of my desire was such a willful thing.

Willfulness is all about effort and control. It's a necessary thing in many ways. Without willfulness we would become paper in the wind. We would never get anything done. We would lack conviction. We wouldn't even manage to feed or clothe ourselves.

Willfulness is gumption, and gumption is good. In willfulness, we set our mind and heart on something and apply ourselves in the direction of our desire. In willfulness, we roll up our sleeves and get to work; we overcome obstacles with the strength of our innovation.

Willfulness plays an essential role even in spirituality. "Study to show yourselves approved."[272] "Stand firm."[273] "Make every effort to keep the unity of the Spirit through the bonds of peace."[274] "Then we will no longer be infants, tossed back and forth by the waves, and blown here and there by every wind of teaching and by the cunning and craftiness of men in their deceitful scheming. Instead, speaking the truth in love, we will in all things grow up into him who is the Head, that is, Christ."[275] All of these verses call for willfulness, the dogged pursuit of Christ's way.

Once we know God's will we are wise to do it, and doing God's will is a willful thing. Doing God's will in the face of opposition is even more willful. The apostles Peter and John showed willfulness when they responded to death threats against them by saying, "Judge for yourselves whether it is right in God's eyes to obey you rather than God. For we cannot help speaking about what we have seen and heard."[276]

But here's where it gets tricky. Willfulness works fine until we get to that place where we can't say for sure that there's an alignment between our will and God's. What's more, willfulness as an orientation of mind, will, and emotion dislodges us spiritually. I use the word "dislodge" in an almost literal way because our ultimate lodging is "in Christ" who invites us to "abide" in him[277] and "rest" in him.[278] A willful spirit can't abide, can't rest. Only a willing spirit can.

We can see willingness of spirit in Samuel's response to God's voice in the middle of the night: "Speak, for your servant is listening."[279] We can read it in King David's heartfelt invitation: "Search me, O God, and know my heart, test me and know my anxious thoughts. See if there is any offensive way in me, and lead me in the way everlasting."[280]

The most extraordinary expression of this willingness of spirit, however, is Jesus, who lived not "on bread alone, but on every word that comes from the mouth of God."[281] "My food," he once told his disciples, "is to do the will of him who sent me and to finish his work."[282]

We see this willingness of spirit put to the ultimate test in the immediately preceding reading in Matthew, and we see Jesus pass the test. In the Garden of Gethsemane, with imminent prospects of suffering and death, Jesus' willingness of spirit prevailed. "Father, if you are willing, take this cup from me; yet not my will, but yours be done."[283]

That's not the end of it. Jesus' last recorded words on the cross represent willingness in the final surrender of dependence and trust. "Father, into your hands I commit my spirit."[284]

I said earlier that the difficulty of truly hearing God increased as my longing to hear God increased, because the strength of my desire was such a willful thing. You may well be able to relate to this. When we want something, we fix our imaginations on it; we stoke the flame of our desire for it; we do what we can to get it. If our desire is strong, we may find ourselves obsessing about it and straining after it, sparing no expense to claim it for ourselves.

Unfortunately, this works against us rather than for us when it comes to God. We can't make God come to us by dint of effort, by the exertion of will. Instead, we must learn to wait on the Lord.[285]

"Wait for the Lord;
be strong and take heart
and wait for the Lord."[286]

It really is tricky business, then, this business of waiting on God in willingness of heart. It runs counter to every instinct that comes into play in the urgency of God's absence. It calls for letting go when everything in us wants to grasp and cling.

One of the hymns that made it possible for me to ease my grip on life in the quiet hours of the dawn was a hymn penned by the pietist Katharina von Schlegel in the tumult of the Thirty Years' War that racked Central Europe in the eighteenth century. "Be Still My Soul" expresses circumstance-defying peace of mind that can only come when one is well-rooted in faith:

Be still, my soul! The Lord is on thy side;
Bear patiently the cross of grief or pain;
Leave to thy God to order and provide;
In every change He faithful will remain.
Be still, my soul! Thy best, thy heavenly Friend
Through thorny ways leads to a joyful end.[287]

The morning disciplines of prayer, song, and Scripture could not perfectly or permanently bring me to the stillness of the waiting, willing, listening heart, but they pointed me in the right direction. They gave me oases of rest, and over time they did make God's transforming work possible.

Most likely we will experience God when our agendas have been wiped off the dry erase board, when everything we think, feel or want has been taken to the cross.

thirty-seven

Matthew 26:47–56

(47)While he was still speaking, Judas, one of the Twelve, arrived. With him was a large crowd armed with swords and clubs, sent from the chief priests and the elders of the people. (48)Now the betrayer had arranged a signal with them: "The one I kiss is the man; arrest him." (49)Going at once to Jesus, Judas said, "Greetings, Rabbi!" and kissed him.

(50)Jesus replied, **"Friend, do what you came for."**

Then the men stepped forward, seized Jesus and arrested him. (51) With that, one of Jesus' companions reached for his sword, drew it out and struck the servant of the high priest, cutting off his ear.

(52)**"Put your sword back in its place," Jesus said to him, "for all who draw the sword will die by the sword. (53)Do you think I cannot call on my Father, and he will at once put at my disposal more than twelve legions of angels? (54)But how then would the Scriptures be fulfilled that say it must happen in this way?"**

(55)At that time Jesus said to the crowd, **"Am I leading a rebellion, that you have come out with swords and clubs to capture me? Every day I sat in the temple courts teaching, and you did not arrest me.** *(56)***But this has all taken place that the writings of the prophets might be fulfilled."** *Then all the disciples deserted him and fled.*

Across the millennia of human existence we have wished we could touch you, you who are Spirit, the Majestic yet elusive Presence. How ironic that when finally given the chance to do just that, we end up "laying hands on you" rather than embracing you.

I have wondered at times how you will be able to achieve your ultimate will without finally circumventing human freedom—my curiosity being driven by the assumption that a coerced conclusion to the drama of human history is inconsistent with the nature of Holy Love. This story may offer the clue I need to understand it. You are the Brilliant Tactician who uses our energy and momentum toward your ends, like the Supreme Marshal artist who takes an opponent's blows by moving with them and using their momentum against them.

The wonder of your way is that, in playing the role of Supreme Marshal Artist, you use our energy not against us, but for us. You take us off-balance only to put us right. And this, ironically, puts us off-balance in yet another way: it shocks our sensibilities as those who fight you and expect you to fight back. It throws us into a new world where love, not war, wins, only to discover that this "new" world is the only real world that ever existed. The rest is insanity, as we created it.

Self-giving love will always, ultimately, win, especially since it has the capacity of resurrection, the power of eternal renewal and return!

Throw it down, and it keeps coming back.

You, the loving Lord, are born again and again and again. I can never defeat you. I can never defeat your coming, your claiming, your conquest of my life. Nor do I want to!

Embrace us, Lord, as we lay our hands on you. Disarm us with your Love. Redeem us in our fleshly foolishness by yielding yourself in flesh and blood.

Disarmed

"Disarm us with your Love. Redeem us in our fleshly foolishness by yielding yourself in flesh and blood." So ended my entry the morning of my prayerful reading of Matthew 26:47–56.

I had been so angry at God, so frustrated by God's refusals to respond to my pleas, so exasperated by God's passivity despite my concerted efforts to light the fire of God's concern. Everything about God's way in the world fueled my fury.

The anger of those who sent guards to arrest Jesus paralleled my own animosity. Had there been some way physically to flail away at God, I probably would have done it.

So how does Jesus respond? He hands me a pair of boxing gloves and says, "Hit away." He places himself at my mercy and lets me dump all of my doubt, disappointment, and despair on him. He places himself at my mercy and just takes it. He takes everything I have to throw at him.

It puts me in mind of a story I first heard through John Claypool, the Baptist-then-Episcopalian preacher whose confessional preaching touched so many. Taking the title of his communion meditation from Peter De Vries's novel, *The Blood of the Lamb*, he related De Vries's story of a young girl dying by inches of leukemia, as narrated by her father, who struggles with his faith during the ups and downs of her health and medical treatment.[288]

During one of the girl's hospital stays, she's watching television clips of old comedies and comments on a pie-throwing segment. "Have you ever noticed when the little guy throws the pie into the face of the big guy, the big guy just stands there and takes it? He even waits for it, his face sort of ready. Then when he gets it, he still waits a second before wiping it out of his eyes, doing it deliberately, kind of solemn, as if the whole thing is a ritual."[289]

These comments come back into play when, months later, the daughter loses her battle for life. Having stopped that very morning to pray at a church near the hospital, her father gets news of her turn for the worse from a nurse coming into the church after work. In his rush to get to the hospital, he leaves on the pew a birthday cake that had been prepared just for her. Later, fresh from the devastation of her death, he returns to the church and finds the cake in its box, right where he left it.

As he stumbles out of the sanctuary, the absurdity and tragedy of the circumstances overcome him. In an explosion of grief, he takes the cake out of its box and heaves it into the face of the crucifix located above the church entrance. His shock at what he has done gets swept up in what happens next:

> Through scalded eyes I seemed to see the hands free themselves of the nails and move slowly toward the soiled face. Very slowly, very deliberately, with infinite patience, the icing was wiped from the eyes and flung away . . . Then the cheeks were wiped down with the same sense of grave and gentle ritual, with all the kind sobriety of one whose voice could be heard to say, 'Suffer the little children to come unto me . . . for of such is the kingdom of heaven.'"[290]

Claypool, reflecting on this story, observed that God is the "big guy" taking what we, the "little guy," throw at him. God, whose strength could overwhelm us, absorbs our frustration, our confusion, our distrust, our fury, and doesn't hit back. Instead, God absorbs it and takes it to the grave. God, in Christ, willingly takes it to the cross, gets sucked into the vortex of death, and thus transforms all of the pain and brokenness of the world.

When this realization hit home for me again, it took the anger right out of me. I experienced the self-giving love of God with renewed effect and remembered that God was *for* me, not *against* me. As a sheep before her shearers is silent,[291] so Jesus' silence through my dark night was a saving silence—a love that would lead me and bless me and never let me go.

thirty-eight

Matthew 27:46

*(46) About the ninth hour Jesus cried out in a loud voice, **"Eloi, Eloi, lama sabachthani?"**—which means, **"My God, my God, why have you forsaken me?"***

I experience a strange consolation this morning: You know exactly what it's like to suffer God's absence. You know what it means to feel the gravitational pull of true despair. There's a black hole of hopelessness that can suck us in if we let it. It occurs not in response to the Divine frown—even judgment takes place in God's company at least, which means we've still got God with us. The black hole of hopelessness occurs beyond judgment, when God simply walks away.

This is your time to suffer the separation of our sin, my sin, the sin of the whole screwed-up world for all time. I have been stuck in this experience of your absence without recourse to complaint. It could be said that I'm just getting what I deserve.

You, on the other hand, deserve better but suffer this separation anyway. In the mystery of salvation, you, the Triune God, choose to experience the death, the separation of sin, so as to overcome this separation for all time, for all who receive you.

Here I am, then, and I will cling to you as you suffer the Father's forsaking. Lord Jesus, take me down with you, for in you I have my only hope that God-forsakenness will end in joy.

A final note of hope: I know that your cry of dereliction from the cross comes from Psalm 22, which ends in hope: "You who fear the Lord, praise him! All you descendants of Jacob, honor him! Revere him all you descendants of Israel! For he has not despised or disdained the suffering of the afflicted one; he has not hidden his face from him but has listened to his cry for help."[292]

Stubborn Confession

A friend of mine, Chris Thacker, has coined a phrase for the faith we declare when times get tough. He calls it our "stubborn confession."

I particularly like this way of talking about the water-resistance of our faith in the deep seas of grief and disappointment. There's something sturdy, even noble, about the refusal to discard conviction when the tides of trouble roll in. Stubborn confession has a Timex quality to it. As the old watch commercials used to say, "It takes a licking and keeps on ticking."

During the months of my treading water in the ocean of unanswered prayer, I clung to anything that would float, anything that could keep my faith alive. There was much I didn't know: God's will, my future, whether there was still hope for me. My mind doubted many things, including God's very existence. Yet my heart kept sounding its confidence in God, my mind kept rehearsing the things I believed—or at least still wanted to believe.

No, it wasn't just what I *wanted* to believe; that makes it sound like there was something willful going on. Instead it was as though those convictions had a life of their own. They refused to die. The weight of my disillusionment couldn't sink them. No matter how exhausted I got in the struggle they refused to go under.

The number one source of my stubborn confession was Scripture, and I am grateful beyond words that I was mentored by people who believed in memorizing as much of it as I could. Some of my favorite verses came readily to mind when I needed them most, affirming things that circumstances had cast into the shadows:

- "I know the plans I have for you, plans for welfare and not calamity, to give you a hope and a future."[293]

- "In all things God is at work for good for those who love him, for those who are called according to his purpose."[294]

- "Trust in the Lord with all your heart, and lean not on your own understanding; in all your ways acknowledge him, and he will direct your paths."[295]

- "Be anxious for nothing, but in everything, by prayer and supplication, let your requests be made known to God; and the peace of God which passes understanding will guard your minds and your hearts in Christ Jesus."[296]

I was particularly inspired by the biblical prophet Habakkuk, who could be called the patron saint of stubborn confession. I'm not sure I would have remembered his hope-against-hope declaration of faith had it not been for a teaching series I did on the Old Testament prophets during my days in the spiritual wilderness. His declaration moved me, coming as it did at a particularly difficult time in the life of Israel. Despite everything going wrong and everything that *could* go wrong, Habakkuk insisted, ". . . yet I will rejoice in the Lord, I will be joyful in God my Savior."[297]

I quoted Habakkuk's confession of faith to myself repeatedly. He hung in there. He refused to abandon his relationship with God. He refused, as Job did later despite his wife's urging, to "curse God and die."[298] Listen to Job's stubborn confessions:

- "Though he slay me, yet will I hope in him"[299]
- "And as for me, I know that my Redeemer lives, and at the last He will take his stand on the earth."[300]

I wanted to curse God, but the voices of Habakkuk, Job, and others wouldn't let me. If they could hang in there, so could I.

The second source of my strength was music. The songs of faith, some of them learned in childhood, some of them later, cradled me in their arms. They held me. They comforted me. They lifted me beyond the reach of cynicism and doubt.

What is it about music that makes it so powerful? How is it that music can touch a place in us that words alone can never reach? There were times when I was at the border of despair, passport in hand, ready to cross over into the land of unfaith, that a song would take me home again: "Be Still My Soul"; "It Is Well with My Soul"; "A Mighty Fortress"; "I Know Whom I Have Believed."

Music could make me weep. Reaching beyond my defenses as a disappointed disciple, it would remind me of God's love. It would liberate the child of faith in me that the ravages of time had kidnapped and held hostage.

The ultimate exemplar of this resiliency for me was Jesus. All I had to do was contemplate his life and death to know what it means to remain true to God no matter what. In the darkest hours of his life, after a lifetime of thankless service and the abandonment of his friends, Jesus experienced total God-forsakenness. It was as if the lights went completely out. In the midst of it he cried, "My God, my God, why have you forsaken me?" Despite all evidence to the contrary, he clung to his faith and finally released himself in death into the grace of God. "Into your hands I commit my spirit,"[301] he said, and then he took his final breath.

Another aspect of this worth noting: Our stubborn confession comes easier in the company of others who join us in the declaration of faith. Given the ambivalence I have felt sometimes toward

Christian community, it helps me to remember just how powerful it can be.

In the summer after my adventures in the red letters of Jesus, our church experienced disaster. The bus carrying our youth and youth sponsors to camp had a tire blow-out, and the bus flipped three times before coming to rest on the side of the highway. Everyone on board was injured. Several were flung through windows. Two ended up under the bus, critically injured. Another one died at the scene.

In the hours and days following, our church came together frequently to worship and pray. I will never forget the power of our worship, the strength of our singing, the confidence of our praying. Rallying together we felt the strength of our unity and love and the assurance that God was greater than anything that life or death could throw at us.

The strength of our common life, woven together in Scripture, prayer and song, became an unbreakable cord during those days that otherwise could have frayed the individual threads of our faith and weakened them until they snapped. We were further strengthened by a worldwide company of believers who communicated with us by mail, e-mail, Facebook and other means.

Three weeks later, when our prayers for a miracle for twelve-year-old Maggie Lee Henson met the terrible news of her death, we rallied together again. Her funeral became a celebration of her life and an expression of our confidence in God. Through prayer, song and proclaimed word, we offered our stubborn confession. No bumper-sticker bromides; no careless clichés to oversimplify the muddled anguish of the moment: Just the simple and dogged confession that God's love would prevail. We clung to the promises of God that line the margins between time and eternity.

I don't know how a person can sustain faith in isolation. I know I can't. There's a strength of heart and mind and voice in the company of the committed that steels us against adversity and the inevitable curveballs that life throws our way. There's a reassurance in the stories and warmth of faith's fellow strugglers that keeps hope alive.

I would have walked away from faith more than once had it not been for this. Scripture, song, and the company of other believers—a stubborn confession that would not let me go.

thirty-nine

Matthew 28:1–10

(1)*After the Sabbath, at dawn on the first day of the week, Mary Magdalene and the other Mary went to look at the tomb.*

(2)*There was a violent earthquake, for an angel of the Lord came down from heaven and, going to the tomb, rolled back the stone and sat on it.* (3)*His appearance was like lightning, and his clothes were white as snow.* (4)*The guards were so afraid of him that they shook and became like dead men.*

(5)*The angel said to the women, "Do not be afraid, for I know that you are looking for Jesus, who was crucified.* (6)*He is not here; he has risen, just as he said. Come and see the place where he lay.* (7)*Then go quickly and tell his disciples: 'He has risen from the dead and is going ahead of you into Galilee. There you will see him.' Now I have told you."*

(8)*So the women hurried away from the tomb, afraid yet filled with joy, and ran to tell his disciples.* (9)*Suddenly Jesus met them.* **"Greetings,"** *he said. They came to him, clasped his feet and* *worshiped him.* (10)*Then Jesus said to them,* **"Do not be afraid. Go and tell my brothers to go to Galilee; there they will see me."**

I imagine the earthquake on Easter morning as the extraordinary moment of your waking to resurrected Life. What was it like for you in those first moments of awareness? Your eyes open as a thrust of the Spirit's breath fills your lungs. Your brain leaps into gear. Father, Son and Holy Spirit experience vivid intimacy and joy. You experience yourself in your transformed existence.[302]

This had to be a moment of ecstatic fulfillment, and there had to be, to the nth degree, a heightened sense of the pleasure you felt after your baptism when the Father said: "This is my Son in whom I am well pleased!"[303]

You have accomplished all that was placed before you. You have remained true through the absolute agony of the worst of it. Your Father has remained true as well. You now awaken with but a little more to do in your incarnation, and this you will do as Conquering Lord, beyond human life's limits and temptations and pain.

It is in a resurrected state that you greet the two Marys and send them on their way with a happy assignment: "Go and tell *my brothers and sisters . . .*"

We had run away. We had deserted you. Our disloyalty had separated us from you before your death had separated us from you. Still, you call us *your brothers and sisters*. You doubly own us, even after we had disowned you. You own us once: "My," you say. You own us twice: "Brothers and sisters," you say. How much clearer could you possibly be that our hope rests not in our faithfulness but in yours.

My hope—the good news that secures my destiny, now and forever—rests in your initiative toward me. You own me, forever and all time. On the back side of the darkness, on this side of my utter loss of innocence, you call me "brother" and thus redeem me for you and your purposes. All is forgiven. All is made new again.

I will reclaim my status as your brother, for the simple reason that you have reclaimed me! I am not too good to accept this unmerited favor. In fact, it's what I've longed for most! I will reclaim my status as your Beloved!

Life, indeed, is good!

Beloved[304]

A fresh experience of God's love truly did happen for me on that second-to-last morning of my red-letter prayer experiment in Matthew. The cloud of vocational unknowing didn't budge, despite the breeze of God's grace; but the dark sense of spiritual alienation did.

Sitting right where I had in the early mornings for months—in my leather chair in the family room—and with the soft light of the tableside lamp to illumine my reading, I opened my Bible where the bookmark fell. A sense of anticipation swam just at the surface of my awareness. The slow, methodical process of walking with Jesus and listening to Jesus, one statement at a time, had brought me to the resurrection story with an alert kind of stillness.

I had thrilled to his power and authority; I had been gripped by his wisdom; I had battled him over the questions in my heart. At the apex of my anguish, I had been disarmed by his anguish—conscious of how willingly and lovingly he had yielded himself to disaster. That experience had quieted me; it had silenced the racket in my head and supplanted it with awe. In his arrest and crucifixion, I had sensed that he carried my hopes with him. I held my breath and waited for what would happen next.

On the morning of my experience of first Easter, the distance between my today and that yesterday diminished almost entirely. I felt like an eyewitness to the intimate first moment when Jesus, the faithful Son, and God, the faithful Father, embraced in oneness again. That feeling of being an eyewitness continued as I heard Jesus doubly own the disciples. I felt doubly owned myself.

To say that this culminating moment was a literary experience doesn't capture what it meant to me. The margin between imagination and spirit became porous. Grace broke through. I had the sense—not the literary sense, but the actual sense—that a light of love had spilled across me. I felt God's embrace. I felt God's joy. I experienced the unmerited, inexpressible delight of God *in me*.

I had felt ignored, dismissed, discarded. For months that turned into two years, I suffered what felt like God's absence. God finally broke through that morning with reassurance that none of this was actually true. God broke through with the brightness and tenderness of pure acceptance. God smiled on me, and thereby gave a helium lift to my spirit. God answered the plea that psalmist David had put into words for me as the constant refrain of my longing:

Create in me a pure heart, O God,
  and renew a steadfast spirit within
  me.
Do not cast me from your presence
  or take your Holy Spirit from me.
Restore to me the joy of your salvation
and grant me a willing spirit, to
  sustain me.[305]

I can't speak for anyone else but, as has been established clearly over the course of this book, I have struggled all of my life with a sense of inadequacy. It doesn't matter how much success I've had or how poised I've become. My genuine self-confidence is frequently unsettled by the sense that I don't measure up.

Of the many Greek and Hebrew words for *sin*, the one that registers most deeply with me is *hamartia*, which literally means "to miss the mark." Picture an archer aiming at a target, with arrow in position, bowstring drawn taut, then releasing the arrow toward the target and missing the bull's-eye. The apostle Paul uses this word for sin in his famous observation that "All have *sinned* and fallen short of the glory of God."[306]

Recovering perfectionist that I am, concern over missing the mark, over falling short, has dogged me as long as I can remember.

Did this lifelong concern originate in my inherent personality and temperament, in my upbringing under the influence of a perfectionist mom and a hard-driving dad, in the Sunday school and worship lessons of my childhood, in a world with report cards of all kinds, or in a lifetime of willful (and sometimes witless) behavior that took me off course? I would guess all of these factors have come into play.

Whatever the sources of my existential insecurity, I accept responsibility for my part in allowing this concern frequently to thwart my relationship with God. Dread that God might give me a failing grade keeps cropping up. It even causes me to avoid God at times. Anticipating God's rejection, I take preemptive steps to turn from God before God can turn from me.

I continuously have to relearn God's grace and relax into God's love. It never ceases to amaze me that I enjoy God's unconditional, unbreakable affirmation.

How many times and how many ways have I experienced break-throughs of God's grace? How many defining moments have I had that could have forever short-circuited this syndrome of insecurity?

Even now, pondering this question, I have come up with a two-page list of serendipities, beginning with a conversation I had with my Baptist Student Union Director my junior year at Baylor. Decisions I had made had hurt others and alienated people who mattered to me. My guilt felt overwhelming and left me wondering if God would ever forgive me and use me again.

From his own experience with guilt and shame[307] Lonnie shared with me words someone else had passed along to him when he needed them most. "The older I get," he said, "the more I realize how capable I am of the worst things imaginable. But it doesn't matter how deep my brokenness goes; God's love goes deeper still and he is able to lift me up and set things right. I have learned to trust that God's love will never fail me. It will never fail you either. Never forget what the apostle Paul wrote: 'God demonstrates his own love toward us in that, while we were yet sinners, Christ died for us.'"[308]

Years later, reading Lewis Smedes's extraordinary book, *Shame and Grace*, I had another breakthrough of seismic proportions, coming to terms with the shame beneath my guilt and the fear it induced. Smedes wrote movingly of the power of God's grace to erase our shame and the fear of rejection it brings:

> The grace of God comes to us in our scrambled spiritual disorder, our mangled inner mass, and accepts us with all our unsorted clutter, accepts us with all our potential for doing real evil and all our fascinating flaws that make us such interesting people. He accepts us totally as the spiritual stew we are . . . For the whole shadowed self each one of us is, grace has one loving phrase: you are accepted. Accepted. Accepted. Accepted.[309]

As already mentioned earlier in the book,[310] I remember sitting outside on the campus of Fuller Theological Seminary in Pasadena, California, and reading these words. They made me weep. I experienced God speaking to me in those moments and, with pen in hand, I recorded what my heart heard God say. Those words have continued to encourage me ever since.

I could go on about the people and books and experiences in nature that delivered God's grace to me just when I needed it most. Suffice it to say, I have enjoyed an embarrassment of riches in this regard.

Nevertheless, my soul still forgets it. The lying voices in my unsteady heart continue to speak, growing louder as time goes by in the absence of God's fresh reminders. I am, in other words, human.

That's why God's multi-year silence so unnerved me. It's also why God's coming to me near the end of my experience in Matthew proved so palpable and transformative.

In the introductory chapter of *Prayer: Finding the Heart's True Home*, Richard Foster tells the story of a friend of his having trouble controlling his young son at the mall. Every effort to get him to behave failed until, inspired by desperation, the father gathered up his son into his arms, held him close, and began singing an off-key, made-up love song to him.

The tactic worked. The rest of the way through the mall and all the way out to the car, the son remained utterly still and attentive, listening to his father love him in song. Then, as the father placed him in his car seat, the little boy spoke for the first time. "Sing it to me again, Daddy! Sing it to me again!"

Foster compares this father-son experience with prayer. "With simplicity of heart we allow ourselves to be gathered up into the arms of the Father and let him sing his love song over us."[311]

I have never outgrown this need for God to sing a love song over me. I hope I never do.

forty

Matthew 28:16–20

(16)*Then the eleven disciples went to Galilee, to the mountain where Jesus had told them to go. (17)When they saw him, they worshiped him; but some doubted. (18)Then Jesus came to them and said,* **"All authority in heaven and on earth has been given to me.** *(19)* **Therefore go and make disciples of all nations, baptizing them in the name of the Father and of the Son and of the Holy Spirit,** *(20)***and teaching them to obey everything I have commanded you. And surely I am with you always, to the very end of the age."**

Moses, in his final address to the people of Israel, concluded by saying, "Choose Life."[312] You conclude by saying,

"All authority in heaven and on earth has been given to me . . ." My time with you has come as one long lesson in your unmatchable power and authority. All the power and authority of heaven is focused in your one unequaled life.

"Therefore go and make disciples of all nations . . ." The blessing and the calling come hand in hand. I am saved. I am sent.

Thus I live. And there will be no limit to the lengths to which I will go.

"**Baptizing them in the name of the Father and of the Son and of the Holy Spirit and teaching them to obey everything I have commanded you . . .**" The student becomes the teacher, ready or not, which keeps sending me back to my lesson book, lest I neglect any of the "everything" you have commanded me to share with others.

"**And surely I am with you always, to the very end of the age.**" There it is. There is your response to the longing with which I began this red-letter journey. Just before the period at the end of your final sentence on earth, you say to me, "Greg, I *am* with you!

- Now and forever!

- Wherever your feet take you!

- However your mind directs you—or misdirects you!

"Your eyes, ears, mouth, nose, hands, head, heart, and gut, whether centered and settled, homed in or homeless and seeking, reside in the pleasure of my company. You abide with me, in me, and I in you perpetually, come what may.

"Release yourself from the needless struggle to have and hold onto what is already yours. Why grasp at the wind when you are already in my grasp? Why continue to struggle after the Life that is already yours, my gift to you, in me, for all time? Simply *be*, restful and responsive. The growing and going will flow naturally as you do. Taste and see. Enter into the feast of heaven . . . and keep singing, 'Y'all come!'"

Life is good!

Life Is Good

The final days of my devotional experiment in Matthew brought a turning of the calendar and with it a new lease on life. My last reading solidified my reawakened sense of God's grace. I had felt God's forgiveness in the days before. I felt God's company now. Refreshed by a renewed sense of God's presence and heartened by Christ's indomitable love, I experienced a warm light penetrating my previously darkened mind.

During a holiday visit to Kansas City, Priscilla bought two new T-shirts on the front of which appeared the words, "Life is good." These three words struck home with me, and I quietly decided that I would recall this motto every day that year as a reminder to keep a more positive frame of mind. I committed myself in faith to trust and obey God as the path to the good life.[313] I established it as my intention to engage in life-affirming, self-giving activity however I could.

A few weeks later, I came across a book created by brothers Bert and John Jacobs, the team behind the Life is good® clothing brand. I couldn't resist purchasing it. Through illustrated wit and wisdom, the Jacobs brothers point to opportunities for happiness all around us. Colored line drawings of a smiling "Jake" and his dog, "Rocket," the characters on their products, accompany the sayings.

I would have rolled my eyes at these lighthearted sight- and sound bites not long ago; but a doorway in me had come unlatched, and self-protective skepticism had flown out the window on the wind that rushed in.

Here are three examples from the book that spoke to me, given my recent experience. The image of helmeted Jake on a carefree bike ride accompanies the statement, "Do what you like. Like what you do." Rocket, in an ear-pinning, convertible-car ride gives fresh meaning to the words on the opposite page: "If you don't go, you don't see." Jake fishing from a boat with Rocket on board sets up the observation that "The pursuit is the reward."[314]

"The pursuit is the reward."

Without my even realizing it, I had released my obsessive struggle for clarity and connection. This happened simply by walking with Jesus into his experience of the cross and resurrection. Focused on him rather than myself, I abandoned my agendas and therein experienced a rebirth of hope, a new confidence in Christ, a rest and joy in willingness of heart.

I welcomed happiness. I relaxed in the renewed simplicity of trust. I quit pressing God so much to answer the unanswered question of my vocational future (I didn't quit entirely; but I got better about it!). God granted me a fresh capacity to embrace the day . . . and the people who populated my world.

Clarity would come later but the saving grace ("Life is good") came by following Jesus.

It took me almost another year to realize that God had actually carried me through the stages of grief. Elisabeth Kübler-Ross may have popularized a five-stage understanding of grief,[315] but the processes of denial, anger, bargaining, depression and acceptance lie at the heart of the ancient biblical way of spiritual transformation. Something in us must die if we are to live.

No, it's more than that. We must die if we are to live. "I have been crucified with Christ," the apostle Paul wrote, "nevertheless I live. Yet not I, but Christ lives in me, and the life I now live in the flesh I live by faith in the Son of God, who loved me and gave his life for me."[316]

Evangelical Christianity tends to concentrate on the great conversion by which a person who is not a Christian becomes a Christian ("You must be born again," said Jesus[317]); but life with God actually involves an ongoing series of big and small conversions by which "old things pass away; behold all things become new."[318]

I shouldn't have been surprised, then, that renewal came hard. Renewal came hard because dying came hard. My prayerful walk with Jesus through the Gospel of Matthew inevitably took me to his death, and mine, on the cross. My unreasonable expectations of God had to die; my unreasonable expectations of myself and the church and life in general had to die too. Ultimately, I had to suffer the agony of yielding my life again; I had to let God be the potter while I was the clay.[319] This was a dying process, and it led me through all of the stages of grief and ultimately to the Garden of Gethsemane where, in a prayer of relinquishment, I came to rest, after the pattern of Jesus, in faith-based acceptance.

This didn't answer all of my questions or erase the complications of my imperfect, unfinished life. Instead, it allowed me to let God be God, beyond what I could understand or control. It allowed me to gain a new measure of acceptance of self, with implications for loving self for God's sake.[320] It released me into my now with greater contentment and gratitude.

Then, having relaxed my vocational agendas (having at least bracketed them out emotionally), it put me in a position to receive, to hear, vocational clarity. This became a serendipitous by-product instead of the obsessive goal of the journey.

"The pursuit is the reward."

At the outset of this book I said that what followed would be as much about the search for truth as it would be about finding it. I said that sometimes, it turns out, the journey is the destination in disguise. This, as it turns out, is one of the most important things I learned through my journey in the dark.

Putting it this way may sound a little like Jake-and-Rocket-style wisdom, but it measures up well against a core conviction of biblical faith. The author of Hebrews writes, "Now faith is the assurance of things hoped for and the conviction of things not seen."[321] His subsequent honor roll of faith illustrates this hopeful way in the lives of biblical greats. "All of these people were still living by faith when they died. They did not receive the things promised; they only saw them and welcomed them from a distance."[322] In complete agreement, the apostle Paul penned these simple, timeless words: "The just shall live by faith."[323]

I have a tendency to keep falling back into a destination-driven life, with all goals accomplished, all problems solved, and all questions answered. God keeps reminding me that we experience life's dynamism in the ongoing interplay of Being and Becoming, Doing and Resting, Seeking and Knowing. As long as we live, we cycle between these polarities of our existence as a current of electricity cycles between positive and negative magnetic poles.

God's first gift to us is Being, finding rest in God and unconditional acceptance. By faith, we experience ourselves as God's beloved. We experience God's delight.

God's second gift to us is Becoming. Lest we settle into the lethargy and entropy of an unexamined, unexpressed life, God energizes us with purpose and passion. God ignites in us a desire to stretch, grow, create, understand, solve, and contribute. God aims us at a horizon beyond our current reach.

But God always brings us back to Being, lest we exhaust ourselves and lose perspective. Cycling back to Being protects us against pride, disappointment and guilt. In a hyperactive life these grow like weeds and choke the life out of us. The home base of Being keeps us rooted in love. It counteracts the frustration of knowing "in part" with the reminder that what we know matters less than that we "are fully known."[324]

Being and Becoming. Doing and Resting. Seeking and Knowing—and being known. This is life, and it's why the journey *is*, in some ways, the destination in disguise.

Or, as the wise writer of one of my recent fortune cookie fortunes put it, "It is sometimes better to travel hopefully than to arrive."

Life is good.

later: Vocational Clarity Comes

The return of hope and the experience of God's presence occurred just as my Matthew experiment came to an end. Vocational clarity came later—months later, it turned out.

The welcome light of God's love blazed bright when it returned at the coming of the new year. Then it flickered. The renewed sense of God's presence didn't lift the cloud of unknowing; nor, as it so happened, did it offset the fatigue I felt after six solid years at an unsustainable pace of congregational, denominational and civic leadership.

As I mentioned in an earlier reflection piece, I had the good fortune of supportive lay leadership who made it possible for me to get away for two months of reflection and renewal in the spring of 2009. Those in the inner circle of planning knew that I was weighing the option of continued pastoring versus reactivation of the nonprofit Priscilla and I had created in 2001.[325] They knew that I felt nudged toward a more focused pursuit of my passions as a writer and organizational coach, and as a partner with Priscilla in the marriage-education movement.[326] They also heard me say that I couldn't tell whether it was God or fatigue talking. They encouraged me to take a break, hoping that it might reenergize me for pastoral ministry, but accepting that it might confirm the tug I felt in a new direction.

The moment of clarity came for me two-thirds of the way into my time away. It came after an extended time of physical, emotional, relational and spiritual rest. Interestingly enough, God chose "the Word beyond the Word," to borrow a phrase from earlier in this book, to finally reach me.

I had taken Parker Palmer's book, *Let Your Life Speak*,[327] with me on my sabbatical, having read it before and benefited from its conversations on vocation. Settling into a comfortable seat near a picture window at our family home in the mountains of north central New Mexico, I opened it and began to read.

Perhaps the best way to capture what happened next is to share my journal entry from the next morning:

> Mark the date. This was the day when during an afternoon reading of the first two chapters of Parker Palmer's book, I experienced inward confirmation that the time has come to leave pastoral ministry and pursue my vocation in terms truer to my giftedness, my interests, and my limitations.

I experienced this "inward confirmation" as the signal from God I had long awaited. The key to this impression was how deeply I resonated with Palmer's point of view *and* two specific elements of his own story.

Palmer had learned something of great importance from experience and the ongoing influence of the Spirit in his life: namely, that we locate and pursue our true vocation by listening to what our life is really trying to tell us. *Our* life. He had come to the conviction that however God might clarify our calling through others, vocation doesn't come by conforming to an external voice unrelated to who we are. It doesn't ignore the actualities of our life in its invitation to make our contributions to the world around us. It rises up in our aptitudes and our passions. And in the journey of discovering our true vocation, we find clues to it even in the shadows of our weaknesses and failures.

As I said, I resonated deeply with Palmer's point of view. True to everything I had come to believe about vocation, it spoke to me right then in a particularly compelling way. It settled me into a quiet place away from the clamoring of other voices—voices real and imagined, of people past and present, and even a constructed voice of my own that had been trying to shoehorn me into the life I had been leading. His point of view prepared me to retrace my life, looking with fresh openness for the clues to vocation that surfaced in its incidentals.

I knew that I had a longer story to rummage through than ever before—longer by far than when I first landed on the professional dimension of my vocation in high school; longer even than my last serious reconsideration of vocation seven years earlier, when returning to pastoral ministry after a one year hiatus. I knew that if I were open to it, this very fact would serve me well. A longer story meant a higher likelihood of repeat themes that would point the way, some of them positive and some of them not.

I felt honestly and deeply open to whatever my life wanted to tell me. I knew it would take me back to strengths and passions and aptitudes and achievements that felt affirming. In keeping with what Palmer's book was saying, I also knew that it would take me graciously, but firmly, to other clues about my vocation in the shadows of my weaknesses and failures.

To a significant degree I had already begun the process. Through the full length of my dark-night experience, and even before, I had been praying vocational questions and excavating my life for answers. Vocational clues, like photos and film clips, lay strewn across the table in my imagination. This may explain why my dawning moment came so quickly in the reading of Palmer's book. His life's journey of discovery, so essential to his book, provided reference points for my own journey. At two points in particular, his story spoke so powerfully to themes in my life that I was thrust with stunning force to a new place of vocational clarity.

The first point in his story that struck me seems relatively minor when compared with other defining moments in his life. Well along his way in living vocationally, he looked back at his childhood and saw, for the first time, the connection between his boyhood interest in being an ad man, like the father of one of his friends, and his "lifelong fascination with language and its power to persuade, the same fascination that has kept me writing incessantly for decades."[328] I highlighted this statement, feeling the surge of an inward "Yes!" in my own vocational spirit. It beautifully expressed my persistent and still somewhat pent-up passion for using my writing as an avenue of service to the world.

What appealed to him about the power of words was their power to "persuade." The synonym I used more often to describe my passion was "influence." This had been true since my freshman year at Baylor when the word surfaced in a series of audio tapes on Christian leadership that our campus minister played in a gathering of up-and-coming campus leaders. Listening to the tapes, I knew I wanted to be a person of influence for God. That day I had written the word "influence" in my notes and put my sense of life mission on paper for the first time: "My mission is to help people experience an abundant life—John 10:10."

In the course of my adult life, writing had come to play an increasingly important and satisfying role in this sense of mission. Through articles and columns I had addressed the realities of life and pointed people toward God. I had even taken more than one stab at writing a book, but had been hampered by how all-consuming I allowed the rest of my life to remain. Writing kept falling to the margins, increasingly important to me, but not urgent enough to preempt any of the other things I was doing.

The inward affirmation in that moment with Palmer's book felt like the writing-influencing passion finally shouldering its way forward and claiming its place among my vocational priorities.

I had a second, deeply compelling epiphany as I read what Palmer had to share about a grim period of depression in his life. His ability to find his way out of that dark place had been served in part by the ego-piercing admission to himself that he had not been wired for life inside educational institutions. He had served in more than one setting but fear had gotten the best of him—fear that his scholarly limitations would be exposed. He had avoided this painful insight with sweeping judgments about the arrogance, corruption and irresponsibility of academia; but when he dug deeply into what his life was telling him, he had to own up to the truth. Rather than continuing the exhausting and distressing life this underlying issue had produced, he came to peace with his weakness, accepting that he was better off and more fruitful working with educational institutions from the outside, in a consultative role. He experienced grace in his fear, seeing that by closing one door it had allowed him to turn toward other doors that still stood open.[329]

I felt a kind of thunderclap of recognition in what he shared. His self-discovery hadn't led him to turn his back on institutional life; it had pointed him toward a new way of relating "to institutions with which I have a lifelong lover's quarrel."[330] Slightly altered, his admission could just as easily have been my own. His admission related to educational institutions; mine related to the local church. I knew that I had had a lifelong lover's quarrel with the church, and my desire to leave pastoral ministry—an on-and-off theme across the length of my pastoral history—related, as it did for him, to fear of failure and a checkered history of success.

His perspective was permission-giving to me. I didn't have to keep fighting this. I didn't have to remain caught in the debilitating psychic stew of congregational leadership because of the false voice of what I "ought" to be able to do. I had badgered myself for too long.

I deeply appreciated Palmer's ability to articulate this discovery of his that so closely matched my own. My soul felt released from a prison of unrealistic expectation when I read what he wrote. It felt like a divine *"Aha!"*

As a matter of application, what all of this meant for me was that I could have a new and more creative relationship with Christians and the Church. I could love congregations, challenge congregations, and continue to serve congregations as a consultant, as a coach, as a preaching and teaching minister, and as a writer.

Taking things one step further, I could even look beyond the local church to fulfill my "be-a-preacher" calling. At a certain level I had known this all along; it had already come into play in my civic involvements, my marriage movement involvements with Priscilla, and the launching of our nonprofit in 2001. Nonetheless, this transformative moment allowed me to release myself at a new level to the broader implications of my calling. Those three words—"be a preacher"—were a simple way of saying "use your influence as a voice for life in Christ," and I could do this with a new sense of freedom, using the tools that are actually in my bag: preaching, teaching, writing, advising, counseling, keynoting and more.

Words fail me in the effort to describe the sense of elation that settled over me in this *Aha!* moment. The gift of clarity had finally come, and I could see God's fingerprints all over it.

I had spent more than two agonizing years in a spiritual eclipse. I had spent decades walking through a vocational fog. My longing for God and God's guidance had gone begging for so long that I had forgotten to expect it at all.

I could scarcely absorb what was happening when the fog cleared. I could scarcely absorb it but I could *feel* it, and the grace note— sweet and improbably long—was joy.

I don't intend for this afterword about my moment of clarity to sound like a fairytale ending—"And he lived happily ever after." Were I able to do so, I would draw an arrow from the end of this chapter to the end of the previous entry, "Life Is Good." That chapter concludes with the observation that we experience life's dynamism in the ongoing interplay of Being and Becoming, Doing and Resting, Seeking and Knowing. In other words, we lead unfinished lives, and since God's grace holds us every step of the way, we might as well enjoy the ride.

I believe this now more than ever. Clarity came. I acted on it. Life has moved on.

This hasn't erased all of my questions or eliminated life's complications but it has, for the time being, resolved the crisis of vocation and faith that propelled me toward my devotional experiment. Where this all leads, only God and time will tell.

I hope you won't mind, however, if I end by telling you that I am savoring where it has led so far.

Notes

All quotations of Scripture are from the New International Version (NIV), unless otherwise noted.

1   Robert Frost, "The Death of the Hired Man," in *The Poetry of Robert Frost* (New York: Holt, Rinehart, & Winston, 1979), p. 38.

2   I was most deeply influenced by Thomas Kelly in the shaping of this understanding of spirituality. Thomas Kelly, "The Simplification of Life," in *A Testament of Devotion*. (New York: Harper & Row, 1941), pp. 115, 116.

3   Genesis 2:7.

4   Acts 17:28.

5   1 Kings 19:12.

6   Mark 9:14–27.

7   Isaiah 59:1–2.

8   St. John of the Cross, *Dark Night of the Soul* (London: Baronius Press, 2006).

9   For James Fowler's seminal presentation of his thinking, see: *Stages of Faith: The Psychology of Human Development and the Quest for Meaning* (San Francisco: Harper & Row, 1981). I have been most deeply influenced by his subsequent work, *Becoming Adult, Becoming Christian: Adult Development and Christian Faith* (San Francisco: Harper & Row, 1984).

10   As a starting point, see, Ludwig Feuerbach, *The Essence of Christianity*, George Eliot, trans. (New York: Prometheus Books, 1989). For a serious Christian treatment of Feuerbach's perspective, see: Hans Kung's analysis in, *Does God Exist? An Answer for Today*, trans. Edward Quinn (New York: Doubleday & Co., 1980), pp. 191–216.

11   Determined to take this alternative seriously, I decided to read the bestsellers of those being called "the New Atheists." I read Richard Dawkins, *The God Delusion* (New York: Mariner Books, 2006); Daniel Dennett, *Breaking the Spell: Religion as a Natural Phenomenon* (New York: Penguin Group, 2006); Sam Harris, *The End of Faith: Religion, Terrorism and the End of Reason* (New York: Norton, 2004); and, John W. Loftus, *Why I Became an Atheist: A Former Preacher Rejects Christianity* (Amherst, NY: Prometheus Books, 2008). Dennett's book distinguished itself among these four because of its even-handedness. Unlike Dawkins and Harris, Dennett resists the temptation to take cheap shots at those who dare to believe in God. He focuses on making a case for a naturalistic worldview.

12   Hebrews 4:12.

13   John 10:10.

14   Frederico Fellini, in *The Atlantic* (Dec. 1965). Fellini recognized that every painting, every sculpture, every concerto, every book on the shelf conveys something

of the artist's life, something of the artist's soul. It tells us something of their life's joys and sorrows, something of who they are, something of what moves them and matters to them. It leaves trace marks of the story of their life.

When we step into the world of the sacred, the autobiographical elements become even more compelling. After all, those who write, compose, paint, perform, or craft to the glory of God thereby invite us to see God through their eyes. The lens of their experience becomes the lens through which we filter our own hopes and fears about time and eternity.

Chapter One

15   For the contemporary reader's sake, I have replaced the King James Version (KJV) references of my original journal entries with New International Version (NIV).

16   **BLACKBIRD** © 1968 Sony/ATV Music Publishing LLC. All rights administered by Sony/ATV Music Publishing LLC, 8 Music Square West, Nashville, TN 37203. All rights reserved. Used by permission.

17   John 10:10.

18   Thomas R. Kelly, A *Testament of Devotion* (New York: Harper & Row, 1941), p. 115.

19   Matthew 13:45–46.

Chapter Two

20   Deuteronomy 8:3; 6:13, 16.

21   Galatians 5:22–23.

22   Genesis 18:16–33.

23   Genesis 28:20–22.

24   Exodus 35:15–17.

25   Malachi 3:10.

26   Deuteronomy 30:11–20.

27   John 14:23–27.

28   Joshua 1:5.

29   Psalm 37:4.

30   Proverbs 3:5–6.

31   Romans 10:9.

32   Revelation 3:20 (NRSV).

33   Matthew 6:33.

34   Matthew 28:20.

35   Romans 6:23a.

36   Romans 3:23.

37   Romans 6:23b.

38   Matthew 4:7 (Dt. 6:16).

39   Jeremiah 29:13.

40   Proverbs 3:5–6.

41   John 14:23.

Chapter Three

42   Frederick Buechner, *Wishful Thinking: A Theological ABC* (New York: Harper & Row, 1973), p. 119.

43   Fowler, *Becoming Adult, Becoming Christian*, p. 95.

44   Ibid., pp. 95–96.

45   Rick Warren's book, *The Purpose Driven Life: What Am I Here For?* (Grand Rapids, MI: Zondervan, 2002), became a phenomenal best seller with its biblically-centered vision of the human vocation. I greatly admire this book and have referred to it repeatedly since first reading it. Still, I prefer the idea of a purpose *centered* life to the idea of a purpose *driven* life.

Chapter Four

46   See Richard J. Foster with Kathryn A. Helmers, *Life with God: Reading the Bible for Spiritual Transformation* (New York: HarperOne, 2008).

47   Psalm 51:7.

48   Psalm 66:10.

49   Matthew 5:3, 8.

50   Philippians 4:8–9; emphasis added.

Chapter Five

51   Edwin Friedman, *Generation to Generation; Family Process in Church and Synagogue* (New York: Guilford Press, 1985), pp. 27, 39, 208–209.

52   Friedman, p. 209.

53   John 13:3.

54   1 Corinthians 10:13; Philippians 4:12; James 1:2–4.

55   "The Gambler," Kenny Rogers, 1978. Don Schlitz, songwriter; Sony/ATV Tunes; D/B/A Cross Keys Publisher.

Chapter Six

56   Luke 11:5–10.

Chapter Seven

57   Matthew 5:6; 6:33.

58   Matthew 5:21-22, 38–42, 43–47.

59   Matthew 6:19–34.

60   G. K. Chesterton, *What's Wrong with the World* (reprinted USA: Feather Trail Press, 2009), Part I, Chapter 5, "The Unfinished Temple."

61   I must credit Elizabeth O'Connor, *Journey Inward, Journey Outward* (New York: Harper & Row, 1968) for her influence on this journal entry. Having meditated frequently on the first chapter of her book (pp. 1-9), I drew reflexively from her insights into this way that is hard, that few find, that leads to life.

62   "Unbeatable Biscuits; The secret is in the fold." *GQ Magazine*, August 2004, p. 66.

63   Cecil B. De Mille, quoted in Stephen R. Covey, *Principle-Centered Leadership* (New York: Summit Books, 1990), p. 94.

64   Ecclesiastes 2:10.

65   Ecclesiastes 2:11.

66   Pippert, p. 97.

Chapter Eight

67   John 20:21.

68   1 Corinthians 12:27.

69   2 Corinthians 12:9.

70   Matthew 16:23.

71   Matthew 20:20–28.

72   Matthew 19:27.

73   Matthew 13:36.

74   Matthew 14:13–21; 15:32–38.

75   Matthew 4:1–11.

76   Matthew 21:12–13.

77   Matthew 5:43–47.

Chapter Nine

78   Matthew 6:25ff.

79   This term for God comes from Hebrew tradition and literally means "God will see" or "God will provide." See the Bible's founding example of this in Genesis 22:14.

80   Francis Greenwood Peabody, "A Religion of Adventure; Creed of Courage as Opposed to the Churchdom of 'Safety First'" (*New York Times*, October 17, 1920), pp. 2, 10.

81   Jeremiah 29:4–7.

82   Donald Kaul, "A Lesson in Real Life" (*Kansas City Star*, Thursday, April 9, 1993), p. C15.

Chapter Ten

83   Di Freeze, "Chuck Yeager: Booming and Zooming (Part 2)," *Airport Journal*, Dec. 2003.

84   Lewis B. Smedes, *Shame and Grace; Healing the Shame We Don't Deserve* (HarperSanFrancisco, 1993), p. 107. He writes, "Inside our shame broods the worst of all fears, a fear that is the sting of death itself, the fear of rejection."

85   Elizabeth O'Connor, *Journey Inward, Journey Outward* (New York: Harper & Row, 1968), pp. 3, 4.

86   2 Timothy 1:7.

Chapter Eleven

87   Maria Beesing, et al. *The Enneagram: A Journey of Self-Discovery* (Denville, NJ: Dimension Books), pp. 5–13, 19–23.

88   2 Corinthians 12:7–10.

89   Ecclesiastes 4:9–12.

Chapter Twelve

90   Paul Ricoeur, *The Symbolism of Evil* (Boston: Beacon Press, 1967), pp. 349f.

Chapter Thirteen

91   A training organization for lay people providing one-to-one Christian care to hurting people.

92   David Paap, "What Does It Cost to Care?" The National Small Group Conference, Orlando, FL, February 21, 1989.

93   Paap identified seven costs that caring people are willing to pay: (1) Caring people take the needs of others seriously; (2) Caring people develop plans to respond to the needs of others; (3) Caring people are willing to bear the pain of another person; (4) Caring people are willing to trust people with their feelings; (5) Caring people sacrifice their own agendas; (6) Caring people pay the price of skill development; (7) Caring people are willing to experience continual conversion to the mission of the church.

94   John Maxwell, *Failing Forward: Turning Mistakes into Stepping Stones for Success* (Nashville: Nelson, 2000).

Chapter Fourteen

95   Matthew 10:20.

96   Matthew 5:17–48.

97   Joel Barker, *Future Edge* (New York: William Morrow, 1992).

98   Acts 10:45–46.

99   Acts 11.

100   Acts 15.

101   Acts 15:15–18.

102   Numbers 22:28–30.

Chapter Fifteen

103   Douglas L. Anderson, ed. *Christian Classics: The Confessions of St. Augustine* (Nashville: Broadman Press, 1979), Book 1, Chapter 1, p. 23.

104   *The Message*, p. 1766.

105   Rudolph Otto, *The Idea of the Holy*, trans. John W. Harvey (London: Oxford Press, 1943), pp.80–84.

106   Isaiah 6:5.

107   Max Lucado, *Just Like Jesus* (Waco, TX: Word, 1998).

108   Mark 5:1–20; focal verse, 15.

109   The Navigators; P.O. Box 6000, Colorado Springs, CO 80934-6000; www.navigators.org

110   Richard Foster, *Celebration of Discipline*. New York: Harper & Row, 1978.

111   See particularly, Thomas Kelly, *A Testament of Devotion* (New York: Harper & Row, 1941), 121–123; and, Brother Lawrence, *The Practice of the Presence of God* (New Kensington, PA: Whitaker House, 1982).

Chapter Sixteen

112   1 Corinthians 13:12.

113   The term "fellow strugglers" is an allusion to John Claypool's book, *Tracks of a Fellow Struggler*. (Waco, TX: Word Books, 1974.) The material in this book is drawn from Claypool's sermons during his daughter Laura Lue's battle with leukemia and after her death. In the book and throughout his years of ministry, Claypool modeled a healthy balance of transparency and hope.

114   John 10:28–29.

115   Matthew 5:3.

Chapter Seventeen

116   In Matthew 13:18-23, Jesus explains this parable, clarifying that the "seed" is his "message of the kingdom," his "word" being proclaimed.

117   John Wimber, *Power Evangelism* (Ventura, CA: RegalBooks, 1986), p. 42.

118   Genesis 3:8.

119   2 Chronicles 16:9.

120   Isaiah 59:1.

121   Numbers 6:25.

122   Isaiah 6:8.

123   1 Kings 19:12–13.

124   John 3:3, 5–7.

125   Isaiah 6:9, 10; Matthew 13:1–17.

126   Kenny Loggins and Jim Messina, "Watching the River Run," Gnossos/JasperillaPortofino, 1973.

127   Lyrics by L. Casebolt, based on John 4:13–14.

Chapter Eighteen

128   I have lost the article, but Wayne Dyer's perspective on this matter can be found in several of his books, including, *You'll See It When You Believe It: The Way to Your Personal Transformation* (New York: W. Morrow, 1989).

129   John 20:25.

130   John 20:27.

131   John 20:29, emphasis added.

132   Josh McDowell, *The New Evidence That Demands a Verdict* (Nashville: Thomas Nelson, 1999), pp. 155-163; based on C. S. Lewis, *Mere Christianity* (New York: HarperCollins, 2001 paperback edition), p. 52.

133   I have been most profoundly influenced in my own reflections on the historicity of the resurrection by Professor Frank Tupper and, through him, the German theologians, Wolfhart Pannenberg and Jürgen Moltmann. For a more popular treatment of this, read Lee Strobel, *The Case for Christ* (Grand Rapids: Zondervan, 1998).

134   Brain research has led to the conclusion that the two sides of the brain control two different "modes" of thinking. The left hemisphere is the logical, analytical side; the right hemisphere is the seat of affection and thinks intuitively and holistically.

Chapter Nineteen

135   Kyle Yates Sr. related this story from the Scottish pastor, Dr. John McNeil, in *Psalms of Joy and Faith* (Nashville: Broadman, 1973), p. 73.

136 Ignatius of Loyola, trans. Anthony Mottola, *The Spiritual Exercises* (New York: Doubleday, 1964).

137 Foster, *Prayer*, p. 15.

138 Ibid., p. 19.

Chapter Twenty

139 Genesis 12:1–5.

140 Exodus 2–4.

141 Acts 9:1–30.

142 George Bullard is a ministry partner and the strategic coordinator of The Columbia Partnership. He is author of multiple books, including one that served as an essential tool for FBC, Shreveport during this period of future-shaping work: *Pursuing the Full Kingdom Potential of Your Congregation* (Lake Hickory Resources, 2005).

143 Hebrews 11.

144 I first saw a variation of this quote on a banner in the sanctuary of a church in Bossier City, LA.

Chapter Twenty-One

145 Matthew 25:31–46.

146 Gary Haugen, "Just Courage: Charging the Darkness," Willow Creek Association Leadership Summit, August 7, 2008.

147 Gary Haugen is President and CEO of International Justice Mission (www.ijm.org) and author of *Good News about Injustice: A Witness about Courage in a Hurting World* (Downers Grove, IL: IVP, 10th Anniversary edition, 2009); and *Just Courage: God's Great Expedition for the Restless Christian* (Downers Grove, IL: IVP, 2008).

148 To learn more about Teach for America, go to their website: www.teachforamerica.org.

149 To learn more about the Prison Entrepreneurship Program, go to their website: www.prisonentrepreneurship.org.

150 For more information about Fuller Center for Housing, go to their website: www.fullercenter.org.

151 James 2:14–16; I John 3:16–18.

152 Matthew 25:31–46.

153 Luke 4:14–21.

154 John 2:1–11.

Chapter Twenty-Two

155 This personality pair and the three pairs that follow come from the Myers-Briggs Personality Type Indicator, based on the work of Carl Jung. For a popular, in-depth treatment of this approach to personality, see David Keirsey, *Please Understand Me II* (Del Mar, CA: Prometheus Nemesis, 1998). Religious leaders can benefit from a study by Roy M. Oswald and Otto Kroeger, *Personality Type and Religious Leadership* (Washington, D.C.: Alban Institute, 1988).

156 Maria Beesing, et al. *The Enneagram; A Journey of Self-Discovery* (Denville, NJ: Dimension Books, 1984) served as my initial introduction to the enneagram

and looked closely at patterns of avoidance. I have also benefitted from Kathleen Hurley and Theodore Dobson, *My Best Self: Using the Enneagram to Free the Soul* (HarperSanFrancisco, 1993).

Chapter Twenty-Three

157   James 1:2–4.

158   Psalm 23:4; John 14:21–23.

159   This is an allusion to Harry Emerson Fosdick's chapter, "Prayer as Dominant Desire," in *The Meaning of Prayer* (New York: Association Press, 1946), pp. 133–151. On p. 146, Fosdick says, "The universe itself responds to a man's insistent demands upon it. Even the forces of the spiritual world align themselves, however reluctantly, with a man's controlling prayer [or 'central craving,' p. 145].")

160   Psalm 6:2–3.

161   Psalm 17:8–9.

162   Psalm 32:3–4.

163   Ecclesiastes 1:2.

164   Ecclesiastes 1:16.

165   Ecclesiastes 2:3.

166   Ecclesiastes 9:1.

167   Matthew 16:24–25.

Chapter Twenty-Four

168   See, for example, Exodus 33:20; Isaiah 6:5.

169   1 John 4:16–17.

170   1 John 4:18.

171   J. B. Phillips, *Your God Is Too Small* (New York: Touchstone, 1952).

172   Annie Dillard, *Teaching a Stone to Talk* (New York: Harper & Row, 1982), pp. 52–53.

173   Psalm 111:10; Proverbs 9:10.

174   Acts 17:24, 28.

Chapter Twenty-Five

175   Frederick Buechner, *Telling the Truth: The Gospel as Comedy, Tragedy, and Fairy Tale* (New York: HarperCollins, 1977), p. 98.

176   Hebrews 11:6.

177   Matthew 17:20–21.

178   Matthew 7:7–8.

179   Exodus 2:23–25.

180   Exodus 14:21–31.

181   2 Chronicles 20.

182   These miracles are essential to the story of Jesus as recounted in the Gospels.

183   Exodus 13:20–22.

184   1 Kings 19:12.

185   Matthew 17:19.

186   Mark 9:24.

187   See note 133.

188   Hebrews 11:13.

Chapter Twenty-Six

189   Ephesians 6:12.

190   Psalm 37:4.

191   Jeremiah 29;13.

192   Matthew 7:7–8.

193   Matthew 7:11.

194   Mark 9:23–24; Hebrews 11:6.

195   John 14:13–14.

196   1 Thessalonians 5:17; Luke 18:1–8.

197   Exodus 2:24–25.

198   Matthew 7:11.

199   Matthew 6:8.

200   Matthew 10:29–31.

201   Matthew 6:25–34.

202   Matthew 17:20–21.

203   Isaiah 59:1–2.

204   Hebrews 11:6; James 1:5–8.

205   Luke 18:1–8.

206   James 4:3.

207   James 5:16.

208   Oscar Wilde, *An Ideal Husband,* Act II, in *The Complete Works of Oscar Wilde* (New York: Harper Perennial, 2008), p. 506.

209   Peter Berger, *The Heretical Imperative* (New York: Doubleday, 1980).

210   Daniel 3:17–18.

211   Habakkuk 3:17–19a.

212   Acts 4:18–20.

213   Luke 22:42–44.

214   Mark 15:34.

215   Luke 23:46.

216   Matthew 19:26.

217   Matthew 6:25–34.

218   E.g., 1 Corinthians 10:13; Romans 5:1-5; James 1:2–4, Romans 8:28.

Chapter Twenty-Seven

219   Galatians 5:22–23.

220 Dietrich Bonhoeffer, *Life Together* (New York: Harper & Row, 1952), pp. 77–78.

221 Ralph Keyes, "We, the Lonely People," in *Annual Editions; Focus: Urban Society*, Jacqueline Scherer, ed. (Guilford, CT: Duskin Publishing Group, 1978), pp. 21–27.

222 A television series in the 1980's, set in a Boston pub that celebrated unconditional friendship. As the theme song put it: "Sometimes you want to go / Where everybody knows your name, / and they're always glad you came. / You wanna be where you can see, / our troubles are all the same. / You wanna be where everybody knows / Your name."

Chapter Twenty-Eight

223 Psalm 139:23–24.

Chapter Twenty-Nine

224 Charles Dickens, *A Christmas Carol* in *Five Christmas Novels* (New York: Heritage Press, 1939), p. 81.

225 The sweet spot on a tennis racket is the area at the center of the strings a player aims for when striking a ball. It's the area from which a player can generate the most power.

226 See Chapter 3: "Vocation and the Silence of God."

227 Marcus Buckingham and Donald O. Clifton, *Now, Discover Your Strengths* (New York: The Free Press, 2001), inside front jacket. The Gallup Organization research behind this book has led to multiple books and some exciting tools that people and organizations are using to transform their life and work.

228 Parker Palmer, *Let Your Life Speak* (San Francisco: Jossey-Bass, 2000), pp. 98–103.

229 Stephen Covey, *The Seven Habits of Highly Effective People* (New York: Simon & Schuster, 1989), pp. 287–307.

Chapter Thirty

230 Carl Jüng, quoted in Richard Foster, *Celebration of Discipline* (San Francisco: Harper & Row, 1978), p. 13.

231 *Celebration of Discipline*, pp. 15–32.

232 John Ortberg, *The Life You've Always Wanted; Spiritual Disciplines for Ordinary People* (Grand Rapids: Zondervan, 1997), pp. 81–96. For more on "Slow movements" that are making their way into the mainstream of European and American culture, see Carl Honoré, *In Praise of Slowness; How a Worldwide Movement Is Challenging the Cult of Speed* (HarperSanFrancisco, 2004). Honoré reports on expressions of this mindset that are impacting offices, factories, neighborhoods, kitchens, bedrooms, hospitals, and schools, thus redefining the way people eat, work, relate, and raise their kids.

233 Ortberg, p. 84.

234 Ortberg, p. 88.

235 In Paula Steichen, *My Connemara* (New York: Harcourt, Brace & World, 1969), p. 49.

Chapter Thirty-One

236   *Evidence That Demands a Verdict* (Location: Campus Crusade for Christ, 1972).

237   Philippians 4:13.

238   William Shakespeare, *The Tragedy of Hamlet, Prince of Denmark*, Act 3, scene 2, line 230.

239   I had to laugh at Daniel Dennett's artful dodge when dealing with the origin of the world. Dennett, in my opinion, is the most compelling of the "new" atheists. He is brilliant, and for the most part he resists the temptation to caricature the opposition. Still, he gets tangled in his own logic when dealing with step one of the world as we know it: "What does need its origin explained is the concrete Universe itself, and as Hume's Philo long ago asked: Why not stop at the material world? *It*, we have seen, does perform a version of the ultimate bootstrapping trick; it creates itself *ex nihilo* ["out of nothing"], or at any rate out of something that is well-nigh indistinguishable from nothing at all." (Dennett, p. 244). I'm sorry, but it doesn't matter how microscopically small the first bit of matter was, it was still "something" rather than "nothing"!

240   19th century atheist Ludwig Feuerbach's way of describing faith in God; see footnote #10.

241   I put "imaginary" in quotes because we get the impression during the movie that Harvey might actually be more than just a figment of Elwood's imagination.

242   Dennett, p. 245. "If what you hold sacred is not any kind of Person you could pray to, or consider to be an appropriate recipient of gratitude (or anger, when a loved one is senselessly killed), you're an atheist in my book."

243   An elderly farmer in a church I pastored during seminary years had nothing but disdain for TV weathermen. "If I want to know the weather," he said, "I stick a rope out my window. If it comes back wet, I know it's raining."

244   Exodus 3:14.

245   Isaiah 55:8–9.

246   1 John 4:16.

247   I continue to be grateful for the rich body of work being created by theologians, biblical scholars, pastors, and others to address the mystery of God's providence. Among these, I would commend a book by my major professor during graduate work: E. Frank Tupper, *A Scandalous Providence: The Jesus Story of the Compassion of God* (Macon, GA: Mercer University Press, 1995).

Chapter Thirty-Two

248   This is a reference to Parker Palmer's book, *Let Your Life Speak*. I had read this book shortly after its release. Though I didn't know it on the morning of this particular journal entry, a rereading of this book in the early spring of 2009 would prove decisive.

249   Brer Fox molds tar into a human-like figure and uses it to lure Brer Rabbit into a trap in "The Wonderful Tar-Baby Story," Joel Chandler Harris, *Animal Stories* (New York: Nelson Doubleday, 1954), pp. 16–18.

250   West Wing, Season Two, Episode 22, "Two Cathedrals."

251   "God grant me the serenity to accept the things I cannot change, courage to change the things I can, and wisdom to know the difference." Reinhold Niebuhr's famous prayer has entered into the lexicon of contemporary culture.

252   Madeleine L'Engle, "Act III, Scene ii," in *The Ordering of Love: The New and Collected Poems of Madeleine L'Engle* (London: Shaw, 2005).

253   M. Scott Peck, *The Road Less Traveled* (New York: Touchstone, 1978), p. 28.

Chapter Thirty-Three

254   Philippians 3:10.

255   Isaiah 59:1–2.

256   Matthew 13:13–15.

257   Matthew 5:21–22.

258   Matthew 5:27–30.

259   Matthew 5:33–37.

260   Matthew 5:8.

261   Judges 6-8.

Chapter Thirty-Four

262   Martin Handford, *Where's Waldo*, 2nd Edition (Cambridge, MA: Candlewick Press, 1997). This best-selling children's book offers page after page of illustrated scenes in which a red and white shirted Waldo stands somewhere hidden in the mad action and the crowd.

263   1 Corinthians 10:13; author's translation, emphasis added.

264   Martin Luther King, Jr., *Address to the Southern Christian Leadership Conference*, August 16, 1967.

Chapter Thirty-Five

265   Rainer Maria Rilke, *Letters to a Young Poet*, trans. M. D. Herter Norton (New York: W. W. Norton & Co., 2004), p. 45.

266   Chapter 5, "Nonanxious Presence."

267   Henry McCloud and John Townsend, *Boundaries; When to Say Yes, How to Say No to Take Control of Your Life* (Grand Rapids: Zondervan, 1992).

Chapter Thirty-Six

268   Romans 5:8.

269   1 Corinthians 10:13 (NASB).

270   Matthew 11:28–30.

271   Gerald May, *Will and Spirit: A Contemplative Psychology* (New York: HarperCollins, 1982).

272   2 Timothy 2:15.

273   Ephesians 6:14.

274   Ephesians 4:3.

275   Ephesians 4:14–15.

276   Acts 4:19–20.

277   John 15:1.

278   Matthew 11:28.

279   1 Samuel 3:10.

280   Psalm 139:23–24.

281   Matthew 4:4.

282   John 4:34.

283   Luke 22:42; cf. Matthew 26:39, 42.

284   Luke 23:46.

285   Isaiah 40:31; Psalm 27:14; 130:5; Isaiah 30:18; Acts 1:4.

286   Psalm 27:14.

287   For anyone interested in music-related devotion I would recommend *The One Year Book of Hymns*, compiled and edited by Robert K. Brown and Mark R. Norton (Wheaton, IL: Tyndale House, 1995). William J. Petersen and Randy Petersen provide a devotional telling of the stories behind each of the hymns in this 365-day collection.

Chapter Thirty-Seven

288   John Claypool, "The Blood of the Lamb," Northminster Baptist Church, Jackson, MS, August 19, 1979; Peter De Vries, *The Blood of the Lamb* (Chicago: University of Chicago Press, 1961).

289   A variation of Claypool's rendition and the original from the novel: DeVries, pp. 191–192.

290   DeVries, p. 237.

291   Isaiah 53:7.

Chapter Thirty-Eight

292   Psalm 22:23–24.

293   Jeremiah 29:11.

294   Romans 8:28.

295   Proverbs 3:5–6.

296   Philippians 4:6–7.

297   Habakkuk 3:16.

298   Job 2:9.

299   Job 13:15.

300   Job 19:25 (NASB).

301   Luke 23:46.

Chapter Thirty-Nine

302   1 Corinthians 15:51ff.

303   Matthew 3:17.

304   The title of this entry owes itself to Henri Nouwen, who, as well as any of my literary mentors, understood what it means that we are the beloved of God. See, for instance, his book, *Life of the Beloved: Spiritual Living in a Secular World* (New York: Crossroads, 1992).

305   Psalm 51:10–12.

306   Romans 3:23; italics added.

307   Somewhere years ago, someone clarified for me the distinction between guilt and shame. One relates to doing; the other relates to being. Being proves the deeper of the two issues. We feel guilt for what we do. We feel shame for who we are. Guilt has to do with deserving. Shame has to do with worth.

308   Romans 5:8.

309   Smedes, p. 117.

310   Chapter 17, "The Still Small Voice."

311   Foster, *Prayer*, pp. 3–4.

Chapter Forty

312   Deuteronomy 30:19.

313   Proverbs 3:5–6.

314   Bert and John Jacobs, *Life is Good. Simple Words from Jake and Rocket* (Des Moines, IA: Meredith Books, 2007).

315   Elisabeth Kübler-Ross, *On Death and Dying* (New York: Scribner, 1969).

316   Galatians 2:20 (author's translation).

317   John 3:7.

318   2 Corinthians 5:17.

319   Isaiah 63:8.

320   On an occasion I can't now remember, pastor-preacher-theologian John Claypool spoke of the love of self for God's sake as the highest form of love, higher even than the love of God for God's sake. He credited the 12th century monastic, Bernard of Clairvaux, for this insight. See Bernard of Clairvaux, *On the Love of God*, Classics of Faith and Devotion (Portland, OR: Multnomah, 1983).

321   Hebrews 11:1.

322   Hebrews 11:13.

323   Romans 1:17.

324   1 Corinthians 13:12; see also 1 Corinthians 8:2–3.

Later

325   For more, go to www.GregoryLHunt.com.

326   For more about this work, go to www.BetterMarriages.org.

327   Parker J. Palmer, *Let Your Life Speak; Listening for the Voice of Vocation* (San Francisco: Jossey-Bass, 2000).

328   Palmer, p. 14.

329   Palmer, pp. 26–30.

330   Palmer, p. 36. I like this expression. It places dissatisfaction firmly within the bonds of a lifetime love and commitment. It remains rooted in good will.

Book Club Discussion Questions

- This book addresses the concerns of anyone who has ever searched in vain for God's presence, power and guidance. Has there been a time in your life when your yearning for God has gone unanswered? What was it like for you? What did you do about it? How did the situation resolve itself?

- In what ways, if any, have you experienced God's presence, power and direction in your life? How important is this to you?

- Greg mentions five possible explanations for his experience of the silence of God:

    1. Faltering faith

    2. Some moral obstacle

    3. A "dark night of the soul"

    4. Faith development

    5. Projection of the imagination

    Which of these makes the most sense to you? Can you think of other explanations?

- Greg's crisis of faith connected with a crisis of calling. What role does your faith play in career decisions and the choices you make about the way you prioritize your time?

- Would you say that you are more of a "Nomad" or a "Nester"? (Chapter 9) What impact has this had on the course of your life? How has it affected your relationship with God? How has it affected your relationship with others? How have you incorporated the opposite tendency into your life?

- Greg talks about how his fears of failure and rejection played into his situation. What do you fear the most? How have your fears impacted your relationship with God and your choices in life? How have you overcome your fears? What would you like to do at this point in your life to conquer your fear?

- In chapter 15, Greg writes about spiritual rest and asks, "Why does this prove so elusive an experience, if Jesus wants it and I want it, too?" What have you found to be the biggest obstacles to spiritual rest, and how can a person overcome these obstacles?

- Jesus' compassion and his spirit of selfless service inspired Greg during his dark night of the soul. What recommendations would you offer to someone who wants to become a more compassionate, selfless person?

- Does prayer make a difference? What role has prayer played in your life?

- Greg observes that "sometimes, it turns out, the journey is the destination in disguise." What does he mean by this? Do you agree or disagree? What might you do at this time of your life to strike a healthy balance between being "purpose driven" and "enjoying the ride"?

About the Author

 Greg Hunt is a highly regarded speaker, consultant, and writer. He leverages his wide-ranging work in the worlds of church, community, business, academia, life coaching and relationship education to help people think holistically and purposefully about their lives, relationships, and work.

In September, 2009, after thirty-plus years of pastoral ministry, Greg transitioned into a new expression of his vocation as President of Directions, Inc. Directions is a nonprofit he and his wife, Priscilla, founded to serve organizations, couples and individuals in creating a more life-friendly world. Together, Greg and Priscilla travel extensively, facilitating faith-based and non-sectarian couple retreats, workshops and conferences.

They call metro Kansas City home. They have two married children and two granddaughters.

For more about Greg and his work, go to www.GregoryLHunt.com.

Other Books by Bettie Youngs Books Publishing Co.

The Maybelline Story
And the Spirited Family Dynasty Behind It

Sharrie Williams

A woman's most powerful possession is a man's imagination.
—Maybelline ad, 1934

In 1915, when a kitchen-stove fire singed his sister Mabel's lashes and brows, Tom Lyle Williams watched in fascination as she performed what she called "a secret of the harem"—mixing petroleum jelly with coal dust and ash from a burnt cork and applying it to her lashes and brows. Mabel's simple beauty trick ignited Tom Lyle's imagination, and he started what would become a billion-dollar business, one that remains a viable American icon after nearly a century. He named it Maybelline in her honor.

Throughout the twentieth century, the Maybelline company inflated, collapsed, endured, and thrived in tandem with the nation's upheavals. Williams—to avoid unwanted scrutiny of his private life—cloistered himself behind the gates of his Rudolph Valentino Villa and ran his empire from a distance. Now, after nearly a century of silence, this true story celebrates the life of an American entrepreneur, a man whose vision rocketed him to success along with the woman held in his orbit: Evelyn Boecher—who became his lifelong fascination and muse. Captivated by her "roaring charisma," he affectionately called her the "real Miss Maybelline" and based many of his advertising campaigns on the woman she represented: commandingly beautiful, hard-boiled, and daring. Evelyn masterminded a life of vanity, but would fall prey to fortune hunters and a mysterious murder that even today remains unsolved.

A fascinating and inspiring story, a tale both epic and intimate, alive with the clash, the hustle, the music, and dance of American enterprise.

A richly told juicy story of a forty-year, white-hot love triangle that fans the flames of a major worldwide conglomerate.
—Neil Shulman, associate producer, *Doc Hollywood*

ISBN: 978-0-9843081-1-8 • $18.95
In bookstores everywhere, online, or from the publisher:
www.BettieYoungsBooks.com

Out of the Transylvania Night

Aura Imbarus

An epic tale of identity, love, and the indomitable human spirit.

Communist dictator Nicolae Ceausescu had turned Romania into a land of zombies as surely as if Count Dracula had sucked its lifeblood. Yet Aura Imbarus dares to be herself: a rebel among the gray-clad, fearful masses. Christmas shopping in 1989, Aura draws sniper fire as Romania descends into the violence of a revolution that topples one of the most draconian regimes in the Soviet bloc. With a bit of Hungarian mysticism in her blood, astonishingly accurate visions lead Aura into danger—as well as to the love of her life. They marry and flee a homeland still in chaos. With only two pieces of luggage and a powerful dream, they settle in Los Angeles where freedom and sudden wealth challenge their love as powerfully as Communist tyranny.

Aura loses her psychic vision, heirloom jewels are stolen, a fortune is lost, followed by divorce. But their early years as lovers in a war-torn country and their rich family heritage is the glue that reunites them. They pay a high price for their materialistic dreams, but gain insight and a love that is far richer. *Out of the Transylvania Night* is a deftly woven narrative about finding greater meaning and fulfillment in both free and closed societies.

Aura's courage shows the degree to which we are all willing to live lives centered on freedom, hope, and an authentic sense of self. Truly a love story!
—Nadia Comaneci, Olympic gold medalist

If you grew up hearing names like Tito, Mao, and Ceausescu but really didn't understand their significance, read this book!
—Mark Skidmore, Paramount Pictures

This book is sure to find its place in memorial literature of the world.
—Beatrice Ungar, editor-in-chief, Hermannstädter Zeitung

ISBN: 978-0-9843081-2-5 • $14.95

In bookstores everywhere, online, or from the publisher:
www.BettieYoungsBooks.com

On Toby's Terms

Charmaine Hammond

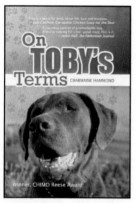

When Charmaine and her husband adopted Toby, a five-year-old Chesapeake Bay retriever, they figured he might need some adjusting time, but they certainly didn't count on what he'd do in the meantime. Soon after he entered their lives and home, Toby proved to be a holy terror who routinely opened and emptied the hall closet, turned on water taps, pulled and ate things from the bookshelves, sat for hours on end in the sink, and spent his days rampaging through the house. Oddest of all was his penchant for locking himself in the bathroom, and then pushing the lid of the toilet off the tank, smashing it to pieces. After a particularly disastrous encounter with the knife-block in the kitchen—and when the couple discovered Toby's bloody paw prints on the phone—they decided Toby needed professional help. Little did they know what they would discover about this dog. *On Toby's Terms* is an endearing story of a beguiling creature who teaches his owners that, despite their trying to teach him how to be the dog they want, he is the one to lay out the terms of being the dog he needs to be. This insight would change their lives forever.

Simply a beautiful book about life, love, and purpose.
—Jack Canfield, Coauthor *Chicken Soup for the Soul* series

In a perfect world, every dog would have a home and every home would have a dog—like Toby!
—Nina Siemaszko, actress, *The West Wing*

This is a captivating, heartwarming story and we are very excited about bringing it to film.
—Steve Hudis, Producer, IMPACT Motion Pictures

ISBN: 978-0-9843081-4-9 • $14.95

In bookstores everywhere, online, or from the publisher:
www.BettieYoungsBooks.com

Diary of a Beverly Hills Matchmaker

Marla Martenson

The inside scoop from the Cupid of Beverly Hills, who has brought together countless couples who have gone on to live happily ever after. But for every success story there are ridiculously funny dating disasters with high-maintenance, out-of-touch, impossible to please, dim-witted clients!

Marla takes her readers for a hilarious romp through her days as an L.A. matchmaker and her daily struggles to keep her self-esteem from imploding in a town where looks are everything and money talks. From juggling the demands her out-of-touch clients, to trying her best to meet the capricious demands of an insensitive boss, to the ups and downs of her own marriage to a Latin husband who doesn't think that she is "domestic" enough, Marla writes with charm and self-effacement about the universal struggles all women face in their lives. Readers will laugh, cringe, and cry as they journey with her through outrageous stories about the indignities of dating in Los Angeles, dealing with overblown egos, vicariously hobnobbing with celebrities, and navigating the wannabe-land of Beverly Hills. In a city where perfection is almost a prerequisite, even Marla can't help but run for the BOTOX every once in a while.

Marla's quick wit will have you rolling on the floor.
—**Megan Castran, international YouTube Queen**

Sharper than a Louboutin stiletto, Martenson's book delivers!
—**Nadine Haobsh,** *Beauty Confidential*

Martenson's irresistible wit is not to be missed.
—**Kyra David, author,** *Lust, Loathing, and a Little Lip Gloss*

ISBN: 978-0-9843081-0-1 • $14.95

In bookstores everywhere, online, or from the publisher:
www.BettieYoungsBooks.com

It Started with Dracula
The Count, My Mother, and Me

Jane Congdon

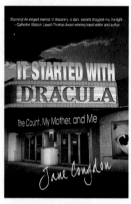

The terrifying legend of Count Dracula silently skulking through the Transylvania night may have terrified generations of filmgoers, but the tall, elegant vampire captivated and electrified a young Jane Congdon, igniting a dream to one day see his mysterious land of ancient castles and misty hollows.

Four decades later, she finally takes her long-awaited trip—never dreaming that it would unearth decades-buried memories of life with an alcoholic mother. Set in Dracula's backyard, the story unfolds in a mere eighteen days as the author follows the footsteps of Dracula from Bucharest, to the Carpathian Mountains and the Black Sea. Dracula's legend becomes the prism through which she would revisit her childhood, and lay claim to a happiness she had never known.

A memoir full of surprises, Jane's story is one of hope, love—and second chances.

Unfinished business can surface when we least expect it. *It Started with Dracula* is the inspiring story of two parallel journeys: one a carefully planned vacation and the other an astonishing and unexpected detour in healing a wounded heart.
—Charles Whitfield, MD, bestselling author of
Healing the Child Within

An elegant memoir of discovery, of dark secrets dragged into the light.
—Catherine Watson, Lowell Thomas
Award-winning travel editor and author

An elegantly written and cleverly told real-life adventure story, proving that the struggle for self-love is universal. An electrifying read.
—Diane Bruno, CISION Media

ISBN: 978-1-936332-10-6 • $15.95

In bookstores everywhere, online, or from the publisher:
www.BettieYoungsBooks.com

Amazing Adventures of a Nobody

Leon Logothetis

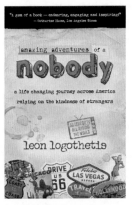

In a time of economic anxiety, global terror and shaken confidence, Englishman Leon Logothetis, star of the hit series *Amazing Adventures of a Nobody* (National Geographic Channels International, Fox Reality), shows us what is good about mankind: the simple calling people have to connect to others.

Tired of his disconnected life and uninspiring job, Leon Logothetis leaves it all behind—job, money, home, even his cell phone—and hits the road with nothing but the clothes on his back and five dollars in his pocket. His journey from Times Square to the Hollywood sign relying on the kindness of strangers and the serendipity of the open road, inspire a dramatic and life changing transformation.

Along the way, Leon offers up the intriguing and charming tales gathered along his one-of-a-kind journey: riding in trains, buses, big rigs and classic cars; sleeping on streets and couches and firehouses; meeting pimps and preachers, astronauts and single moms, celebrities and homeless families, veterans and communists.

Each day of his journey, we catch sight of the invisible spiritual underpinning of society in these stories of companionship—and sheer adventure—that prove that the kind, good soul of mankind has not been lost.

A gem of a book: endearing, engaging and inspiring!
—Catharine Hamm, *Los Angeles Times*, travel editor

Masterful storytelling! Leon begins his journey as a merry prankster and ends a grinning philosopher. Really funny—and insightful, too.
—Karen Salmansohn, AOL Career Coach, and Oprah.com Relationship Columnist

ISBN: 978-0-9843081-3-2 • $14.95

In bookstores everywhere, online, or from the publisher:
www.BettieYoungsBooks.com

Living with Multiple Personalities

Christine Ducommun

Christine Ducommun eloquently shares her story of her descent into madness, struggling to regain her sanity as four personalities vie for control of her mind and protect her from the demons of her childhood. A story of identity, courage, healing, and hope.

Christine Ducommun was a happily married wife and mother of two, when—after returning to live in the house of her childhood—she began to experience night terrors, a series of bizarre flashbacks, and "noises in her head." Eventually diagnosed with dissociative identity disorder (DID), Christine's story details an extraordinary twelve year ordeal of coming to grips with the reemergence of competing personalities her mind had created to help her cling to life during her early years. Therapy helps to reveal the personalities, but Christine has much work to do to grasp their individual strengths and weaknesses and understand how each helped her cope and survive her childhood as well as the latent influences they've had in her adult life. Fully reawakened and present, the personalities struggle for control of Christine's mind and her life tailspins into unimaginable chaos, leaving her to believe she may very well be losing the battle for her san- ity. Christine's only hope to regain her sanity was to integrate each one's emotional maturity while jettisoning the rest, until at last their chatter in her head could cease. Anyone who has ever questioned themselves—whether for a day, a week, or longer—will find themselves in this stunning probe into the often secret landscape of the mind.

A powerful and shocking true story. Spellbinding!
—Josh Miller, Producer,
The Christine Ducommun Story,
(a made for TV movie)

ISBN: 978-0-9843-0815-6 • $14.95

In bookstores everywhere, online, or from the publisher:
www.BettieYoungsBooks.com

Bettie Youngs Books

We specialize in MEMOIRS
. . . books that celebrate
fascinating people and
remarkable journeys

VISIT OUR WEBSITE AT
www.BettieYoungsBooks.com